Comparative Political Economy

Why do unemployment, inflation, and growth rates vary across political economies? Why are some capitalist societies more equitable than others? Why is public spending higher in some countries than others? Drawing on insights from political science, economics, and business, this book addresses these and other related questions in the context of advanced capitalist democracies.

The first part of the book investigates how macroeconomic performance and policy outcomes such as public spending, tax revenue, and trade openness are shaped by various economic and political institutions as well as democratic politics. The second part probes the effects of economic performance and social changes on domestic politics. At the end of each chapter, key terms, review questions, and a short list of recommended readings are included.

Each chapter is designed to familiarize readers with core concepts, theoretical arguments, and empirical evidence related to different substantive themes. With in-text focus boxes and short case studies, this book is ideal for anyone seeking a rigorous introduction to the comparative political economy of advanced political economies, and will be a valuable text on courses in political economy, comparative economics, and related areas.

Prosper M. Bernard, Jr., a former Fulbright scholar, has held academic appointments in the United States and Canada. He is currently an adjunct assistant professor at the City University of New York and New York University. He has published several books and scholarly articles.

Comparative Political Economy

Theory and Evidence

Prosper M. Bernard, Jr.

Routledge
Taylor & Francis Group
LONDON AND NEW YORK

First published 2022
by Routledge
2 Park Square, Milton Park, Abingdon, Oxon OX14 4RN

and by Routledge
605 Third Avenue, New York, NY 10158

Routledge is an imprint of the Taylor & Francis Group, an informa business

British Library Cataloguing-in-Publication Data
A catalogue record for this book is available from the British Library

Library of Congress Cataloging-in-Publication Data
Names: Bernard, Prosper M., Jr., 1972– author.
Title: Comparative political economy: theory and evidence/Prosper M. Bernard, Jr.
Description: 1 Edition. | New York: Taylor and Francis, 2021. | Includes bibliographical references and index.
Identifiers: LCCN 2021012160
Subjects: LCSH: Comparative economics. | Expenditures, Public. | Economic policy. | Commercial policy. | Social change.
Classification: LCC HB90.B476 2021 | DDC 338.6/046—dc23
LC record available at https://lccn.loc.gov/2021012160

ISBN: 978-0-367-18949-5 (hbk)
ISBN: 978-0-367-18951-8 (pbk)
ISBN: 978-0-429-19946-2 (ebk)

DOI: 10.4324/9780429199462

Typeset in Bembo
by Apex CoVantage, LLC

Contents

Figures

Tables

Focus boxes

Acknowledgment

The idea of writing this book has been in my mind for quite some time. It was hatched about ten years after teaching political economy at the graduate level at New York University. I am now in my 15th year, and I have to say that this experience has brought much enjoyment and satisfaction in my professional life.

In the course of this book project, a number of people have been kind enough to give advice, feedback, and encouragement. I would like to thank John Bowman for providing general and specific comments on each chapter of the nearly finished manuscript. John taught me political economy when I was a doctoral student a long time ago. I trace my interest in political economy back to those years, and I am very grateful for his help with this book. I would also like to thank Tony Spanakos for commenting on different parts of the manuscript and offering helpful suggestions regarding the writing style. Several people provided very helpful comments on specific chapters. I would like to thank Roshen Hendrickson for her comments on Chapters 2, 3, and 6; Ming Xia and Richard Hunter for their comments on the introductory chapter; and Berry Lalioti for her extensive comments and advice on Chapter 7. I have also benefited immensely from several online databases. Their organizers, most of whom are academics, deserve a special thanks for their service to academia and the public at large.

At Routledge I would like to thank Chloe James, Eleni Steck, and Natalie Tomlinson for their guidance at each step of the editorial and production process. Caroline Lalley as copy editor offered helpful suggestions that helped improve the final manuscript. I would also like to thank Andy Humphries and Anna Cuthbert, the previous editorial team responsible for shepherding the book project in its early stages.

Lastly, my greatest appreciation goes to my wife, Myrna Kcomt. She has been a constant source of support and encouragement as I balanced teaching, the occasional consulting gigs, and this book project. Contrary to what she thinks, it is because of her that this project came to fruition sooner rather than later. If only I had met her sooner in life. I dedicate this book to her.

Hartsdale, New York
January 2021

CHAPTER

1

Introduction to the study of comparative political economy

As a subfield of political science, comparative political economy (CPE) analyzes the differences in economic outcomes and policies across countries and time. It focuses on the comparative performance of modern capitalist economies—probing in particular the factors that contribute to the different patterns of distributive, redistributive, and collective outcomes across countries. CPE scholars are especially interested in the following questions: Why are some countries more prosperous than others? Why do unemployment and inflation rates vary across political economies? What accounts for the cross-national variance in GDP growth and income growth? Why are some capitalist societies more equitable than others? What accounts for the differences in the level and composition of taxation and public spending across countries and over time? These questions define the analytical parameters of the study of comparative capitalism. A key objective of this book is to address them in the context of advanced capitalist democracies.

These questions direct our attention to the interaction of markets and government, two different means of ordering and organizing human endeavors. Let's first describe, in an abstract way, the key properties of each. The logic of the market is to channel resources (capital, labor, land, and entrepreneurship) to the most competitive and profitable economic activities. To achieve that end, markets function more or less as decentralized allocative mechanisms: market exchanges are free and voluntary in the sense that the actions of firms and individuals are motivated by self-interest rather than compliance to non-market commands. Leading economists such as Adam Smith (1723–1790), Friedrich Hayek (1899–1992), and Milton Friedman (1912–2006) championed market capitalism over alternatives because it allocated resources efficiently, fostered competition and innovation, and created opportunities for individuals to promote their material interests.

On the other hand, the logic of the government is to exercise authority on behalf of the interest of the public. Governments, particularly in democratic systems, can be effective agents of the public by virtue of their ability to define and compel appropriate market behavior, monitor and enforce compliance, allocate public resources, and protect the personal rights of citizens in the economy (Hacker and

DOI: 10.4324/9780429199462-1

Pierson 2016; Vogel 2018). Governments use a variety of tools to promote the public interest as defined by the democratic process—laws, regulations, public spending, taxation and licensing, public ownership, among other tools. In effect, the government functions like a centralized allocative mechanism: members of a society acquiesce to the commands of public officials, trusting that society is better off under the guidance of "an informed, efficient, and humane government" than to be left to their own devices (Wolf 1993: 3).

We have, of course, described the market and the government in idealized ways. Markets are depicted as if they always function perfectly; the government is characterized as a benevolent agent of the public. If each offered a perfect means of organizing human endeavor, then societies would choose market over government, or government over market. In fact, it is because both are flawed that modern democratic capitalist systems have opted for some kind of market-state mixture. Next, we briefly elaborate how governments and markets affect each other.

How governments affect markets

The first row in figure 1.1 spotlights key positive and negative effects associated with government intervention in the economy. Positive effects mean that the exercise of public authority in the economy improves distributive, redistributive, and/or collective outcomes; negative effects imply the opposite. The effects vary by the degree of gains or losses and by their durations, some being short lived others lasting much longer.

Market failures

Governments perform an instrumental role in the economy when they fix market failures. If governments decided not to address these problems, markets would cease to function efficiently. The negative effects would be significant—slower productivity and innovation, poorer quality of life, many unhappy consumers, and slower growth. It is for these reasons that even the most ardent defenders of market capitalism have agreed that market failures have to be corrected by the government from time to time.

Market failures can be defined as conditions in which markets fail to achieve efficient outcomes. Outcomes are Pareto efficient if no actions are available that can make somebody better off and no one else worse off. When outcomes are inefficient, it implies that an economy's available resources are not being used to their fullest

	Positive effects	Negative effects
Government → Economy	*Fixing market failures* *Distributional equity* *Demand management*	*Government failures* *Election-motivated manipulation*
Economy → Government	*Economic voting* *State capacity*	*Rent-seeking* *Political capture*

FIGURE 1.1 Typology of political economic effects

potential and that there are opportunities to improve the well-being of society. Markets are competitive when barriers to entry are low and control is diffused among firms. The lack of competition can lead to inflated prices, limited consumer choices, and inferior products and services—all of which undermine the well-being of society.

There are several types of market failures. For example, public goods such as public transportation, clean air, street lighting, national defense, the police and justice system, roads, and knowledge would be undersupplied if left solely to markets given that they are for the most part non-excludable and non-rival in consumption. Non-excludable means that people cannot be denied the ability to consume such goods; non-rival refers to the idea that a person's ability to consume such goods does not impair others' ability to do so. It is the fact that people can consume public goods even though they have not paid for them (sometimes called the ability to "free ride") that discourages markets from supplying such goods and has led governments to provide them using different delivery methods.

Another type of market failure involves externalities which exist when the negative or positive effect of an action falls on people other than those responsible for carrying out that action. If polluters are not required to shoulder the cost of their actions, polluting will go unabated and it is the people living around them who will bear the cost even though they are not responsible for degrading the air quality. If companies are not compensated somehow for training their workforce, fewer companies will do so and the productivity of the national workforce will suffer. Governments typically use regulations to combat negative externalities. They use subsidies and tax incentives to encourage firms to perform activities that are known to lead to positive externalities. Governments have assumed a great deal of responsibility in nurturing an educated workforce by establishing public educational systems and supporting higher education as well.

Markets can also fail when individuals and firms face information asymmetries. A transaction might fall through if a seller fails to disclose sufficient information about a product or service. For example, someone might walk away from buying a used car if the seller fails to produce a report of the car's history. Similarly, a seller might refuse to sell a product or service if the potential buyer fails to disclose enough information about their qualifications. For example, life insurance providers might refuse to sell this product if the consumer fails to reveal her health history. Lack of information might lead consumers, investors, and firms to make bad decisions—decisions they otherwise would not have made had more information been available. Governments can create information-rich environments by mandating and standardizing product and service description, holding someone liable for misstatements and misreporting, and requiring firms to make regular financial disclosures.

Fixing market failures speaks to a broader point—namely, markets need public governance. Markets are complex institutions; to function effectively they need to be supported by a robust set of laws, regulations, and standards. From property rights protection, to anti-price fixing and anti-insider trading legislation, to consumer safety standards, to accounting standards, to antitrust enforcement, to disclosure requirements, to environmental protection regulations, these and other governmental tools prevent markets from succumbing to their inherent flaws. Reflecting this view, Vogel (2018: 2) notes, "there is no such thing as a free or perfect market," rather market institutions "must be created and sustained by the visible hand of the government."

Distributional equity

The association between growth and equity is often portrayed as a trade-off. The trade-off argument is summarized here by Pontusson (2005: 4):

> governments may create a more equal distribution of income and consumption . . . but in so doing they inevitably distort market forces and undermine efficiency, which in turn leads to slower growth, less employment, and lower average standards of living.

The growth-equity trade-off is often discussed in the context of the interplay between capitalism and democracy. There are two aspects of capitalism that contribute to socioeconomic inequality. One is that the main catalyst of the individual drive to be productive, innovative, and efficient is the expectation of unequal distribution of rewards. If everyone expected equal rewards, what would be the point of working harder than others or investing in higher education? It is the expectation of higher returns when individuals go above and beyond the norm that fuels market behavior. When individual efforts are aggregated upwards into macroeconomic outcomes, the result is economic growth coupled with unequal sharing of prosperity. The inequality effects of capitalism are also attributed to the fact that capitalism commodifies the labor of individuals. Specifically, the well-being of individuals is dependent on their market participation (for more see Chapter 2; also see Esping-Andersen 1990). Not only does capitalism tend to bring all human activities into its orbit, the valuation or worth of one's contribution in the marketplace varies greatly across groups and individuals.

The egalitarian effects of democracy stem from the needs and desires of the majority. The logic of democracy is to promote the will of the majority, which typically represents the lower and middle classes. The majority espouses policy preferences that are distinct from those of the affluent class because these groups face different economic circumstances. In modern times, democratic majorities have advocated the idea of a moral economy—one in which human dignity, egalitarianism, and social rights are prioritized over market outcomes (Streeck 2011). In response, democratic governments have created social safety nets and market regulations that redistribute income and wealth, protect people against income losses, and impose social obligations on capital. Democracy has also penetrated the walls of companies via laws that promote codetermination, an industrial relations arrangement that gives workers an effective voice in the workplace and, in some cases, corporate boards (for more see Chapter 2).

A commonplace view of the relationship between capitalism and democracy is that they are in tension with one another. The rising concentration of income and wealth in the top echelon of societies in the early 1900s (symbolized by the "Roaring Twenties") and in recent decades in the United States (characterized as the "New Gilded Age") are stark reminders of the inegalitarian dynamics of capitalism—of rising unequal prosperity. For many, the historical evidence reveals how democratic capitalist systems are unsustainable—time and again capitalism subordinates democracy to the dictates of market operations. The 30 years following World War II ("the golden age of capitalism"), when prosperity was shared across income groups, "should be recognizable as truly exceptional," as Streeck (2011: 5–6) observes. The periods before and after represent "the normal condition of democratic capitalism—a condition ruled by an endemic conflict between capitalist markets and democratic politics."

An alternative view is that democracy and capitalism can coexist, delivering both equality and economic growth. The golden age of capitalism illustrated how democracy can harness capitalism without suffocating productivity, innovation, and output growth, leading to shared prosperity. In fact, comparative political economists have found that since the 1970s several democratic capitalist countries, notably those in the Nordic region, have been more successful than Anglo countries such as Canada, the United Kingdom, and the United States, at fostering shared prosperity.

The variations in the institutional configuration of advanced capitalist countries is central to understanding why there are persistent cross-national differences among these countries with respect to levels of growth, equality, and employment. In the Nordic countries, markets are "embedded" in an institutional framework maintained by laws and social practices which has been flexible enough to avoid stifling the dynamism of markets but strong enough to protect people against the excesses of markets (Pontusson 2005; Thelen 2014). In these coordinated capitalist systems, governments encourage market development using a variety of tools that we described earlier, coordinate their policy actions with groups representing employers and labor, and invest in education and fixed capital projects (both of which help ease market operations). The social safety net plays an instrumental role in coordinated capitalism (for more see Chapter 2). Certain social policies induce wage restraint among organized labor, encourage individuals to invest in occupational- and firm-based skills, and facilitate business investment. In short, this alternative view of the relationship between capitalism and democracy holds that coordinated capitalist systems have a better track record of fostering equitable growth than uncoordinated capitalist systems like those of Anglo countries.

Smoothing out business cycles

The Great Depression (1929–1939) put into full relief the fragility of markets. It called into question the notion that markets could recover on their own. Keynesianism was born out of the experiences of that decade. This school of economic thought holds that the government should intervene in the economy when aggregate demand cannot recover on its own. By undertaking robust countervailing policy measures, the government can ease the transition from recession to recovery. Whether it is stimulating the economy through monetary expansion (lowering the interest rate and easing access to credit) or fiscal expansion (increasing government spending and lowering taxes) or by mixing both economic instruments, the overriding goal of these stimulus measures is to encourage companies to rehire and to spur household consumption.

Since the Great Depression, governments have practiced demand management whenever economic activities have slowed. In response to the

Great Recession (2007–2009) and the recession caused by the COVID-19 pandemic in 2020, governments around the world unveiled stimulus packages that provided income support to households, job retention assistance, and loans and guarantees to firms in financial trouble. Monetary authorities lowered interest rates and shored up their national financial systems by providing liquidity support. This type of support spurred lending by banks and encouraged funding of household and commercial activities. During the height of the Great Recession, some governments undertook extraordinary and controversial measures like "bailing out" banks—meaning they assumed temporary control of them or served as a backstop to financial institutions facing liquidity problems. Ultimately, these measures stabilized financial and consumer markets, setting the stage for an economic recovery.

IN FOCUS BOX 1.1 GOVERNMENT RESPONSES TO COVID-19

As of early 2021, national economies are still reeling from the COVID-19 pandemic that started in early 2020. Governments have implemented various measures to shore up employment, provide income support to households, and help firms ride out the economic fallout of the pandemic. Figure 1.2 provides data on the size of the fiscal responses of national governments in 12 countries. The responses are divided into two categories. Governments have provided temporary deferrals of tax payments and other forms of tax relief to households and firms; allocated more funds to their health care systems; and increased spending on measures such as extended unemployment benefits, wage subsidies, and targeted cash transfers to households and firms. Further, governments have provided liquidity support to financial and non-financial firms in the form of loans, guarantees, and equity injection.

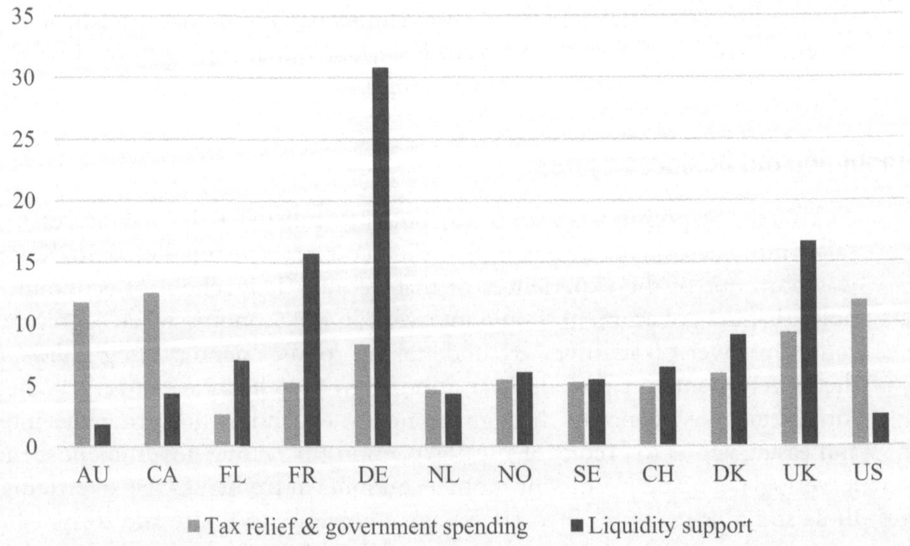

FIGURE 1.2 Fiscal responses to COVID-19 as of late 2020 (% of GDP)

In France, Germany, and the United Kingdom, liquidity support figures large in how governments in these countries have responded to the economic fallout of the pandemic. On the other hand, the bulk of the fiscal response in Australia, Canada, and the United States has taken the form of government spending coupled with tax relief. Another difference concerns how governments have promoted job retention. Numerous governments in Europe have implemented "short-time work policies" (STW) which directly compensate workers when work hours are cut. STW measures help firms adjust their workforce without having to resort to layoffs. In the United States, the Paycheck Protection Program (PPP) provides forgivable loans to small- and medium-sized firms to help them keep employees on the payroll.

Government failures

In the three previous sections we considered how governments can positively affect the economy. In the next two sections we look at how the economy can be adversely affected by the actions of the government. This area of inquiry has been greatly influenced by public choice theory, a branch of economics that focuses on how the incentives and motivations of public officials can lead them to act in ways that are deleterious to the economy. Public choice theorists provide important insights into how the institutional environments within which public officials operate induce distinct behaviors, a point we will return to later in this chapter. In this section we focus on government failures, which refers to the notion "that government processes do not have mechanisms for promoting efficiency that are as powerful as the market's" (Rhoads 1985: 69). The focus here is on how bureaucratic agencies operate. In the next section, we will focus on how elections—a key element of democracy—incentivize elected representatives to manipulate the economy in ways that have long-term negative effects.

Government failure arises from two factors that, in turn, contribute to "low-powered" incentives. First, the governmental apparatus is not subject to the types of competitive pressures that firms in the private sector face. Exposure to competition is crucial for incentivizing agents to perform at their best; it serves as a catalyst for optimal effort. In the private sector, competition forces firms to be innovative, cut costs, and improve the quality of services or products. Firms who compete effectively in turn reap the rewards—a higher profit margin, larger market share, and an increase in shareholder value. The lack of competition within the governmental apparatus and the absence of financial rewards for outstanding work, reduce the incentives of public agencies to be cost-minded and efficient in their use of public resources, and to strive for customer (public) satisfaction.

Second, bureaucratic agents do not face the full consequences of their actions—generally, an agent is not personally and materially rewarded for a wise decision or punished for a bad one. In the private sector, a bad or good corporate decision directly affects a company's bottom line. A poor decision can lead to demotions and layoffs within management; wise decisions may lead to promotions and higher pay. Because there is no effective way of aligning the public cost/benefit of a public agency's actions to its personal cost/benefit, public officials face lower incentives to consistently strive to improve the quality of public services and the means by which they deliver them (Dixit 1998).

It is for these reasons that public choice theorists call into question the government's ability to efficiently allocate resources. Governments are notorious for cost overruns when they undertake public infrastructure projects. In the wake of privatization reforms—selling of government-owned companies to buyers in the private sector—that took place in the 1980s and 1990s in countries around the world, it became evident how inefficient and costly several state-provided services were in comparison to when those services were delivered by the private sector. Similarly, the outsourcing of public functions—contracting out to the private sector services that hitherto were provided by the government—has generated in some cases sizable cost savings for governments, suggesting that the private sector is more efficient than the public sector at delivering various services to the people. Various studies have also chronicled how bureaucratic agencies tend to "justify costs rather than reducing them," leading to budget growth, and how some regulations create unexpected adverse effects over time (Rhoads 1985: 69; Wolf 1993). In short, government failures impose costs on the economy—for example, burdensome and inefficient regulations on industries and higher taxes to finance a larger public sector, all of which impact investment, competitiveness, and economic growth.

Economic manipulation

Public choice theorists have also explored how the election calendar can incentivize incumbents to manipulate the economy to reap short-term political gains. A pre-election economic expansion followed by a post-election contraction is commonly referred to as an election cycle. Election-motivated manipulation might look harmless; after all, voters may benefit materially from an election-timed expansion. However, voters are likely to face economic pain in the wake of elections as officials take measures to combat the inflation that the pre-election expansion caused. Such costs to voters may ultimately eclipse whatever material gains they reaped in the run-up to elections.

To be sure, the size of the economic costs related to elections (and democracy in general) varies across democratic capitalist countries because of their different institutional compositions. This is an area of analysis we will explore in detail in Chapters 3 and 4. Specifically, the motive to manipulate the economy before elections is shaped by various institutional factors—for example, degree of electoral competition and prospect of reelection. Moreover, the ability of elected representatives to manipulate the economy varies across countries based on the degree of central bank independence, level of capital mobility, among other factors.

What we should emphasize here is that although the economic costs of democracy can vary in size, these costs arise because of the principal-agent (P-A) problem inherent in modern democracies. In democracies, the "principals" (the citizenry) delegate authority (that is, the right to rule) to "agents" (government officials) whom they have selected through elections. Moreover, government officials, now acting as principals, delegate power to bureaucratic officials to implement and enforce laws and policies on behalf of elected officials. The P-A problem in both scenarios stems from the inability of principals to ensure that the actions of their agents are always aligned with their interests. The crux of the problem is that agents possess information about their intentions and actions that their principals do not have. Agents may use such information advantage in ways that undermine their principals' key interests. While control mechanisms exist to minimize agent costs, which we discuss later in this chapter, they may not be effective enough to curb agents' discretion and to induce them to exert all of their efforts on behalf of their principals.

How the economy impacts the government

Many scholars have investigated how capitalist development is conducive to democracy. Schumpeter remarked that "modern democracy rose along with capitalism, and in causal connection with it . . . modern democracy is a product of the capitalist process." Similarly, Dahl observed that "it looks to be the case that market-oriented economies are necessary . . . to democratic institutions, though they are certainly not sufficient" (Quoted in Almond 1991: 468). What these and other scholars observed was a historical association between the rise of capitalism—specifically the emergence of a market society—and the transition to and consolidation of democracy. Instead of investigating the relationship between the economy and government at the macro-historical level, this section draws insights from public policy analysis and public choice theory to discuss how markets positively and negatively affect what governments do (the second row in figure 1.1).

State capacity

Sustained economic development and growth can facilitate the expansion and maintenance of state capacity. State capacity is defined here as "a set of administrative, fiscal, and legal capabilities that allow politicians to effect the translation of policies into binding and authoritative public policies" (Beramendi et al. 2015: 13). The relationship between the economy and state capacity has been the subject of extensive investigation (e.g., Dincecco 2017). There is an abundance of evidence suggesting that the level of state capacity has a profound effect on economic development. At the heart of this relationship is the idea that strong state capacity can be leveraged to remedy market failures and to provide effective governance of markets which, in turn, leads to economic prosperity. Here, we seek to briefly explore how economic prosperity reinforces state capacity—particularly, the ability of the state to provide for the needs of its citizens through social welfare provisioning. This is a topic we will discuss in Chapter 7.

There are two mechanisms by which prosperity can bolster this form of state capacity. First, based on insights from Wagner's Law, the ability of governments to collect taxes increases as economic conditions improve. This is because the willingness of people to pay more taxes increases as individual incomes rise. The expansion of tax collection, in turn, enhances the government's fiscal capacity which can be leveraged to provide a wider range of public social transfers and services. Second, an affluent society can afford to have a more generous welfare state. Affordability here means that a government has the ability to channel more public resources toward social welfare without having to defund other state activities.

The expansion and retrenchment of the welfare state seen over the past seven decades closely follow changes in economic conditions. Huber and Stephens (2001: 83) find that growth in GDP per capita during the postwar period was positively related to welfare state expansion. As they put it, "a stronger resource base . . . [made] it easier to construct a comprehensive and generous social safety net and to provide a variety of social services." Slower growth rates in the postindustrial era (since the 1970s) have directly impacted states' capacity to maintain their social welfare commitments. As Pierson (2001a: 83) observes, "it is the slowdown in growth that lies behind much of the current concern about OECD countries. If 3 to 4 percent economic growth had continued over the past quarter-century, many of our current problems would never have materialized."

Economic voting

The ability of elected officials to stay in office often hinges on how the economy is performing under their watch. When the economy is performing well, incumbent officials stand a better chance of getting reelected; during bad economic conditions, the risk of electoral defeat grows for incumbents. Economic voting, a topic we address in Chapter 5, draws attention to how the economy influences what government officials do via the mechanism of democratic accountability. As agents of citizens, elected representatives in democracies are subject periodically to the evaluation of the voting population. One way of thinking about elections is that they function as a means of holding incumbents responsible for how they handle the economy during their elected terms. This democratic institution, in essence, helps curb potential moral hazard by elected representatives, a risk that arises due to the inability of voters to directly monitor the actions of their representatives. If incumbents know their prospects of reelection are based on how the economy is performing, then they are more likely to make policy decisions that promote the economic interests of voters.

There appears to be a contradiction between the logic of economic voting—the economy promotes good government via electoral accountability—and the logic of election cycles—incumbents seek to manipulate the economy to improve their reelection prospects. Recall that these are theoretical claims based on key assumptions which may not hold in reality. We have already entertained reasons why election cycles may not occur. It is also important to note that how voters evaluate the economy (retrospectively or prospectively) and how well informed they are, can affect how the economy impacts what governments do via the medium of elections. We will review these points in greater detail in Chapters 4 and 5.

Rent-seeking and capture

Market power can be converted to political power and used to advance the interests of organized business at the expense of the public interest. In this section, we briefly discuss how the political influence of business can be leveraged in ways that end up harming the economy and worsen inequality via rent-seeking and "corrosive" capture. This area of study has been heavily influenced by public choice theorists who have asserted that the democratic process can lead to policy outcomes that undermine collective gains and lead to the redistribution of wealth away from the democratic majority. This result stems from two interrelated dynamics. On the one hand, they argue that the political motives of elected representatives induce them to cater to business groups, supplying rents to them in exchange for election support.

On the other hand, the outsized influence of business groups can lead them to dominate the policymaking process, rendering it less responsive to the public interest.

Some public choice theorists have described the democratic state as "some passive reflector of interest group demands . . . [whereby] the political system provides a quasi-market setting for brokering wealth transfers and extorting rents" (Mitchell and Munger 1991: 518 and 523). This pessimistic view sharply contrasts with perspectives that understand the state as a mitigator of market failures and as a promoter of collective gains. These alternative perspectives assert that democratic governments are sufficiently independent to discern the public interest and to take legislative actions to promote it.

Rent-seeking is a type of business activity aimed at distorting market dynamics. Its purpose is to generate profits that exceed what companies would otherwise obtain under competitive market conditions. Firms that obtain rents, in essence, redistribute existing market value in their favor by denying other firms the ability to enter a market or to expand their business. Rents may come in the form of regulations that keep potential market entrants at bay and lock-in market privileges for insider firms. One of the economic effects of rent-seeking, as Lindsey and Teles (2017) note, is that it leads to "upward redistribution" of wealth; in other words, the market distortions caused by regulations worsen economic inequality by concentrating more wealth at the top. Another effect, which Olson (1982) and Lindsey and Teles (2017) chronicle, is that rents interfere with capitalism's process of creative destruction. Rents can stifle technological innovation by curbing competition, can interfere with market creation by discouraging resource reallocation, and can ultimately suppress economic growth.

The political influence of business reaches beyond rent-seeking as several political scientists have noted. Bartels (2017), Gilens (2005), Hacker and Pierson (2011), among others have shown that the policy outcomes especially in the United States, but also increasingly in Europe, are biased in favor of the preferences of business. What they point to is commonly referred to as "corrosive" capture: a process in which "organized firms render regulation less robust than intended in legislation or than what the public interest would recommend." It is common for capture to result in "the reduction of costly rules and enforcement actions that cut into profits," not just the accretion of rents (Carpenter and Moss 2013: 16–17). From the energy sector, to the financial sector, to the food sector, the capture of the policymaking process by powerful industry lobbies in the United States has left an indelible mark on these sectors' regulatory structure. For example, the deregulation of the financial sector starting in the 1980s, which occurred under the intense lobbying and electioneering efforts of business groups, set in motion dynamics in the real estate market that ultimately culminated in its crash in 2007. Recent rollbacks in the 2010 Dodd-Frank Wall Street Reform and Consumer Protection Act, which established transparency and oversight regulations in the financial sector, suggest that corrosive capture remains prevalent in this public policy domain.

Doing comparative political economy

Much of what comparative political economists do involves investigating how the interaction between the choices of actors and institutions leads to different patterns of cross-national economic performance and policies. Since the "economic turn" in the study of comparative politics, CPE scholars have been much more attentive to how the aggregation of actors' choices impact outcomes (Levi 2000). By "economic turn," we mean that CPE scholars have used microeconomic tools and methods to shed light on the microfoundations of the political economic phenomena they are studying—specifically, investigating how individual preferences and attitudes are formed and how individual choices are aggregated upwards into policy outcomes. A brief example will illustrate how the use of economic methods—particularly choice-theoretic reasoning—has enhanced our analytical leverage in the study of various topics in CPE.

Political science scholars have long suspected that the distribution of income is related to the level of redistribution in democracies, as illustrated in figure 1.3. At the macro-level, more inequality (measured using the gini coefficient) has appeared to be associated with more redistributive spending (measured as public social spending as a percentage of GDP) (see Kenworthy and Pontusson 2005). What was missing until the pioneering works of Meltzer and Richard (1981) and Romer (1975) was an analytical framework to explore the microfoundations of this macro-level phenomenon (for more, see Chapter 7). Democracies empower the majority (lower- and middle-income voters), the group of citizens who stands to gain the most from redistribution. Briefly, the Meltzer-Richard-Romer (MRR) model asserts that when incomes in a society become more unequally distributed—such that the median income falls further and further below the average income—popular demand for redistribution increases. Here, choosing more redistribution rather than less is based on a benefit-cost calculation: the expected increase in one's current material well-being from redistribution relative to the efficiency costs of taxation. It turns out, however, that individual preferences over redistribution are shaped by other factors that we will discuss in Chapter 7. The other contribution of the MRR model and other similar models is that it elaborates how individual preferences translate into redistributive outcomes through partisan-electoral channels. Institutional channels play an important role because they can either facilitate or obstruct the translation of public preferences into policy outcomes.

We can extract from this example several general insights that are featured in CPE research. First, CPE scholars often assume that individual behavior is instrumental insofar that the choices actors make are intended to maximize the achievement of their interests. Individual interests can be self-regarding or other-regarding. Self-regarding interests focus on wants or needs that affect one's own condition or state, such as financial security, safety, prestige, and power. Other-regarding interests are wants that affect others and often arise when people identify with particular groups—racial, ethnic, or national. Behavior that stems from other-regarding interests is commonly referred to as altruism. The MRR model assumes voters' choices are guided by self-regarding interests. Recent models of redistribution, however, hold that some voters exhibit altruistic behavior toward in-group members, leading them to support redistribution even though that stance can lead to a higher personal tax burden. Moreover, other models assume that self-interested individuals seek to maximize their future rather than current utility. People tend to evaluate the utility of social policies that protect them against labor market risks in this manner.

Second, CPE is keenly aware of the importance of strategic interaction in shaping economic performance and policy outcomes. Political and economic actors take

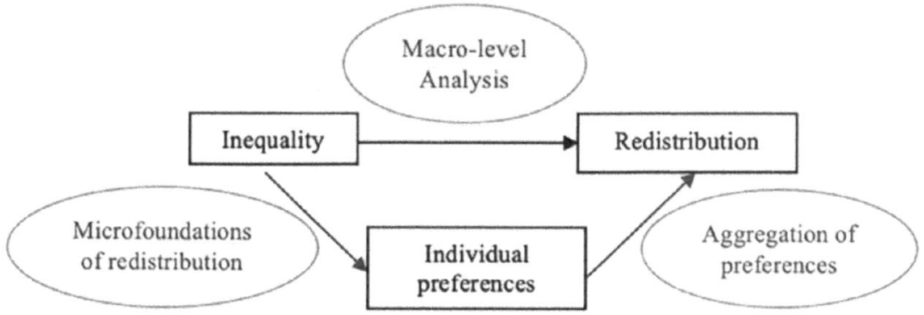

FIGURE 1.3 Macro- and micro-level analysis of redistribution

account of what others are likely to do before they choose among the options they have. The moderation of wage demand, which helps keep inflation in check and unemployment down, is partly determined by the strategic interaction between labor unions. Where labor is poorly organized—that is, fragmented into a large number of small wage bargaining units—wage moderation is difficult because each tries to outdo the other in securing a higher nominal wage contract to protect their real purchasing power.

Wage moderation is also determined by the strategic interaction between labor and employers. Labor representatives are more likely to agree to wage moderation if they know that employers plan to channel the labor cost savings into productivity-improving and job-creating investments (for more see Chapter 2). Clearly, the organizational characteristics of these producer groups as well as the institutional context within which they interact have important implications not just in terms of how they interact (coordinated or uncoordinated) and how they define feasible courses of action, but also in how they define their interests. Shifting to election and partisan cycles, scholars have argued that the occurrence of such cycles is partly influenced by the expected reaction of central bankers to fiscal expansion. If a central bank stands ready to counteract a pre-election expansion or partisan-induced expansion, then incumbent politicians and parties are more likely to abstain from such a policy action (for more see Chapter 4).

Finally, institutions figure prominently in the study of CPE. Much has been written about the institutional varieties of contemporary capitalist economies. Various typologies have been used to classify advanced political economies based on differences in the institutional configurations that structure and govern the workings of their economies: liberal, statist, and corporatist political economies (Katzenstein 1985; Zysman 1983); Nippo-Rhenish and Anglo-American models (Gourevitch 1996); liberal market, coordinated, and mixed market economies (Hall and Soskice 2001; Hall and Gingerich 2004); non-liberal and liberal capitalist economies (Streeck 2002); and most recently wage-led, consumption-led, and export-led growth regimes (Baccaro and Pontusson 2016). Using these and other typologies, CPE scholars have sought to show how different patterns of economic performance and policy outcomes are traced to the institutional diversity among advanced capitalist democracies.

Institutions matter because they shape the actions of people. As Hall and Taylor (1996: 939) note, "it is through the actions of individuals that institutions have an effect on political outcomes." There are two ways to think about the relationship between institutions and the choices of actors. The first approach holds that institutions "structure agents' choices" as Blyth (2009) notes; or another way of putting it, they represent "exogenous constraints" on the behavior of actors in the political and economic realms, as Shepsle (2006) points out. Accordingly, institutions are defined as "the formal rules, compliance procedures, and standard operating practices that structure the relationship between individuals in various units of the polity and the economy" (Hall 1986: 19).

These institutions have an obligatory character in that actors are expected to comply with formal rules. They also establish relations of authority among actors and have mechanisms of enforcement. Institutions define what is appropriate and inappropriate behavior and permissible and prohibited actions. Because institutions narrow the range of feasible actions, have mechanisms to enforce compliance, and provide information about the behavior of others, the actors that interact within them are able to form expectations about the present and future behavior of others, thereby affecting the outcome of strategic interaction. Shepsle (1989: 137) and other rational-choice institutionalists have claimed that such institutions induce an equilibrium, that is, an institutional status quo that "is *invulnerable* in the sense that no other [institutional] alternative . . . is preferred by all the individuals" who possess the ability to effect change. Historical institutionalists, on the other hand, are more inclined to think that institutions persist due to path-dependent dynamics—a form of self-reinforcement in which the possibility of deviating from an institution-induced order becomes increasingly smaller the longer it exists (Pierson 2000).

Another approach considers institutions as "chosen structures" that help actors achieve mutual gains (Blyth 2009). Accordingly, institutions are purposefully and voluntarily created by actors to help them overcome a social dilemma—that is, a situation in which individually rational behavior makes everyone worse off. Social dilemmas are manifested in cooperation, coordination, and commitment problems. The failure to achieve optimal outcomes in these scenarios is partly caused by the presence of transaction costs. Dixit (1998: 38) defines transaction costs as "anything that impedes the specification, monitoring, or enforcement of an economic [or a political] transaction." There are several forms of transaction costs. First, limited foresight, lack of information, and uncertainty can result in incomplete contracts that leave many contingencies unspecified. Second, information asymmetry and opportunism can lead to moral hazard, adverse selection, and time inconsistency—problems commonly associated with principal-agent relationships. Third, investment in relationship-specific assets and time inconsistency can lead to a hold-up problem (see In Focus Box 1.2 for definitions of these concepts). In the face of such transaction costs, actors are unable to make credible commitments and unwilling to engage in collective action. According to the current understanding of institutions, actors create self-enforcing governance structures—common practices and voluntaristic, though formal arrangements—that help them to economize on transaction costs. Instead of conceiving institutions as constraining action, this approach understands institutions as enabling action. They help actors overcome obstacles to collective action (Hall and Thelen 2009).

IN FOCUS BOX 1.2 KEY CONCEPTS IN NEW INSTITUTIONAL ECONOMICS

Opportunism refers to self-interested behavior which inclines actors to shirk, deceive, and conceal information. It corrodes trust and renders commitments less credible. Actors may act opportunistically when contracts are incomplete (i.e., lack precise rules that prohibit various types of actions) and when they are involved in relations in which their principals do not have the information they have.

Moral hazard and *adverse selection* are caused by hidden actions and concealed information by agents, and illustrate the conflict of interest that can exist between a principal and an agent in the absence of effective control mechanisms. *Moral hazard*, a type of agent cost, arises from the inability of a principal to verify if an agent is exerting all of his efforts on the principal's behalf. If the agent knows that his principal cannot fully monitor his actions, a self-interested agent has an incentive to shirk and take other actions that are beneficial to him but not his principal. *Adverse selection*, another type of agent cost, arises from the inability of a principal to know the true qualities of someone with whom he is about to enter into a contractual arrangement. The prospective agent has an incentive to hide his flaws or exaggerate his competence; the result is that the agent knows things about himself that the principal does not.

Time inconsistency is a type of relational dynamic in which the best policy in any circumstance is sacrificed for a policy that is expedient at the present time. Price stability is considered to be the best economic policy objective at any time. It is for that reason that government officials signal their commitment to this policy. However, government officials facing elections might strategically time tax cuts or increase short-term targeted public spending to reap immediate political gains. These fiscal expansionary measures can spur growth but also cause inflation. When actors face incentives to back away from an optimal policy after it is announced, they have difficulty making commitments that others deem credible.

Relationship-specific assets represent a type of asset whose value is tied to a specific contractual arrangement, usually between an upstream and a downstream firm. This asset type has limited marketability outside the arrangement it was originally created for—it is considered a sunk cost. A firm that invests in this asset type is exposed to the risk of a *holdup* by another firm in that it might seek to change the terms of the agreement in ways that reduce the returns on relationship-specific assets. In politics, aspects of the holdup problem arise when legislators delegate authority to the bureaucracy—specifically, invest agencies with the power to implement legislation. Legislators face the possibility that these agencies may misuse or abuse their authority, which would reduce the political returns that legislators were expecting when they created these delegated arrangements.

Varieties of capitalism

It is hard to think of another recent political economy approach that has been as influential in the study of comparative capitalism as the varieties of capitalism (VoC) approach. Developed by Hall and Soskice (2001), the VoC approach combines both understandings of institutions—they create opportunities for and place constraints on actors; and they are chosen structures while also serving as repositories of shared understandings that promote common expectations among actors. The VoC approach explores the microfoundations of the institutional diversity of capitalist economies by focusing on the actions of firms in the face of social dilemmas.

In that respect, the VoC approach differs from several other CPE approaches that have offered macro-level explanations for the cross-national differences in economic outcomes. For example, the corporatist literature, which we discuss in Chapter 2, spotlights how differences in the organizational capacities of labor in conjunction with the presence of social democratic governments have shaped cross-national differences in distributive, redistributive, and collective outcomes. Katzenstein's (1985) work on "democratic corporatism" showed how the combination of the coordinative capacities of labor, a culture of cross-class compromise, and a consensus-style democratic politics afforded smaller European economies an institutional advantage over their larger European counterparts and the United States in terms of economic performance during the turbulent decade of the 1970s. The VoC approach is also different from the "national policy style" approach associated with works by Shonfield (1965), Hall (1986), and Zysman (1983) for example. This genre of analysis traces divergent economic policies and outcomes to differences in national cultures, interventionist capacities of states, and patterns of state-society relations.

At the heart of the VoC approach is the question of how firms go about addressing various coordination and commitment problems they encounter when interacting with workers, owners, suppliers, and clients. For example, how do firms coordinate their actions with labor to ensure moderate wage changes and improve workplace productivity? How do firms cultivate the skill-sets required for their product market strategy? How do firms obtain finance? How do firms get the intermediate goods and technologies they need? Some of these problems are related to dynamics captured by principal-agent interactions while others stem from hazards relating to transaction costs. In short, if firms cannot create effective governance structures to help them minimize agency costs and transaction costs, national productivity, innovation, and prosperity suffer.

According to the VoC approach, firms overcome these problems by gravitating toward one of two modes of coordination, as illustrated in table 1.1. Firms in liberal market economies (LMEs) tend to coordinate via competitive market arrangements characterized by arm's-length relations and formal contracting, and also tend to avoid long-term commitments with other parties. Moreover, price signals and considerations of marginal returns dictate the type of contractual arrangements firms use to govern their interactions with other parties. On the other hand, firms in coordinated market economies (CMEs) tend to coordinate their endeavors via strategic interaction, consisting of institutional practices conducive to deliberative and network-based relationships. This institutional environment fosters trust, long-term strategizing, and co-investment. As table 1.1 shows, these two coordination modes are associated with distinct institutional practices in five spheres of the political economy. The existence of distinct coordination modes between LMEs and CMEs stems from the different institutional settings found in these two types of capitalist economies. When firms seek to coordinate their actions with other parties, their choice of coordination type is based in part on the preexisting formal institutions as well as on their "experience with a familiar set of actors and the shared understandings that accumulate from this experience" (Hall and Soskice 2001: 13).

TABLE 1.1 A comparison of the institutional features of LMEs and CMEs

Liberal Market Economies	Coordinated Market Economies
Industrial relations: uncoordinated, firm-level wage bargaining; weaker employment protection.	**Industrial relations**: coordinated, industry- or multi-industry level wage bargaining; stronger employment protection.
Skills formation: general skills system; limited employer involvement in skills development.	**Skills formation**: occupational-, industry-, and/or firm-based skills system; employer and industry involvement in skills development (in-house training; apprenticeship).
Corporate governance: shareholder model characterized by its dispersed ownership structure, high degree of minority shareholder protection (MSP), and relatively larger equity markets.	**Corporate governance**: stakeholder model defined by its concentrated ownership structure, lower degree of MSP, and relatively smaller equity markets.
Inter-firm relations: weak employers' organizations foil collective action and coordination efforts, militate against information and technology sharing.	**Inter-firm relations**: encompassing employers' associations facilitate information-sharing, technology transfers, and coordination to enhance industry growth and competitiveness.
Employee-firm relations: limited "voice" opportunities for workers vis-à-vis management; protection of managerial prerogatives.	**Employee-firm relations**: formal "voice" opportunities for workers in works councils and corporate boards.

A key claim of the VoC approach is that institutional complementarities emerge between the institutional practices found in the five domains of the political economy. The complementarity of two institutional practices means that the performance of one is enhanced by the presence of the other. We will explore the complementarity between industrial relations and corporate governance in Chapter 2. The existence of institutional complementarity reinforces the differences between LMEs and CMEs, but also bestows distinct comparative institutional advantages according to the VoC approach. For example, Hall and Soskice (2001) claim that the institutional practices associated with LMEs tend to encourage radical innovation—which lead to new product and service lines—and to ease adjustment to market changes by facilitating reallocation of capital and labor. On the other hand, CMEs tend to have an advantage in incremental innovation—gradual improvements in the manufacturing of products—and in diversified quality production—a production strategy that requires a workforce with occupational- and firm-specific skills and collaborative labor-employer relations in the management of the workplace.

The plan of this book

This book seeks to provide readers with a comprehensive survey of selected topics in comparative political economy. A unique feature of this book is that it evaluates a wide range of research against data collected on 12 affluent OECD countries: Australia (AU), Canada (CA), Denmark (DK), Finland (FL), France (FR), Germany (DE), the Netherlands (NL), Norway (NO), Sweden (SE), Switzerland (CH), the United Kingdom (UK), and the United States (US). Moreover, this body of research is evaluated using data covering a period from the early 1980s to the mid-2010s, enabling us to determine whether arguments based on earlier data have been able to stand the test of time. Throughout the book, scatterplots are used to help readers visualize how key variables central to a theoretical argument correlate with each other. The scatterplots include the best-fit (or regression) line, correlation coefficient (r), and statistical significance level (sig) when the correlation reaches a conventional level of .05 or less.

In each chapter, relevant data are collected for the 12-country sample. The sample is clustered into three groups of equal size. The Anglo countries include Australia, Canada, the United Kingdom, and the United States. The continental European group includes France, Germany, the Netherlands, and Switzerland. The Nordic group comprises Denmark, Finland, Norway, and Sweden. Readers familiar with the VoC literature will notice that Anglo countries are commonly labeled as liberal market economies, while the other two country clusters are labelled as coordinated market economies, with the Nordic cluster distinguished from other CMEs as Pontusson (2005) does. Moreover, those familiar with Esping-Andersen's (1990) three welfare state types will recognize the overlapping between that scheme and the one used in this book. Indeed, the research on the comparative capitalism of advanced OECD countries often uses country classifications similar to the one used throughout this book. To be clear, the classification of countries used in this book serves simply as a heuristic tool to organize and present data. The book does not advance a specific explanation about why and how countries cluster into three groups, nor does it claim that the clusters themselves are causally related to specific macroeconomic or policy outcomes.

When surveying the research in any field of study, a particular framework has to be used to help determine what areas of inquiry to explore. In this book, chapter topics were selected and organized based on a two-fold framework. Part one of the book, which includes Chapters 2, 3, and 4, investigates the effects of institutions and democratic politics on economic performance and policies. As we discussed, institutions do not act, rather they shape human agency by placing constraints on actors, creating opportunities for action, or by inclining them to act in certain ways. In the first part of the book, we will focus on how macroeconomic performance and public policies are shaped by various economic and political institutions as well as democratic politics. Democratic politics is defined here as the maneuvering that incumbent officials and political parties undertake in order to advance their political interests in the context of democratic accountability and representation. In addition to exploring the macro-level relationship between institutions and outcomes, we will also examine the micro-dynamics of macro-level economic outcomes.

Chapter 2 explores the economic institutional variations across advanced capitalist countries and their effects on macroeconomic performance. Not only does the chapter analyze the economic effects of labor and business individually and jointly, it also examines how the interaction between labor market practices and other political-economic institutions such as central banks and corporate governance regimes affect performance. Chapter 3 investigates the effects of different political institutions on economic policy outcomes such as public spending, revenue, and social spending. Specifically, it explores why different political institutional configurations are associated with different policy outcomes. Chapter 4 probes the effects of elections and the partisan composition of government on macroeconomic performance. It explores why, how, and when the electoral and partisan motives of government officials result in policy and macroeconomic cycles.

Part two of the book, which includes Chapters 5, 6, and 7, explores the effects of the economy and society on domestic politics. There are two aspects of domestic politics this section focuses on. One is election outcomes, the other is public policy outcomes. As an area of political economic inquiry, economic voting draws attention to how economic performance affects elections. Public policy outcomes will be investigated from two perspectives. We are interested, first, in studying the effects of socio-economic inequality on the direction and responsiveness of public policies in general and, second, in exploring how societal and economic factors affect the demand for and level of social spending.

Chapter 5 explores the link between the economy and election outcome, focusing in particular on the contingent and complex nature of the association between the economy and election outcomes. Chapter 6 investigates the causes and effects of economic inequality and is designed to complement Chapter 7's analysis of redistribution. In that chapter, we explore the effects of inequality and other factors on individual preferences for redistribution and on the level and type of redistributive spending. The concluding chapter is used to discuss new directions in CPE research. It briefly discusses the burgeoning research on patterns of liberalization, growth models, and populism.

Books that survey the field of comparative political economy do so using different analytical frameworks. This book is no different. It contributes to the study of comparative political economy by shining the spotlight (back) on politics. This book's attention to the nexus between political institutions and democratic politics on the one hand and comparative capitalism on the other is inspired by works such as Keech's (2013) *Economic Politics in the United States*, Persson and Tabellini's (2003) *The Economic Effects of Constitutions*, and Alt and Crystal's (1983) *Political Economics*. By focusing on politics—exploring how political motives, institutions, and bargaining shape economic outcomes and how economic and social factors affect political outcomes—this book draws attention to areas of political economic inquiry that have tended to be left out of recent surveys of CPE.

Key concepts

Adverse selection

"Corrosive" capture

Government failure

Institutions

Market failure

Moral hazard

Principal-agent relationship

Rent-seeking

Time inconsistency

Transaction costs

Varieties of capitalism

Discussion questions

- How is the economy shaped by government actions?
- How are political outcomes shaped by the economy and society?
- What effects do institutions have on the political economy?
- What insights can we gain by studying comparative political economy from a varieties of capitalism perspective?

Further reading

Bowman, John R. 2014. *Capitalisms Compared: Welfare, Work, and Business*. Thousand Oaks: CQ Press.

Explores policy differences among Germany, Sweden, and the United States in several public policy areas such as health, family, labor market, finance, and corporate governance.

Coyle, Diane. 2020. *Markets, State, and People: Economic for Public Policy*. Princeton, NJ: Princeton University Press.

Uses insights from welfare economics to evaluate public policy performance.

Menz, Georg. 2017. *Comparative Political Economy: Contours of a Subfield*. New York: Oxford University Press.

Approaches the study of comparative capitalism by analyzing cross-national institutional diversity within different spheres of modern capitalism.

Vogel, Steven K. 2018. *Marketcraft: How Governments Make Markets Work*. New York: Oxford University Press.

Rejecting the government versus market and the regulation versus competition dichotomies, this book makes the case that effective market governance requires effective government regulations.

PART

I

The effects of institutions and democratic politics on economic outcomes

CHAPTER

2

Economic institutions

How does the organization of the economy affect macroeconomic performance? Is growth, employment, and price stability better in the presence of certain institutional arrangements? In this chapter we will focus on several institutional arrangements related to labor and business. The organizational characteristics of both producer groups, as we will learn, have a profound effect on economic performance. Equally important is that performance is affected by the interaction between different economic institutions.

The chapter is organized as follows. The chapter starts by exploring the features of the labor market that make it distinct from other markets. That discussion will launch us into the first section of the chapter which elaborates on several institutional characteristics of labor and business—namely union density, coverage, labor centralization and concentration, and employer coordination. The second section will focus on the effects of different institutional configurations on economic performance. Moreover, this section will examine how the interaction between labor market arrangements and other political economic institutions such as central banks and corporate governance regimes impact performance.

Readers will immediately notice that the chapter devotes a lot of space to labor market institutions. There are several reasons for this focus. First, the different production regimes we find in advanced OECD countries, which have served as engines of growth and prosperity in those countries, are closely related to different labor market arrangements. This is an empirical observation that guides the varieties of capitalism approach. Second, the vast literature on corporatism, which was born out of scholars' efforts to explain cross-national differences in economic performance on the eve of, during, and after the turbulent decade of the 1970s, spotlights the crucial role that labor organization plays in promoting price stability, output growth, and innovation. What these first two points underscore is that industrial relations, directly or via the complementary interaction with other economic institutions, matter to the economy. Finally, as we will discuss in later chapters, labor market conditions impact politics. For example, popular demand for social protection is influenced by the extent to which workers are exposed to the risk of unemployment.

DOI: 10.4324/9780429199462-2

Further, the partisan cycle literature, which we discuss in Chapter 4, reveals that the ability of Left parties in government to achieve their partisan objectives is conditioned by the organization of labor.

Why is the market for labor different from other markets?

A labor market represents all transactions in which workers exchange their talent, experience, and physical effort for a wage or salary paid by their employers. Labor markets vary in terms of scope. For example, the market for lawn care is local, whereas the market for teachers or accountants is national and even global. Labor markets also differ with respect to competition level. The market for full-time university professors in the United States is highly competitive given that there are limited openings in any given year for a growing pool of freshly minted doctoral graduates. We find the opposite in the market for produce harvesters or for specialized welders—employers in the agriculture or construction industry struggle to fill these types of jobs.

Another way in which labor markets differ has to do with the level of skills and training that is needed to participate in them and their corresponding wage rates. For example, employment in the labor market for pediatric anesthesiologists—a specialty in the medical field that is highly compensated—follows eight years of university education (four of which is spent in a medical program), four years of medical residency, one year in a fellowship program, and passage of the general and pediatric anesthesiology board exams. On the other hand, because employment in the janitorial services market does not require specialized skills, meaning more people are qualified to participate in that labor market, average earnings are much lower.

The fact that one's labor service is being exchanged for money over a period of time makes labor markets unique from other markets. Bowman (2014) identifies three distinct characteristics regarding the commodity of labor. First, because your labor is an integral part of who you are—your dignity, sense of self-worth, financial well-being hinges on it—the market for labor cannot operate without protections that uphold basic human rights. As Bowman (ibid: 172) observes, "unlike other commodities, labor is not produced to sell for a profit, nor can it be discarded or stored when it becomes less valuable on the market." For those reasons, the intervention of the government is required to ensure workplace safety, prevent exploitative work practices, and provide social welfare benefits to cushion workers against market dislocations.

Another distinct characteristic of the labor market is that the interaction between employees and employers exhibits properties commonly associated with the principal-agent model we discussed in the first chapter. To deal with the problem of agency loss, employers can use negative inducements such as demotions, pay reductions for lateness, or dismissal in the event of consistent underperformance. Positive inducements such as bonuses, recognition, promotions, and promise of long-term employment are likely to go a long way in motivating workers to meet their employers' expectations. Inducements like these not only motivate workers to fulfill their duties but also inspire creativity, loyalty, and improve productivity.

A third feature that distinguishes the market for labor is that it is primarily a buyer's market. If it were a seller's market, workers (as sellers of labor services) would get their preferred compensation and other employment terms. Employers would go out of their way to entice people to work for them. Instead, most employees in labor markets find themselves having to accept the employment terms offered out of fear that someone else will end up with the job if they do not accept them. Further, what makes employers' power unique is that it is leveraged to command people to do something—such as providing labor services within specific hours of the day or execute specific tasks on a given day. Contrast this form of market power with a situation in which a customer seeking to buy window shades threatens to go to a competing merchant if she does not get a deeper discount from the current vendor. That vendor (the seller) does not have to give the customer such a discount if it means a financial loss for the business. That ability to walk away with minimal consequences to the seller of window shades rarely exists for employees in the labor market. If workers do not follow their employers' commands, dismissal is inevitable and with it comes the loss of income.

It is because of these features of the labor market that workers since the beginning of the industrial era have organized themselves in order to advance and defend their interests. The organizational strength of labor has played an instrumental role in enabling workers to secure more equitable terms of employment, to elect labor-friendly political parties, and to coordinate with employers on issues such as training and product development. In the next sections, we will explore various institutional characteristics of labor and employers and discuss how economic performance has been influenced in part by the interaction between labor and firms.

Institutional features of labor and employers

Union density and coverage

Unions help workers promote and defend their interest in the economy and in the public policy sphere. One of the central roles of trade unions has been to represent workers in collective bargaining negotiations with employers. Industrial relations institutions shape both the process and outcomes of those negotiations. Here, we will focus on four institutional characteristics that industrial relations scholars have found to have important effects on unions' political power and collective bargaining capacity over wages and working conditions—namely, union density, centralization, concentration, and bargaining coverage.

Union density refers to the share of the working age population that belongs to a union. In table 2.1, union density is measured more narrowly insofar as omitting individuals who are retired, independent workers, students, and unemployed from total union membership. The size of union membership is often used as a yardstick to measure the power of labor for it captures the ability of unions to organize workers in the labor market and signals their capacity to mobilize workers into collective political action.

A look at union density between the 1960s and 1990s reveals three general trends (Wallerstein and Western 2008). First, countries clustered around three groups,

TABLE 2.1 Institutional features of labor markets

	Union Density			**Wage Coordination**			**Bargaining Level**			**Bargaining Coverage**		
	1980s	2010s	Change	1980s	2010s	Change	1980s	2010s	Change	1980s	2010s	Change
Nordic	*71.5*	*62.3*	*−9.2*	*3.9*	*4.0*	*0.1*	*4.0*	*3.5*	*−0.5*	*80.5*	*82.1*	*1.7*
Denmark	77.4	69.0	−8.4	3.9	4.0	0.1	3.9	3.0	−0.9	82.5	79.3	−3.2
Finland	69.9	66.1	−3.8	3.6	4.0	0.4	4.0	4.1	0.1	77.3	86.5	9.2
Norway	57.4	51.7	−5.7	4.2	4.0	−0.2	4.0	4.0	0.0	72.5	72.7	0.2
Sweden	81.2	62.3	−18.9	4.0	4.0	0.0	4.2	3.0	−1.2	89.5	90 .0	0.5
Continental	*25.7*	*15.7*	*−10.0*	*3.3*	*3.3*	*0.0*	*3.1*	*3.0*	*−0.1*	*76.2*	*74.1*	*−2.1*
France	14.4	8.0	−6.4	1.6	2.0	0.4	3.0	3.0	0.0	87.1	98.2	11.1
Germany	34.2	17.8	−16.4	4.0	4.0	0.0	3.0	3.0	0.0	85.0	57.9	−27.1
Netherlands	28.8	18.2	−10.6	3.5	4.0	0.5	3.2	3.0	−0.2	82.7	83.6	0.9
Switzerland	25.2	18.7	−6.5	4.0	3.0	−1.0	3.0	3.0	0.0	50.0	56.7	6.7
Anglo	*36.7*	*20.4*	*−16.3*	*1.8*	*1.3*	*−0.6*	*2.1*	*1.3*	*−0.9*	*55.3*	*32.1*	*−23.1*
Australia	46.2	16.0	−30.2	3.2	2.0	−1.2	3.7	2.0	−1.7	83.9	59.2	−24.1
Canada	34.7	29.6	−5.1	1.5	1.0	−0.5	1.0	1.0	0.0	37.5	28.6	−8.9
United Kingdom	47.2	25.1	−22.1	1.0	1.0	0.0	2.7	1.0	−1.7	78.8	28.6	−50.2
United States	18.5	10.8	−7.7	1.0	1.0	0.0	1.0	1.0	0.0	21.0	12.0	−9.0

Note: averages calculated by the author; averages for the 2010s cover up to 2015 or 2016.

Sources: Visser (2019) for the data on union density, bargaining level, and bargaining coverage; Brady et al. (2020) for the data on wage coordination.

distinguished by their level of union density. The Nordic countries maintained the highest levels of union density. For example, in the early 1980s over two-thirds of the active, dependent, and employed labor force was unionized in Denmark, Finland, and Sweden. Australia, Canada, Germany, the Netherlands, and the United Kingdom had union density rates ranging between 30% and 50%. France, Switzerland, and the United States had union density rates below 30%.

Another trend is that union density rates began to diverge starting in the 1960s. Wallerstein and Western (2008: 214) observe that unionization "varied in a small band between about 30% and 60%" in the 1950s, but by the 1980s the dispersion "had increased to 70 percentage points." While union density rose in Canada and the United Kingdom and all the Nordic countries, unionization on average either remained stable or declined in the other eight countries between the 1960s and 1980s. Whereas the gap between Sweden's and France's union density rates was 46 percentage points in the 1960s, it increased to 67 points in the 1980s due to the significant rise in unionization in Sweden.

The third pattern has to do with the decline of union density since the 1980s. Every country experienced dwindling unionization between the 1980s and 2010s. The largest declines occurred primarily in medium-density countries such as Australia, Germany, the Netherlands, and the United Kingdom, although Sweden also witnessed a 19-percentage point drop in its density rate during that time frame. In contrast, the smallest declines were seen across all three union density groups—specifically, Canada, Finland, France, Norway, and Switzerland.

Why is union density higher in some countries?

Scholars have focused on different factors to account for the cross-national differences in trade union membership. Three political-institutional factors in particular have received a lot of attention—namely, Left government incumbency, union-controlled unemployment insurance, and institutionalized channels of union representation (Ebbinghaus and Visser 1999; Rothstein 1992; Wallerstein and Western 2008). In the postwar era, a mutually reinforcing dynamic existed between industrial workers and Left parties. On the one hand, organized labor was the core constituency of labor or social democratic parties. The electoral victories of Left parties throughout Europe were achieved thanks to the mobilizational strength of unions. On the other hand, labor's close link with left-wing governments, as Lange and Garrett (1985: 798) observe, gave "greater assurance that labor's interests [would] be politically guarded." Countries with longer durations of Left governments usually have had more union-friendly public policies. Importantly, studies have found that the association between union strength and Left government has become weaker over time. The Left-labor alliance that proved instrumental in expanding unionism in the first three decades of the postwar period has gradually unraveled since the 1980s. One factor that has caused this relates to the decision by many Left parties to reposition themselves in order to appeal to middle-class voters. Another factor is that Left parties have increasingly embraced neoliberal economic policies which have eroded union protections.

Trade union membership has also been affected by the presence of the Ghent system of unemployment insurance. The fact that high-union density countries such as Denmark, Finland, and Sweden (as well as Belgium) have had Ghent systems has led some scholars to conclude that "in order to have really strong unions, such a system seems necessary" (Rothstein 1992: 42). Why? In the Ghent system, it is unions not government agencies that administer the publicly subsidized unemployment scheme. While union members are usually automatically enrolled in the unemployment benefit scheme, non-members must visit a union office to sign up for it. As Rothstein (ibid: 41) notes, the fact that "unions can make it difficult for nonunion members to obtain the insurance" serves as an effective material incentive to become union members.

The Ghent system has also bolstered unions' control of the supply of labor by enabling union officials to determine what constitutes suitable jobs for unemployed workers. This means that unemployment benefit recipients are not forced to accept jobs that do not match recipients' skills or that require relocation or, importantly, that pay below union-set wage rates. While critics have claimed that such protections create "rigidities" in the labor market by making it more difficult to fill job vacancies, proponents assert that the regulation of competition among the unemployed is necessary to prevent them from "underbidding" union rates (Rothstein 1992: 41; Wallerstein and Western 2008: 216).

The literature also finds that cross-national differences in union strength are attributed to whether institutional mechanisms that promote union interests in wage negotiations and at the workplace exist. For example, unionization levels tend to be higher where collective bargaining between unions and employers occurs at the national level. Centralized bargaining, the argument goes, helps reduce opposition to unionization from employers in non-union workplaces since they are subject to the same collective wage agreement as unionized firms (Wallerstein and Western 2008). We will discuss the concept of centralization of collective bargaining later in the chapter.

An empirical study by Ebbinghaus and Visser (1999) finds that unions are stronger in workplaces that have union dominated works councils and that operate under closed-shop arrangements. While access to workplaces enhances unions' capacity to recruit and retain members, closed-shops are a means to enforce union membership. Works councils grant workers codetermination rights—namely, consultative, information, and co-decision rights—at the workplace level, which enable them to participate in matters relating to human resource management (such as scheduling, recruitment, and dismissal), work organization, and training and retraining. Whereas codetermination rights in Scandinavian countries have been vested in unions as part of collective bargaining agreements, in continental European political economies such rights are not "exclusively guaranteed" to union organizations, therefore establishing a separate or " 'non-union' based channel for worker representation and consultation in firms" (Ebbinghaus and Visser 1999: 144). Thus, although works councils are found in workplaces above a certain size across Europe, codetermination channels have been found to bolster union density when they are dominated by unions.

The decline of unions

The erosion of union strength since the 1980s can be attributed in part to changes in the three political-institutional factors we examined above and to structural factors such as postindustrialism and technological change. Because Left parties have become less dependent on the support of organized labor, they have become freer to deviate from pro-union positions. Rueda (2006) finds that after Britain's Labour Party separated from unions in the early 1990s, the New Labour adopted employment promotion policies that trade unions had largely opposed in the past. From the perspective of union "insiders," active labor market policies undermined their job protections by introducing more labor market competition.

Some scholars have linked union decline to the electoral losses of Left parties and the concurrent rise of Right parties. Western's (1997) study suggests that the erosion of union strength tends to accelerate after leftist parties lose parliamentary elections. Throughout Europe, many of the reforms that have adversely affected unions, such as those relating to industrial relations and the Ghent system of unemployment insurance, have occurred when Right parties have been in power. In their analysis of the transformation of industrial relations in Europe, Baccaro and Howell (2011) detail how the British Conservative Party's victory in late 1979, led by Margaret Thatcher, set the stage in the 1980s for an all-out deregulatory offensive against the country's labor organizations. Those measures had a devastating effect on organized labor.

Moreover, the Ghent system of unemployment insurance in Denmark and Sweden underwent major changes soon after the electoral victories of center-right coalitions in both countries in 2001 and 2006, respectively. In Sweden's case, the government's decision to raise the fees to enlist in union unemployment funds, raised the cost of retaining union membership because union dues include fund fees.

According to Kjellberg's (2009) analysis, that reform resulted in a 6-percentage point drop in union density by 2008.

Another strand of scholarship associates the decline of unionization with technological innovation and changes in occupational structures. At the heart of structural accounts is the argument that the distributional effects of the transition to the postindustrial era have become increasingly stacked against semi-skilled production workers, the core pillar of trade unionism during the post-WWII Fordist era. The postindustrial era (from the 1970s to the present) is distinct from the Fordist era in three important ways. First, whereas the Fordist era centered around the mass production of standardized goods, the post-Fordist era has been marked by the expansion of the service sector. Second, while Fordist production pivoted on the complementarity between low-skilled labor and mechanized production, the knowledge economy depends on high-skilled workers who complement information and communication technologies (ITCs). Finally, the globalization of production and trade, coupled with the automation of routine production tasks, have hollowed out the manufacturing sectors in advanced political economies. As a result, the share of workers employed in manufacturing today is much lower than it was during the Fordist era (Boix 2019).

These structural changes have challenged unions' abilities to recruit and maintain cohesion among members. First, the erosion of unionization has been occurring against the backdrop of declining manufacturing, which, aside from the public sector, has been unions' main locus of recruitment. Between 1975 and 2007, manufacturing employment as a percentage of the working-age population dropped from 21.8 to 9.3 in Britain, from 16.3 to 9.4 in Denmark, from 17.6 to 9.8 in France, and from 21.4 to 10.9 in Sweden (Boix 2019: 134). Second, the service sector has been more difficult to unionize than the manufacturing sector because it is much more differentiated. It encompasses high-paying, knowledge-intensive industries such as business services and financial intermediation and low-paying, lower-skill industries such as hotels and restaurants, wholesale and retail trade, and personal and protective services. Another point is that the diffusion of ICTs has put a wage premium on general, transferable high-skills such as computing, analytics, accounting, and management, but has depressed the demand for low-skilled labor. This polarizing dynamic in labor markets has undermined the feasibility of wage solidarity, a key objective of industrial unions.

IN FOCUS BOX 2.1 BARGAINING COVERAGE AND DEUNIONIZATION

The decline in unionization, as many industrial relations scholars have noted, has not brought about an equivalent erosion in bargaining coverage. Bargaining (or union) coverage—which refers to the number of workers covered by wage bargaining agreements as a share of all workers with the right to bargaining—is higher than union density as table 2.1 shows. Moreover, cross-national changes in bargaining coverage since the 1980s do not point to a common downward trend. In fact, Finland, France, the Netherlands, Norway, Sweden, and Switzerland experienced coverage rate increases between the 1980s and 2010s. The countries that did see a drop in coverage rates tended to cluster into two groups. Steep decreases in coverage occurred in initially high coverage countries such as the United

Kingdom (dropped by 50.2 percentage points), Germany (27.1), and Australia (24.1). Modest decreases took place in initially low coverage countries such as the Canada and the United States, and in Denmark, which had a high coverage rate in the 1980s.

Figure 2.1, which plots average union density against average bargaining coverage in the 2000s, reveals that there was a great deal of dispersion in coverage rates among low-union density (below 35%) countries. Some countries such as France and the Netherlands have coverage rates that are more than four times their union density rates. The gap between density and coverage is attributed to two main reasons. One reason is that in many countries, employers' associations require that the firms affiliated with them apply the terms of collectively negotiated wage agreements. Further, in the case of France and, to a certain extent the Netherlands, the gap can be attributed to the fact that governments mandate that all firms in an industry adhere to the wage-setting terms that leading trade unions and employers' associations have collectively bargained.

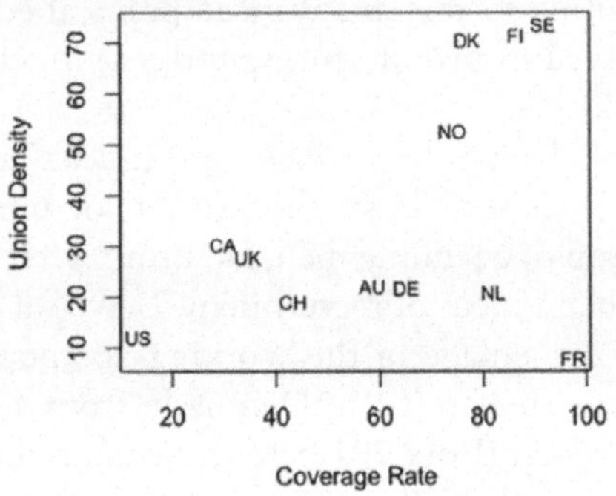

FIGURE 2.1 Average net union density and average coverage rate, 2000s

Source: Table 2.1.

Centralization

Peak-level, economy-wide wage bargaining has been a mainstay of the Nordic political economies in the postwar period. The presence of encompassing unions and employer peak associations has been an effective antidote to the collective action problem that commonly foils wage moderation efforts when unions and employers are disorganized. As we will examine shortly, this feature of industrial relations is linked to strong macroeconomic performance precisely because of its ability to contain wage militancy.

There are two ways to understand centralization. It can be thought of in terms of the level at which wage bargaining between unions and employers takes place. Centralization can also refer to the degree of authority that peak associations exercise over their affiliates and how much authority those affiliates have over local organizations. These two measures may not coincide with each other. For example, a collective agreement negotiated at the national or multi-industry level may not be binding on all workplaces covered by the agreement. This can occur if the negotiators seek to give companies and local unions flexibility in the implementation of the agreement, a trend seen in Nordic countries in recent decades. Table 2.1 reports data on bargaining levels. Scores between four and five mean that bargaining takes place primarily at the multi-industry or national level. A score of three means that bargaining occurs predominantly at the sector or industry level. A score of one signifies that bargaining occurs at the company level, while a score of two means that bargaining shifts between sector and company levels.

Wage bargaining can occur at the national or central level between the peak associations representing labor and employers, which wield some authority over affiliates at the industry and local levels. In the Nordic countries, wage-setting was centralized for the most part until the 1980s. In Sweden between 1956 and 1982, the union confederation, *Landsorganisationen* (LO), and the employers' organization, *Svenska Arbetsgivareföreningen* (SAF), negotiated non-binding, but "decisive" national settlements that shaped subsequent industry- and firm-level wage negotiations affecting private sector blue-collar workers. Although Sweden's "three-tiered system of wage bargaining" was centralized enough to enable employers' and trade union organizations to coordinate their bargaining actions, the system was also designed to allow for flexibility in the implementation of peak level settlements by lower-level bargaining units. As Pontusson and Swenson (1996: 232) observe, "the peak agreements allocated aggregate [wage] increases across sectors, whereas the intrasectoral distribution [that is, setting the level of wage increase among firms within industries] could proceed more or less as the parties to industry-level and firm-level bargaining wished."

In addition to their multi-industry wage-setting system, the Nordic countries are distinguished from other advanced political economies for having strong union confederations. Based on data from 1950 to 1992, Finland (until the early 1970s), Norway, and Sweden scored high in terms of the degree to which union confederations exercised statutory authority over their affiliates. For example, their peak level union confederations had their own strike funds, had veto power over strikes by affiliates ("peace clauses") and over wage agreements signed by affiliates (though not in Sweden), and participated in bargaining rounds at the industry or lower levels (Golden et al. 2008).

Below the central level, wage-setting can take place at the sectoral or industry level. Exemplified by Germany, this style of wage-setting has been commonly used in continental Europe in the postwar period. In Germany, sectoral wage bargaining has taken place at the regional level, with national unions organized around industries playing a central role in wage-setting. The main union confederation, the *Deutscher Gewerkschaftsbund* (DGB), wields no statutory authority on matters relating to the bargaining demands of its industry-based union affiliates. In the postwar period, it was common practice for the collective wage settlements reached between *IG Metall*, the metalworkers union which represents workers in the automobile, engineering, and steel industries, and *Gesamtmetall*, the association representing employers in these industries, to be adopted by other industries. Further, the sectoral agreements that were aligned with the collective agreement struck in the metalworking sector were binding on all firms within those sectors. In short, these features of industrial relations created some degree of centralization in Germany's wage-setting system.

Finally, wage bargaining can be highly decentralized, occurring at the local or company level. In Canada, the United Kingdom (since the early 1980s), the United States, and to a large extent Australia since the 1990s, unions typically bargain with individual companies. Moreover, peak-level union confederations in most of these countries wield no statutory authority over their affiliates. In contrast to its Nordic counterparts, the American Federation of Labor and Congress of Industrial Organizations (AFL-CIO) has no veto power over the actions of its affiliated unions such as the United Automobile Workers union and shop-level organizations.

Changes in wage-setting since the 1980s

Wage-setting decentralization has occurred since the early 1980s in all countries that had adopted in previous decades either peak-level or sectoral/industry level collective bargaining. In the Nordic countries, the general decentralization trend has involved shifting wage determination from primarily the peak- to industry-level and rendering peak-level agreements functionally minimalist. In continental countries, there has been a general pattern toward adding flexibility in the implementation of industry-level agreements by individual firms, which has been facilitated by the inclusion of "opening clauses" in sectoral collective agreements. In the Anglo countries, the pattern has been to decollectivize firm- and plant-level wage-settings, enabling employers to unilaterally determine wage and non-wage matters at the workplace.

Several arguments have been advanced to account for the varying degrees of wage-setting centralization across advanced OECD countries and for decentralization since the 1980s. Here, we will focus on three types of arguments—economic, partisan, and distributional. The economic argument holds that centralization enables labor and employers to reach wage settlement outcomes that have positive macroeconomic effects. Drawing on insights developed by Olson (1982), the more encompassing organized labor is, the greater the incentive for union leaders to take account of the effects of their actions on the economy. The Olsonian logic is based on the premise that when a large share of workers is organized and represented through centralized labor organizations, union leaders moderate their wage demands out of the concern that if they push up wages too much in the short run, higher inflation will follow, ultimately leading to lower real wages and higher unemployment.

The notion that centralized wage-setting incentivizes labor to internalize the externalities of wage militancy (such as wage-push inflation and higher unemployment) proved to be a powerful motive for the support of centralization by labor and employers in the several trade-oriented European economies in the first half of the twentieth century. In Norway and Sweden, for example, workers and employers in the export-oriented metalworking sector threw their support behind centralized wage bargaining in order to constrain the wage militancy of construction workers who were sheltered from international competition. Because many in the construction occupation worked in the export sector, high construction wages pushed up labor cost in that sector. To offset higher labor costs and maintain employment levels, metalworkers had to accept wage reductions.

To deal with this problem, "Basic Agreements" between labor and employer organizations were reached in Norway and Sweden in 1935 and 1938, respectively. These agreements laid out general rules for collective bargaining and strengthened the authority of union confederations over union affiliates particularly on the question of striking. By the second half of the 1950s, both countries had established centralized wage bargaining. It became common practice for economy-wide wage increases to be based on wage growth in the export sector. This system essentially tamed the bargaining actions of construction workers. As Moene and Wallerstein (2008d: 384) point out, "in gaining control over the wage demands of workers in the non-traded-goods sector, metalworkers and their employers were able to force all workers to share the burden of lowering wage costs in the export sector."

The economic argument to centralization not only holds that centralization is an effective means to achieve wage restraint, it also can be harnessed to achieve economy-wide efficiency gains by way of solidaristic wage bargaining. In an effort to reduce wage disparities, solidaristic bargaining seeks to reduce wage differences between high- and low-skilled workers across industries. To achieve this, the wages of low-skilled workers are raised faster than the wages of workers in higher skill groups. While unions have championed solidaristic bargaining out of their commitment to equality, employers have at times supported this practice for economic reasons. Swedish union economists Gösta Rehn and Rudolf Meidner explained, in the early 1950s, how wage compression could enhance efficiency: wage solidarism "helps structural transformation of the economy by squeezing out low productivity, low-wage jobs and making room for firms with good prospects of development" (quoted in Ibsen and Thelen 2017: 413). According to the Rehn-Meidner logic, raising the labor cost of low-skilled workers would force less efficient companies to rationalize production lest they go out of business, while restraining the wages of high-skilled workers would enable competitive companies to funnel more resources to innovation. In sum, wage compression can boost national productivity and facilitate gradual economy-wide wage increases (Moene and Wallerstein 2008d).

If centralization made economic sense for labor and employers in the Nordic countries and the Low countries such as the Netherlands in the postwar period, then why did that consensus dissolve after the 1970s? From employers' perspectives, wage solidarity was feasible so long as there was consistent demand for less-skilled workers, as there was during the Fordist era. In that context, it made sense for organized business to coordinate their bargaining actions with low-wage unions. However, the shift to knowledge-intensive activities and, more generally, the diffusion of computing and information technologies has raised the demand for high-skilled labor while lowering the need for low-skilled workers. The high skill-bias of recent economic changes has pressured employers to raise the wages of skilled workers and to increasingly rely on automation as a substitute for unskilled workers. Employers now prefer to bargain with high-wage and low-wage unions separately.

Moreover, since the 1980s organized labor has become increasingly divided on the merits of centralized bargaining. Union solidarity has suffered as high-skilled workers in the industrial sector have allied with white-collar and professional workers against the practice of reducing inter-occupational wage differences, which continues to be advocated by blue-collar confederations. In addition, union confederations engaged in wage negotiations have been more influenced by the demands of unions in sheltered sectors such as the public service sector who are more inclined to push for higher wages than the traditional blue-collar unions in export sectors. In short, as unions have become more heterogeneous, their willingness to engage in wage coordination has waned.

The partisan perspective on centralization holds that leftist parties have played an accommodative role by incentivizing both labor and employer organizations to coordinate via centralized collective bargaining. As Cameron (1984), Alvarez et al. (1991), and others have pointed out, organized labor's willingness to coordinate with employers has been influenced in part by the expected payoffs of public policies. Specifically, Left governments have tended to pursue public policies that have encouraged voluntary labor restraint. Often depicted as a strategic political trade-off, encompassing labor organizations commit to wage moderation and foregoing the use of strikes in exchange for the public provision of generous social benefits and services.

A similar dynamic has emerged between Left governments and employers. Employers' willingness to coordinate with labor hinges on the public policy benefits they expect to obtain in return. If a generous welfare state were financed primarily through taxes on capital, that burden would negatively affect employers' cost-benefit calculus of coordinating with labor. Therefore, as Beramendi and Rueda (2014: 256) observe, "employers . . . commit to stable investment and long-term growth in return for the social democratic government's promise not to tax their benefits to finance the welfare state." There is evidence showing that countries with higher levels of centralized coordination—which is also associated with more Left governments—place a larger share of the cost of funding social programs on labor (Cusack and Beramendi 2006).

Partisan explanations provide some insights on why decentralization has occurred in recent decades. One argument is that the electoral victories of rightist parties across Europe have changed the political dynamic that once facilitated strategic exchanges between government and labor. Alvarez et al. (1991) have argued that rightist governments are less inclined to compromise with labor because their policy preferences can be achieved largely without labor's support. Another point is that Left governments in recent decades have moved away from policy positions to which they previously committed in order to secure labor's consent. That consent has been difficult to obtain as Left governments have advocated deregulation, welfare retrenchment, and fiscal austerity.

The distributional argument holds that the preexisting level of inequality in a country influences the prospects of adopting centralized collective bargaining. In their study examining the claim that centralized bargaining leads to lower inequality, Scheve and Stasavage (2009) find that inequality was already declining when centralization was adopted in Denmark, the Netherlands, and Sweden. According to the distributional argument, that historical sequence—inequality reduction preceding the establishment of centralized bargaining—is not coincidental.

The distributional logic can be expounded as follows. In a situation of high inequality, the wage compression that occurs due to centralization means that affluent workers miss out on the extra earnings they would have gained without centralization. Moreover, it also means that they must accept a higher "top up" (increment) on the earnings of poorer workers. As a result, affluent workers are better off in an uncoordinated system, while downscale workers are better off in a coordinated system. As Beramendi and Rueda (2014: 254) observe, because inequality worsens the distributional trade-offs of centralization, "there is no incentive for the wealthier sector of labor to join or remain in the confederation." A key takeaway of this argument is that as wage inequality continues to increase in countries such as Denmark and Sweden, efforts to coordinate bargaining actions between higher- and lower-wage unions are more likely to fail.

Concentration

The coordination of bargaining actions between union and employer organizations hinges as much on concentration as it does on centralization (Golden 1993). By level of concentration, we are referring to how the number of unions involved in the wage-setting process affects the collective ability of unions to overcome competition among them. The logic of concentration, as Golden (1993: 441) explains, is "that where unions are few in number and do not compete for members (i.e., where union monopoly is high), they will be better able to coordinate their wage behavior in ways ultimately beneficial to the national economy."

There are two ways of measuring concentration. Interconfederal concentration refers to the number of peak-level union confederations and the proportion of total union members represented by each confederation. Intraconfederal concentration focuses on the number of national unions within each union confederation and their relative share of union members. The term wage coordination, which appears in table 2.1, captures the degree to which unions and employers harmonize their bargaining efforts, which is facilitated by higher levels of concentration. Higher coordination scores mean that a few union and employers' confederations set patterns, guidelines, or enforceable agreements that apply across multiple industries or to the entire national economy. Lower coordination scores signify that there is little deliberate harmonization in the wage bargaining process, resulting in a large number of different wage agreements dotting industries and sectors.

Table 2.2 provides data on interconfederal concentration in Canada, Germany, and Sweden. The three largest trade confederations are listed, and their shares of the total union membership are reported. According to Golden et al. (2008) the three

TABLE 2.2 Interconfederal concentration

	1985	1990	1995	2000	2005	2010	2015
Sweden							
LO	60.0	57.7	56.1	52.6	48.7	44.1	41.7
TCO	31.9	33.0	33.0	34.5	33.4	34.4	36.9
SACO/ SACO-LR	7.5	8.5	10.0	12.9	15.4	17.8	18.4
Germany							
DGB	80.6	81.0	81.8	77.8	78.6	77.3	76.6
DBB	8.3	8.1	9.0	12.0	14.8	15.7	16.3
DAG*	5.2	5.8	4.4	4.6	—	—	—
CGB	—	—	—	—	3.4	3.5	3.4
Canada							
CLC	57.8	58.6	63.2	72.6	72.0	70.0	69.0
CTCC/CSN	5.8	5.2	6.2	6.3	6.4	6.8	7.0
CFL**	5.7	5.2	4.2	—	—	—	—
CEQ/CSQ	—	—	—	2.8	2.8	2.7	2.7

Notes: *DAG merged with DGB in 2001. **CFL merged with CLC in the late-1990s

Source: Visser (2019)

countries each exemplify unique trends that are seen across rich OECD countries. In Denmark, Finland, France, Norway, and Sweden, interconfederal concentration has declined since the 1950s; in particular, the leading blue-collar confederations in these countries have lost union members while white-collar and professional workers confederations have gained members. This pattern is clearly demonstrated in Sweden. The LO, the country's main blue-collar confederation, has seen its share of union members drop from 84% in 1950 to 41.7% in 2015, while TCO and SACO, which are confederations of professional workers, have gained ground leading to a more balanced (less concentrated) distribution of members among the three confederations. Clearly, the LO is a shadow of its former self; a reality attributed to its failure to adapt to the diversification of Sweden's occupational landscape.

Another pattern is illustrated by what has happened in Germany, the Netherlands, Switzerland, and the United Kingdom. In these countries, interconfederal concentration has not changed much from the early postwar years to the 2010s. Their main occupational confederations' high membership shares have been resilient largely because the composition of their union affiliates diversified across an expanding occupational landscape. In Germany, the DGB has represented more than three-quarters of total union members since the early 1950s. Its union affiliates represent workers in sectors such as metalworking; education and science; mining, chemicals, and energy; police; and various white-collar occupations. Although DBB, which represents public service and white-collar workers, nearly doubled its share between 1985 and 2015, the size of the membership gap between it and DGB has remained quite large.

In Canada and the United States, interconfederal concentration has increased since the early 1950s as a result of mergers between rival confederations and the inclusion of new unions serving non-manufacturing occupations (Golden et al. 2008). The Canadian Labour Congress (CLC) was created in 1955 when the Trades and Labour Congress of Canada (TLC)—a confederation representing trade-base unions—and the Canadian Congress of Labour (CCL)—a confederation representing workplace-based unions—merged. Over time, the CLC's scope of union affiliates expanded to include public sector workers, teachers, nurses, and other social services workers. As a result, the CLC's share of total union members increased from 38% in the early 1950s to 69% in 2015.

The Herfindahl index of union concentration is used to measure intraconfederal concentration. Simply put, it tells us the probability that two randomly selected members of a union confederation are associated with the same affiliate. In general, intraconfederal concentration has increased in all 12 countries since the 1970s, as shown in table 2.3. This is due to the fact that, as Golden et al. (2008) remark, "unions have rationalized their organizations by reducing their number of affiliates and concentrating more members in their largest affiliates." However, this general upward trend in concentration has occurred against different backdrops. The Anglo countries have consistently maintained lower concentration levels because a large number of unions have been affiliated with the largest union confederations. For example, between 105 and 70 Canadian unions were affiliated with the CLC from the early 1980s to the late 2000s. Britain's Trades Union Congress (TUC) also had a similar intraconfederal composition.

Concentration levels in Germany, the Netherlands, and Switzerland have increased since the 1980s. Germany's DGB saw its number of union affiliates drop

TABLE 2.3 Herfindahl index of union concentration

	1970s	1980s	1990s	2000s
Nordic	*0.106*	*0.118*	*0.134*	*0.154*
Denmark	0.131	0.132	0.136	0.165
Finland	0.083	0.090	0.098	0.123
Norway	0.091	0.097	0.136	0.160
Sweden	0.120	0.151	0.167	0.166
Continental	*0.125*	*0.148*	*0.161*	*0.221*
France	0.076	0.108	0.124	0.125
Germany	0.159	0.160	0.157	0.249
Netherlands	0.099	0.155	0.185	0.261
Switzerland	0.164	0.167	0.177	0.250
Anglo	*0.033*	*0.039*	*0.059*	*0.077*
Australia	0.019	0.019	0.032	0.065
Canada	0.031	0.048	0.081	0.073
United Kingdom	0.061	0.062	0.088	0.114
United States	0.020	0.025	0.033	0.054

Source: Visser (2019)

from 16 to eight in 2000, but the share of union members in the largest union affiliates suffered little loss as a result. As for the NVV/FNV, the Netherlands' largest union confederation, its membership share increased while it reduced its number of affiliates. Finally, the Nordic countries and France have exhibited concentration levels that range between continental and Anglo averages. Rationalization within Sweden's LO brought the number of affiliates down from 24 in the early 1980s to 15 by the end of the 2000s.

Employers' associations

In addition to being featured centrally in the varieties of capitalism approach, the role of employers' associations figures prominently in the contemporary research on labor market institutions (e.g., Golden et al. 2008; Calmfors and Driffill 1988; Soskice 1990), social democracy (e.g., Moene and Wallerstein 2008d; Swenson 1991), and corporatism (e.g., Martin and Swank 2012; Thelen 1994). At the center of the "bringing capital back in" argument is the idea that employers have played a protagonist role in facilitating centralized coordination with labor. This cross-class alliance has been instrumental in delivering positive-sum economic gains such as higher employment, lower inflation, investment in fixed and human capital, and higher productivity rates.

Why have employers in Denmark, Germany, Norway, and Sweden been willing to coordinate their endeavors with each other and with labor? Swenson (1991) has argued that employer organizations have provided critical support for wage centralization and wage compression. This is an argument that runs counter to the power-resources claim which holds that employers reluctantly adopted centralization in the face of union power and pressure from Left governments. From the perspective of employers in these four countries, participation in encompassing business organizations has facilitated sectoral or peak-level collective bargaining with labor.

Collective bargaining has helped deliver wage restraint. Moreover, consistent with the Rehn-Meidner logic, centralization and wage solidarity have encouraged employers to collaborate in upgrading workforce skills in order to improve workplace productivity.

Another reason companies have preferred to work through encompassing employers' associations is that it discourages rent-seeking by individual firms. Participation in such associations incentivizes members to internalize the adverse effects that import protection, subsidies, and market restrictions could have on overall economic performance. By controlling rent-seeking behavior, business groups and their members can focus on promoting collective benefits such as enhancing economic competitiveness and national innovation (Hicks and Kenworthy 1998).

Third, encompassing employers' organizations help remedy free-riding problems among firms especially as it relates to skills development. Because firms fear that competitors might poach their trained workers, the rational instinct is for firms to invest as little as possible in human capital development. This leads to a shortage of workers with specific skills (such as occupational or industry based) and undermines the ability of companies to pursue production strategies that intensively use these skills such as flexible production or diversified quality production. By fostering mutual trust and long-term commitments among members, strong business groups facilitate the collective provision of training and technological transfers.

Finally, membership in encompassing employers' associations has a cognitive effect on their members' outlook of their role in society. As Martin and Swank (2012: 23) point out, this type of association can have that effect by

> educating employers about the benefits of social policies, exposing managers to the ideas of government and labor policy experts, focusing participants' attention on broader concerns, nurturing norms of 'social partnership', and allowing employers to participate and have a say in the formation of public policy.

The result is that employers associated with those organizations are more inclined to commit to long-termism, support private-public coordination, and foster constructive relations with organized labor.

Table 2.4 provides cross-national data relating to three measures of employer coordination developed by Martin and Swank (2012). Employers' organization is an additive index that includes the degree of concentration of employers in peak associations, degree of authority exercised by peak employers' associations, and extent to which peak associations are integrated into the process of national policymaking. The last feature is commonly referred to as tripartite concertation (see Lehmbruch 1984). The index of macrocorporatism combines the employers' organization index, organizational strength of unions (density and degree of peak association authority), and centralization of collective bargaining. Lastly, the sector coordination index adds finance-firms relations (specifically, the relative reliance of industry on bank finance versus equity finance) and degree of inter-firm cooperation relating to employee training, research and development, industrial development, and export marketing strategy. In short, whereas the index of macrocorporatism measures the capacity of organized employers to coordinate with labor and government at the national level, the index of sector coordination focuses on the extent of collaboration among firms and between employers and labor at sectoral or industry levels. Both measures are

TABLE 2.4 Employer coordination

	Employers' Organization Index		**Macrocorporatism Index**		**Sector Coordination Index**	
	Early 1980s	Early 2000s	Early 1980s	Early 2000s	Early 1980s	Early 2000s
Nordic	*0.70*	*0.66*	*0.97*	*0.87*	*0.64*	*0.39*
Denmark	0.23	0.23	0.89	0.87	0.28	0.28
Finland	0.82	0.82	0.63	0.67	1.05	0.72
Norway	0.92	1.04	1.19	1.24	0.62	0.28
Sweden	0.82	0.53	1.15	0.69	0.62	0.28
Continental	*0.23*	*0.24*	*0.07*	*−0.04*	*−0.21*	*0.20*
France	0.02	0.20	−0.44	−0.43	−0.99	−0.06
Germany	0.76	0.76	0.24	0.18	1.05	0.28
Netherlands	0.20	0.05	0.60	0.27	−1.17	0.28
Switzerland	−0.05	−0.05	−0.14	−0.18	0.28	0.28
Anglo	*−0.93*	*−1.01*	*−0.86*	*−1.11*	*−1.39*	*−0.57*
Australia	0.10	0.20	0.29	−0.29	−1.50	−0.57
Canada	−1.94	−1.94	−1.45	−1.46	−1.50	−0.57
United Kingdom	0.05	−0.36	−0.71	−1.10	−1.07	−0.57
United States	−1.94	−1.94	−1.55	−1.58	−1.50	−0.57

Notes: Time series starts at 1987 for Finland, 1994 for France, and 1986 for the United Kingdom and the United States.

Source: Martin and Swank (2012)

somewhat comparable with neocorporatism and firm-level cooperation, an alternative pair of measures developed by Hicks and Kenworthy (1998).

There is a long history of business coordination in the Nordic countries. Although the Nordic countries score relatively high on both macrocorporatist and sectoral coordination indexes, organized business in Denmark, Norway, and Sweden historically has been more invested in national level coordination. As Martin and Swank (2012), Swenson (1991), and others have noted, the fact that encompassing employers' associations emerged in the late 1800s in Denmark and the early decades of the 1900s in Norway and Sweden but not in other countries is partly owed to the fact that employers were compelled to organize themselves in an effort to stabilize industrial relations in the face of intensifying labor activism. On the other hand, organized business in Germany and Switzerland historically has preferred to nurture sectoral coordination. The fragmentation of organized business in the Anglo countries and France has stunted the development of coordination capabilities at the national and sectoral levels.

IN FOCUS BOX 2.2 CHANGES IN WAGE-SETTING IN SWEDEN AND GERMANY

Sweden's political economy underwent major changes starting in the 1980s. Employers in the export sector, especially those in the engineering industry, grew increasingly dissatisfied with centralized solidaristic bargaining for two reasons. One reason is that the centralized wage-setting system became too rigid over time because unions representing low-wage and public-sector workers succeeded in obtaining greater reductions in inter-occupational wage differences. In Sweden's postwar wage determination regime, employers could adapt solidaristic agreements on pay distribution increases based on considerations of productivity, international competition, and manpower recruitment needs. By the 1970s, this flexibility was lost as several unions doubled down on reducing "wage drift" within firms and across occupations. That resulted in wage-push inflation and onerous constraints on managerial prerogatives (Pontusson and Swenson 1996).

The other reason is that the existing pay incentives scheme in solidaristic wage-setting proved unsuitable for post-Fordist production methods. As Pontusson and Swenson explain, to make diversified quality production work, employees had to develop broader and deeper competencies at the worksite. In particular, they had to handle more sophisticated and multi-tasked machinery, improve production methods while reducing inventory costs, and directly participate in the development of new products. The high turnover rate among skilled workers made it difficult for firms to cultivate such competencies. As a result, employers sought to craft company-based pay schemes that incentivized workers to commit long-term, learn firm-specific skills required to operate new technologies, and be more proactive in production-related processes.

By the 1990s, Sweden's collective bargaining arrangements had become so decentralized that it permitted wide firm-level variations in the implementation of industry- and national-level collective agreements. As Baccaro and Howell (2011: 544) observe, these agreements "became thinner and more minimalist . . . permitting wide discretion at the firm level." To be sure, the decentralization witnessed since the 1980s has not resulted in the wholesale dismantling of the traditional collective bargaining infrastructure. In the face of the economic crisis of the early 1990s and rising incidence of strikes, employers and unions, with some pressure from the state, struck several "industrial agreements." These agreements demonstrated that the two producer groups retained the capacity to coordinate their endeavors at the multi-sectoral level.

Whereas Swedish employers sought more wage flexibility by decentralizing coordination, German employers since the 1980s have sought to free themselves from the postwar coordinative institutions. Thelen (2014) has argued that the changes in the German industrial relations landscape are not the result of employer-led assaults against specific institutions. Instead, they are the result of employers not actively seeking to extend sector-level coordinating practices prevalent in manufacturing to the growing services sector and to the eastern part of Germany after unification. This type of change stemming from the unwillingness of key actors to adapt institutions to changing realities is referred to as "drift." Thus, while coordination remains strong in the industrial core, it is much weaker in the services sector and in the east.

Evidence of drift is ubiquitous. Union density in services has remained well below the unionization rate in manufacturing even though employment in the services sector has increased (Thelen 2014: 51–2). The share of workplaces in the private sector with works councils declined from 52.4% in 1981 to under 40% in 2005, depriving labor of an important channel of consultation with management (Baccaro and Howell 2011: 539). More and more employers are opting for ohne Tarifbindung (OT) memberships in employer associations, which frees employers of binding sectoral agreements. Upwards of 75% of employer association membership was OT in Saxony, a region in eastern Germany. The country's apprenticeship training system, which has maintained strong support among employers in the industrial sector, is barely present in the services sector (Culpepper and Thelen 2008: 36). What is more, stark differences have emerged between western and eastern Germany with respect to the practice of apprenticeship training. Far more employers in eastern Germany have opted for out-of-firm training, meaning that firms are less inclined to collectively fund and manage the provision of training. As a result, state-level governments have had to play a larger role in subsidizing apprenticeship (ibid: 38–40).

Macroeconomic performance and economic institutions

What accounts for cross-national differences in macroeconomic performance? Why are some countries able to achieve better economic performance than others? Proponents of the neoliberal economic view are likely to attribute good performance to the flexible operation of labor markets. Where unions are weak, social protections are low, and wage determination is decentralized, the argument goes, the demand and supply of labor operate efficiently leading to optimal economic outcomes. This is the position that the OECD took in a 1994 report titled *The OECD Jobs Study*, which aimed to identify the main causes of Europe's unemployment problems in the 1980s and 1990s.

Alternatively, comparative political economists have associated economic growth, better employment outcomes, and price stability with different aspects of coordinated capitalism. Institutions that facilitate wage moderation, encourage employers to invest in training, and nurture long-term worker-employer relations can generate performance outcomes that are at par with, if not superior to, those achieved in more market-driven economies.

Figuring out which perspective is right is not an easy task. A glance at comparative data on real GDP growth, inflation, and unemployment in table 2.5 suggests that no country or cluster of countries has consistently outperformed others. While the Anglo economies have had on average higher growth rates over the past four decades, it is the continental and Nordic economies, where coordinated capitalism is more prevalent, that have generally performed better with respect to inflation and unemployment. If one were to compare Germany, Sweden, and the United States, one would be hard pressed to declare one of these countries a clear winner. Perhaps there are patterns we are overlooking by just comparing performance cross-nationally and over time. Analyzing the data with the guidance of different theoretical perspectives might help us to detect patterns.

Next, we will review research that probes the link between economic institutions and macroeconomic performance. The presentation will be divided into four subsections, each focusing on different institutional arrangements: wage determination; policies that affect the operation of labor markets such as employment protection laws, and passive and active unemployment benefits; and the interaction between industrial relations and other economic institutions, namely central banks and corporate governance.

Wage determination institutions

Several scholars have explored how different wage-setting features impact economic performance. Most of the attention has been directed at the roles of centralization

TABLE 2.5 Comparative economic performance

	Real GDP Growth				Inflation				Unemployment			
	1980s	1990s	2000s	2010s	1980s	1990s	2000s	2010s	1980s	1990s	2000s	2010s
Nordic	*2.7*	*2.4*	*1.7*	*1.6*	*7.6*	*2.5*	*1.9*	*1.4*	*4.4*	*8.0*	*5.8*	*6.7*
Denmark	1.9	2.5	1.0	1.4	6.9	2.1	2.1	1.4	6.7	6.9	4.6	6.9
Finland	3.6	1.8	2.0	0.7	7.2	2.2	1.7	1.4	4.8	11.9	8.3	8.4
Norway	2.9	3.6	1.8	1.5	8.3	2.5	2.1	2.0	2.8	4.8	3.5	3.7
Sweden	2.3	1.8	2.1	2.8	7.9	3.3	1.5	0.8	3.3	8.3	6.8	7.8
Continental	*2.3*	*2.2*	*1.4*	*1.5*	*4.1*	*2.3*	*1.6*	*0.9*	*5.6*	*6.7*	*6.3*	*6.4*
France	2.8	2.0	1.4	1.1	7.4	1.9	1.7	1.0	7.6	9.7	8.4	9.9
Germany	2.0	2.2	0.8	2.0	2.9	2.6	1.6	1.2	5.8	7.8	8.9	5.3
Netherlands	2.0	3.3	1.6	1.1	2.9	2.4	2.1	1.5	8.4	6.3	4.4	6.2
Switzerland	2.3	1.2	1.9	1.8	3.3	2.3	1.0	−0.2	0.6	2.9	3.5	4.1
Anglo	*3.0*	*2.8*	*2.2*	*2.3*	*6.9*	*2.8*	*2.4*	*1.9*	*8.5*	*8.1*	*5.9*	*6.7*
Australia	3.4	3.2	3.2	2.7	8.4	2.5	3.2	2.2	7.6	8.8	5.5	5.6
Canada	2.9	2.4	2.1	2.3	6.5	2.2	2.1	1.7	9.4	9.6	7.0	7.3
United Kingdom	2.7	2.2	1.8	2.0	7.1	3.3	1.8	2.0	9.5	8.0	5.4	6.8
United States	3.1	3.2	1.8	2.1	5.6	3.0	2.6	1.6	7.3	5.8	5.5	7.2

Note: averages calculated by the author. The averages for 2010s cover data up to 2016.

Source: Armingeon (2018)

and coordination of wage bargaining. Earlier research exploring the effects of labor market institutions posited that a negative and linear association existed between centralization of wage bargaining and economic outcomes (Cameron 1984; Lange and Garrett 1985). This strand of literature argued that when wage bargaining occurs in fragmented, decentralized, union-dominated settings, each union is inclined to ignore the externalities of their wage demands. "Leapfrogging" is likely to occur in such a context. That is, each union seeks a wage settlement that exceeds the pay increments that other unions in a related industry secured in their own negotiations. This dynamic tends to result in wage-push inflation and eventually higher unemployment. On the other hand, when unions operate within encompassing bargaining institutions, leapfrogging is avoided and peak negotiators are more inclined to internalize the consequences of their wage demands, resulting in lower rates of unemployment and inflation. In short, more centralization is associated with better economic outcomes.

In a much-cited paper, Calmfors and Driffill (1988) challenge the logic of the linear model just described. They contend that an inverted U-shape relationship exists between wage bargaining centralization and unemployment. A key assumption underpinning their argument is the notion that elasticity of demand declines at higher levels of production aggregation. Because demand for a company's products is generally elastic—that is, consumers can find substitutes if its prices rise too much—a firm is limited in its ability to pass the cost of higher wages to consumers. Given that demand elasticity drops at the industry level and even more at the national level (it is harder to find substitutes for an entire range of industry products and more so for economy-wide products when prices rise), firms coordinating at these two levels of aggregation have more room to raise prices in the face of higher labor costs.

Based on this assumption, when wage bargaining takes place at the firm-level (low level of centralization), unions lack the market power to secure inflation-prone pay settlements. On the opposite end of the centralization continuum, where bargaining occurs at the national level, peak union associations wield significant market power which can be leveraged to secure higher wages. However, because unions are encompassing, they are more inclined to take account of the economic effects of their bargaining demands. Where bargaining occurs at the industry level, unions have sufficient market power to demand wage gains but are not encompassing enough that their members bear a sizable share of the economic costs of their actions. In light of these different contexts, Calmfors and Driffill argue that unemployment levels should be lower at low and high levels of centralization, but higher at intermediate levels.

Figure 2.2 graphs the correlation between levels of wage bargaining centralization and unemployment rates in the 1980s and sketches a "hump-shape" curve as hypothesized by Calmfors and Driffill (1988). The positions of several countries with intermediate to high levels of centralization appear to corroborate their hypothesis. However, Canada and the United States, where wage bargaining takes place at the firm-level, should have lower unemployment, while Switzerland and Germany, where industry-level bargaining was common in the 1980s, should have higher unemployment rates according to the logic of the curvilinear model.

A number of scholars, most notably Golden (1993), Franzese and Hall (2000), and Soskice (1990), have argued that wage coordination rather than wage centralization is more relevant in accounting for cross-national differences in economic performance. Specifically, they contend that higher levels of union and employer concentration—that is, a small number of bargaining units that deliberately harmonize their actions—are conducive to better employment outcomes. In a context where there are few leading bargainers and competition among them is absent, there is much greater incentive for them to reach binding collective agreements with an eye on their expected economic effects. Accordingly, wage coordination should be negatively associated with unemployment.

Aside from offering an alternative explanation for comparative macroeconomic performance, another important contribution of this strand of literature is that it has put more focus on the role of employers in the analysis of wage determination. Leading

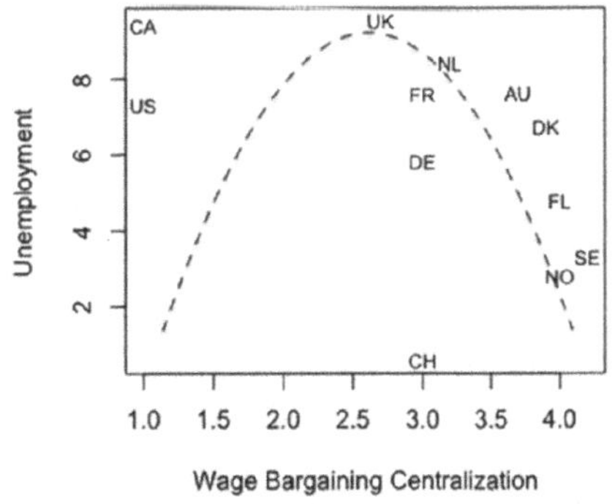

FIGURE 2.2 Unemployment and centralization, 1980s
Sources: tables 2.1 and 2.5.

works by Cameron (1984) and Lange and Garrett (1985) for example have overlooked employer associations. Moreover, while Calmfors and Driffill address employer groups in the context of centralization, they assign greater importance to unions. Soskice's (1990) work on wage coordination spotlights the role of employer associations in bringing about wage restraint, a bargaining outcome that previous literature has tended to attribute largely to unions. Soskice points out that leading business organizations, such as Germany's *Gesamtmetall*, leverage their coordination capacity across industries to ensure that the wage bargaining settlements they negotiated deliver wage increases that are non-inflationary and do not jeopardize their global competitiveness.

Figure 2.3 plots unemployment against wage coordination in the 1980s. Countries that rank low in the degree of coordination such as Canada, the United Kingdom, and the United States tend to have higher levels of unemployment than high coordination countries like Denmark, Germany, Norway, and Sweden. The logic of wage coordination seems to provide more analytical leverage on the question of why unemployment varied across the countries in the sample in the 1980s. In contrasting figures 2.2 and 2.3, we see that the employment situations in Canada, Germany, and the United States fit the coordination argument better than the centralization one.

Still, it would be premature to single out coordination as the main determinant of unemployment as this would require controlling for various other factors, including the possibility that the relationship is sensitive to the time frame being analyzed. Multivariate analyses by Baker et al. (2005), Blanchard and Wolfers (2000), and Nickell et al. (2005) show that the statistical size and significance of the effect of coordination on the unemployment rate not only varies depending on the time period, but also that its impact is conditioned by other factors, specifically union density. While these and other studies consistently find a negative association between coordination and unemployment, Baker et al. (2005), for example, find that coordination's impact is attenuated at higher levels of unionization.

Hicks and Kenworthy (1998) and Martin and Swank (2012) have examined the effects of corporatism on economic performance. Although they define corporatism differently, both studies recognize the central role that the organizational characteristics of labor and business play in making wage coordination possible.

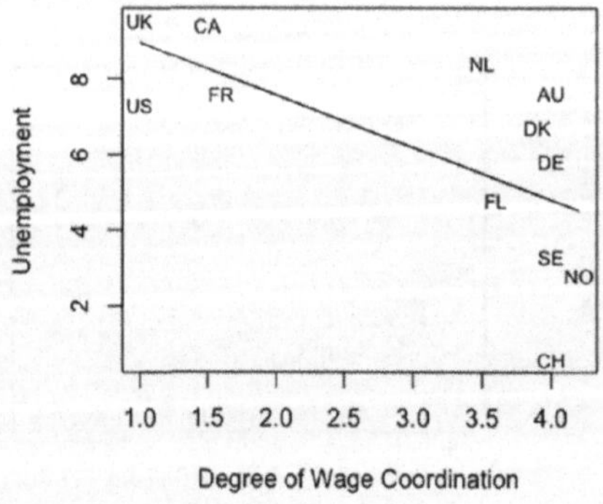

FIGURE 2.3 Unemployment and coordination, 1980s
Note: r = −0.72; sig @ 0.01
Sources: tables 2.1 and 2.5.

Martin and Swank's study shows that the level of macrocorporatism—that is, the degree to which collective bargaining and the organizational strength of producer groups are centralized—impacts economic growth and labor market performance. Their empirical analysis suggests that economic growth is higher in countries with either low or high levels of macrocorporatism. They estimate that annual growth rates in the 2000s were slightly less than 3% in both Canada and the United States (low macrocorporatist political economies) and Denmark and Norway (high macrocorporatist political economies). In contrast, moderately low macrocorporatist countries such as Australia and France experienced annual growth rates of around 2.3% to 2.4%, while moderately high coordinated economies such as Austria and Germany grew at an annual rate of about 2.5%.

Hicks and Kenworthy's (1998: 1654, 1656) study did not find evidence suggesting that corporatism is a key determinant of growth. However, it did find that the corporatist form of coordination curbs inflation (even when controlling for central bank independence), contributes to higher gross fixed capital investment (as a percentage of GDP), and improves trade balance. Their findings also show that corporatism is conducive to low unemployment levels. Martin and Swank (2012: 240) add that in the postindustrial era, coordinated economies have reported lower incidences of long-term unemployment rates and of temporary workers.

Labor market policies

In the previous section, we examined the effects of wage determination institutions on unemployment and growth. In this section, attention shifts to certain aspects of the labor market policy regime that studies have identified as potential determinants of employment outcomes—namely, employment protection laws, generosity and duration of unemployment benefits, and active labor market policies (ALMPs). The neoliberal argument holds that job protection laws, generous unemployment benefits, and higher taxes—what neoliberal economists refer to as "rigidities"—are key sources of unemployment. On the other hand, comparative political economists generally have been skeptical of such claims, pointing to evidence suggesting that certain types of labor market rigidities can help economies achieve optimal employment outcomes (Bradley and Stephens 2007; Rueda 2015).

Employment protection legislation (EPL) limits employers' discretion concerning dismissals. There is not much disagreement among scholars about the employment effects of EPL. In general, EPL weakens demand for labor by raising layoff costs. Firms avoid hiring new workers because strong job protections render hiring decisions largely "irreversible" insofar that firms are constrained in their ability to downsize their workforce during downturns (Siebert 1997: 49). On the other hand, EPL can help stabilize the unemployment rate over business cycles. Employers are more inclined to shorten work weeks rather than resort to layoffs when job protection regulations impose high dismissal costs. Overall, EPL is expected to have a negative effect on employment, but the magnitude should be small given that EPL also helps reduce the number of people out of work (Bradley and Stephens 2007; Nickell 1997).

There are sharper disagreements about how the benefit system impacts labor market performance. Proponents of the neoliberal argument hold that generous unemployment benefits extended over a longer duration lower the personal cost of being unemployed. It also encourages individuals to be "choosy" in their job selection efforts, therefore forcing firms to raise wages to entice the unemployed back to work. Thus, labor supply decisions are affected by the replacement rate of unemployment benefits (the share of earnings covered by benefits), duration of benefits, and reservation wage (lowest wage at which people seek reemployment). According to this line of reasoning, the higher the replacement rate and the longer the duration of benefits, the higher the level of voluntary unemployment (OECD 1997: 52).

Comparative political economists have a more positive view of the effects of the benefits system on the labor market. While CPE scholars agree with neoliberal proponents that generous, long-term unemployment benefits discourage job search and depress labor supply, they, however, recognize the potential benefits of higher replacement rates over a shorter term (Bradley and Stephens 2007). As Estevez-Abe et al. (2001) have noted, generous unemployment benefits provide a necessary cushion for unemployed individuals who possess occupational- and industry-specific skills. Because these skills are less marketable across economic sectors, a generous replacement rate not only compensates for this labor market disadvantage but also provides necessary support during job search which can take longer than for someone with general skills.

To sum up, the CPE view asserts that short-term high replacement rates do not directly contribute to higher unemployment in every circumstance. In economies that rely more on non-general skills, generous benefits are less likely to induce people to quit their jobs given the difficulty in getting reemployed in jobs that fit their skills. Further, although generous unemployment compensation can generate a work disincentive effect, it need not be the case if people view this benefit program as a form of insurance against labor market risks.

Active labor market policies (ALMPs) such as retraining programs, job search assistance, and subsidized employment seek to reintegrate the unemployed into the labor market. Although some neoliberal supporters have questioned the effectiveness of ALMPs, many, including the OECD, have argued that such policies help increase the employment rate. ALMPs proponents also assert that such policies might offset the potential unemployment inducing effect of generous unemployment benefits (Baker et al. 2005; Bradley and Stephens 2007; Nickell 1997).

There is general consensus that taxes on labor may increase unemployment by affecting the demand for and supply of labor. First, because an increase in payroll taxes raises the cost of labor, employers may cut back on hiring or downsize their workforce. Second, an increase in the gap between before-tax wage rate and take-home pay (the "tax wedge") may weaken the incentive to work, especially when the replacement rate of unemployment benefits is high. However, the effects of total taxes (e.g., payroll, income, and consumption taxes) on employment performance has been much debated. Neoliberal proponents are of the view that "the overall tax burden must not just be shifted around but must actually be cut to avoid negative labor market consequences" (Bradley and Stephens 2007: 1494). On the other hand, CPE scholars question this line of reasoning, pointing out that high-tax Scandinavian countries have experienced unemployment rates no higher than low-tax countries such as Ireland and the United States.

How does the evidence match up with the neoliberal (or deregulationist) claims that we have elaborated? Specifically, does the unemployment rate (or employment rate) improve when EPL is relaxed, expenditures on passive and active unemployment benefits are cut, and labor taxes decrease? Focusing on 19 OECD countries between 1980 and 1999, Baker et al.'s (2005) study finds little cross-national evidence to support these claims. For example, Sweden had lower unemployment rates than the United States until the 1990s even though the Nordic country had much more robust job protection rules. What is more, labor market performance proved much better in Sweden than in Spain despite having similar EPLs.

Cross-national data also do not support the argument that there is a positive association between unemployment and labor taxes during this time period. Canada, Ireland, and the United Kingdom had higher unemployment rates in the 1980s than Norway and Sweden even though the Anglo countries had far lower labor taxes. However, a look at over time changes within countries reveals evidence that is aligned with the neoliberal claim. Unemployment rates dropped by more than 3.5 percentage points in the Netherlands and the United Kingdom (when comparing rates between 1980–1987 and 1996–1999) as total labor taxes decreased. On the other hand, labor market performance deteriorated in Belgium and France as taxes rose (see Nickell et al. 2005). Some studies find a positive association between unemployment and EPL, but the estimates of this effect vary widely over time (Baker et al. 2005). Furthermore, while Nickell (1997) finds no association, Baker et al. find that EPL reduced unemployment between 1980 and 1999.

These pooled time-series analyses also generate contradicting results regarding the association between unemployment and replacement rate of unemployment benefits. Bradley and Stephens (2007) report that a higher one-year replacement rate is linked with higher employment levels, but employment drops when the long-term generosity of unemployment benefits increases. In contrast, several studies have found a statistically significant, negative relationship between benefits and unemployment, but the estimates of the effect of benefits vary considerably in these studies (Baker et al. 2005; Nickell et al. 2005; Rueda 2015). The findings on the impact of ALMPs on labor market performance are more conclusive in refuting the neoliberal claim that ALMPs are ineffective job creation tools. Most of the studies referenced in this section find that higher spending on ALMPs is associated with better labor market performance—either lower unemployment or higher employment levels.

Lastly, the empirical studies reviewed here report evidence that is largely consistent with the neoliberal view that taxes on labor worsen labor market performance. However, Baker et al. (2005) find suggestive evidence that the effects of labor taxes vary across different time periods. Further, Bradley and Stephens (2007) report that total taxes as a percentage of GDP is unrelated to employment performance, a finding that contradicts the neoliberal position.

Institutional interaction

Scholars have attributed cross-national differences in macroeconomic performance to the interactive effects between labor market arrangements and other economic institutions. Franzese and Hall (2000) shed light on why some countries with central bank independence (CBI) face a trade-off between low inflation and low unemployment while other countries with the same monetary institutional arrangement have been able to avoid it. There are two effects generated by the independence of central banks that are conducive to low inflation. First, because independent central bankers have a reputation for being averse to inflation, the parties involved in the negotiations of wage and price contracts are more likely to avoid inflation-prone settlements for fear that their actions may be met by tough countermeasures from central bankers. Second, the prospect of provoking central bankers into taking restrictive monetary measures is made more probable given the autonomy of central banks from political influence. In short, the independence of central bankers signals their readiness to wring out inflation.

However, as Franzese and Hall observe, the effectiveness of this signal on the behavior of wage and price bargainers is contingent on how well they can coordinate their actions. They note that in uncoordinated settings, central banks' anti-inflation signals are unlikely to restrain bargaining units because each believes that their individual efforts to obtain higher nominal wage gains will not impact the overall economy. However, if every other bargainer is informed by such a belief—that their individual efforts are too small to affect the whole economy—then wage-push inflation will emerge. Thus, a classic collective action problem arises in uncoordinated settings: although no one likes inflation, because each bargaining unit cannot be certain that others will adhere to non-inflationary nominal wage settlements, each is inclined to add an "inflation increment" into their settlements to hedge against real wage losses that could arise if others reach agreements that are inflationary (Franzese and Hall 2000: 178).

In coordinated wage bargaining settings, however, wage bargainers are more likely to be attentive to central banks' anti-inflation signals. In such a setting, the collective action problem described earlier is avoided because many wage contracts throughout an economy follow the settlement reached by lead bargainers, like Germany's *IG Metall* and *Gesamtmetall*. Their wage-setting agreements have typically served as benchmarks for other industries. The expectation that bargaining units across industries will harmonize their wage-related actions leads each to forego adding an inflation increment. Furthermore, because lead bargainers know that the agreements they reach will be transmitted to other industries, they are much more inclined to internalize the expected effects of their actions on unemployment, inflation, and growth. Moreover, since future macroeconomic conditions ride in large part on the wage settlements negotiated by principal bargainers, they will expect the central bank to comment on such settlements and to signal its readiness to take counteractions if settlements are unsuitable. Such expectations can deter lead wage bargainers from reaching inflationary settlements, obviating the need to use contractionary monetary measures.

Based on the logic underpinning Franzese and Hall's argument, countries with high CBI should have lower inflation rates, but their unemployment levels should vary depending on the extent of wage coordination. Table 2.6 classifies the 12-country sample used throughout this book by their level of CBI and of wage coordination, and reports each cluster's average inflation and unemployment rates between 1980 and 1998. It also provides their "misery" index scores, which is the summation of inflation and unemployment rates. When CBI is high, a change from low to high wage coordination results in a 1.1 percentage point drop in inflation and a 2.3 point drop in unemployment. In looking at the misery index scores across the four country clusters, it is quite clear that the combination of high levels of CBI and wage coordination is conducive to better macroeconomic conditions.

TABLE 2.6 Average inflation and unemployment rates under different institutional arrangements, 1980–1998

	Central Bank Independence			
Coordination of Wage Bargaining	**Low**		**High**	
Low	Inflation:	5.1	Inflation:	4.3
	Unemployment:	8.5	Unemployment:	8.0
	Misery:	13.6	Misery:	12.3
High	Inflation:	5.2	Inflation:	3.2
	Unemployment:	5.9	Unemployment:	5.7
	Misery:	11.1	Misery:	8.9

Country clusters:
Low CBI/low CWB category: Australia, France, and the United Kingdom.
High CBI/low CWB: Canada and United States.
Low CBI/High CWB: Finland, Norway, and Sweden.
High CBI/high CWB: Denmark, Germany, the Netherlands, and Switzerland.

Note: averages calculated by the author, see table 2.5.

Source: adapted from Inequality and Prosperity: Social Europe vs. Liberal America, by Jonas Pontusson (p. 108.)

Corporate governance and labor market coordination

Another area of research on institutional interaction explores the macroeconomic effects of the complementary interplay between labor relations and corporate governance. Institutional complementarity exists whenever the presence of an institution in one domain reinforces the functioning and benefits of an institution in another domain. The efficiency gains generated by complementary institutional configurations, it is argued, translate to better economic performance. Amable et al. (2005), Hall and Gingerich (2004), and Höpner (2005) have argued that combinations of institutional practices in both labor relations and in corporate governance, which facilitate either long-term (strategic) or short-term (market) coordination among actors, are conducive to better economic outcomes.

Certain corporate governance practices, when combined with particular institutional labor relations practices, facilitate strategic coordination. With regard to corporate governance, management is more likely to promote long-termism when corporate ownership and control is concentrated in a few large shareholders, when cross-shareholding is prevalent, and when minority shareholder rights are limited. These institutional practices relieve market pressures on managers by stabilizing sources of finance. These corporate governance features are complementary to labor relations practices that foster long employment tenures, high degree of wage coordination, and centralized collective bargaining. This configuration of institutional arrangements is amenable to production strategies that require employers and workers to co-invest in the development of asset specific skills, co-manage the workplace, and cooperate in upgrading labor productivity. Coordinated market economies such as Austria, Belgium, Germany, and the Nordic countries exhibit characteristics that match this institutional configuration.

On the other hand, short-termism informs managers' decisions when minority shareholder rights are highly protected, corporate ownership is dispersed among a large number of relatively small shareholders, and market capitalization is high. This alternative corporate governance arrangement intensifies market pressures on managers, forcing them to prioritize short-term profitability and arrangements that maximize managerial prerogatives. Accordingly, labor relations featuring weak collectivization, coordination, and centralization are more suitable. This market-based institutional matrix is ideal for production strategies that require managers to adjust their workforce quickly. Liberal market economies such as Canada, Ireland, the United Kingdom, and the United States resemble the characteristics of this institutional combination.

Where institutional practices in corporate governance and labor relations are complementary as described, the resulting efficiency gains should be manifested in the form of better economic outcomes (Hall and Gingerich 2004; Höpner 2005). Focusing on the period between 1971 and 1997, Hall and Gingerich find suggestive evidence that the complementary interaction between the two spheres of political economy increases the national growth rate after controlling for various other determinants. In countries where strategic coordination is dominant (or absent) in corporate governance practices, the growth rate improves as strategic coordination is enhanced (or weakened) in labor relations. In short, Hall and Gingerich's study shows that the macroeconomic impact of labor relations is contingent on the type of coordination in corporate governance.

Conclusion

CPE scholars have long recognized the role that labor market institutions play in shaping countries' macroeconomic performance. One strand of research has focused on the economic effects of different configurations of organized labor and business. As the literature on macrocorporatism shows, the capacity to coordinate within and between producer groups has been instrumental in keeping inflation in check and unemployment low simultaneously. This empirical fact serves as an important reminder that the path to economic success is not limited to one in which societies must adhere strictly to market governance. Another strand of research has explored how certain institutional features of industrial relations, interacting with other political economic institutions, affect economic outcomes. An important takeaway of this literature is that non-market cooperation in industrial relations can yield superior performance when combined with central bank independence and corporate governance coordination.

The decline of organized labor and decentralization of wage-setting arrangements in advanced democracies since the 1970s have prompted scholars to study the long-term economic and political effects of these labor market changes. Does the liberalization of labor market institutions in organized capitalist systems mean that they are going to increasingly function and perform like liberal market economies? We shed some light on this question in the concluding chapter. Moreover, what does the decline of trade unions mean in terms of income distribution? Chapter 6 addresses this question and uncovers evidence suggesting that the increase in inequality in affluent democracies is partly attributed to the erosion of the organizational strength and political influence of unions.

Key concepts

Bargaining coverage

Corporate governance

Drift

Ghent system

Institutional complementarity

Macrocorporatism

Solidaristic wage bargaining

Union centralization

Union concentration

Union density

Discussion questions

- What are the main characteristics of organized labor and organized business, and how have they changed over time?
- Compare and contrast Germany, Sweden, and the United States with respect to union density, bargaining coverage, bargaining level, and wage coordination.
- The neoliberal perspective holds that flexible labor markets and minimal non-market regulations result in better macroeconomic performance. Drawing on data and relevant literature, assess that claim.
- What is coordinated capitalism? Provide an example illustrating how coordinated capitalism works.

Further reading

Hall, Peter A., and David Soskice. 2001. "An Introduction to Varieties of Capitalism." In Peter Hall and David Soskice, eds., *Varieties of Capitalism: The Institutional Foundations of Comparative Advantage*. New York: Oxford University Press.

Introduces the VoC approach, which focuses on how firms coordinate their actions with other stakeholders in different spheres of the political economy.

Katzenstein, Peter. 1985. *Small States in World Markets*. Ithaca: Cornell University Press.

Argues that democratic corporatism, in which coordination among producer groups and government figures large, helped trade-dependent small European states to adjust their production strategies rapidly and flexibly in response to economic changes in the postwar period.

Mares, Isabela. 2006. *Taxation, Wage Bargaining, and Unemployment.* New York: Cambridge University Press.

Argues that Europe's ability to achieve low unemployment and expand welfare generosity simultaneously in the post-WWII period was made possible thanks to a political exchange between organized labor and governments.

Thelen, Kathleen. 2014. *Varieties of Liberalization and the New Politics of Social Solidarity.* New York: Cambridge University Press.

Analyzes how labor market institutions in Denmark, Germany, the Netherlands, and the United States have changed due to liberalization and identifies different paths of liberalization.

CHAPTER

3 Political institutions

How do political institutions affect economic policy outcomes such as public spending, budget deficit, or social welfare spending? Are certain constitutional structures associated with better macroeconomic performance? This chapter explores these questions first by studying the economic effects of two types of constitutional features—namely, forms of government (presidential and parliamentary) and electoral systems (plurality-majority and proportional representation). This will be followed by a selective survey of research that examines the effects of different configurations of political institutions. Let's first address the question of how to study the effects of political institutions.

Studying the effects of political institutions

There are three focuses in the research on the economic effects of political institutions. One strand of research focuses on the link between accountability and economic outcomes (Hicken at al., 2005; Persson and Tabellini 2004b). Accountability means that voters can sanction office holders for failing to advance the public interest to a degree that satisfies the electorate's expectations. When political institutions establish direct lines of accountability between voters and individual incumbents, politicians have a keener interest in avoiding actions that violate the public's trust, such as seeking private gains or deviating from electoral promises (Manin et al., 1999a). To the extent that average voters are averse to higher taxes and wasteful spending, exposure to direct accountability should incline incumbents to pursue more austere fiscal policies. However, arguably, the same incumbents might want to engineer economic expansions prior to elections if they judge that this policy action will help them secure reelection. If so, direct accountability can incentivize office holders to instrumentalize fiscal and monetary policies for political ends. This is an area of inquiry we will explore in detail in the next chapter.

Another line of research focuses on the role of veto points. By veto point we mean any individual or group that can block legislation, or, stated otherwise, whose

DOI: 10.4324/9780429199462-3

consent is needed to change a policy (Tsebelis 1995). Institutional features such as separation of powers, bicameralism, legislative committees, judicial review, and federalism create various veto wielding actors and thus render policy change more difficult. Similarly, the presence of several political parties in government can frustrate efforts to change the status quo, for their partisan prerogatives may get in the way of reaching an agreement. The theory of veto points suggests that the more veto points there are, the greater the degree of policy stability. Further, because multiple veto points help "lock-in" policy decisions, governments with various veto actors can commit more credibly to optimal policies in the long run. Therefore, there should be less volatility in key macroeconomic benchmarks such as inflation, unemployment, and GDP growth. On the other hand, when the consent of multiple veto players is necessary to pass legislation, each player is in a position to demand side-payments which tend to benefit narrow interests (Cox and McCubbins 2001). This can lead to higher public spending and potentially result in budget shortfalls.

Finally, some studies investigate how political institutions affect economic outcomes by aggregating citizens' preferences into public policy decisions (Persson and Tabellini 2004b). While some institutions such as proportional representation and federalism create opportunities for the representation of particularistic interests, others such as single-member districts and parliamentary regimes push groups with varying interests to combine forces. Whether policy outputs benefit narrow or broad interests depends on how institutions structure interest representation. Inclusive and consensus based institutional dynamics tend to be more conducive to policies that advance the general interest; exclusive and competitive decision-making structures tend to result in policies that cater to narrow interests (Crepaz 1996).

Forms of government: presidential and parliamentary systems

There are two general forms of democratic governments. The main distinction between presidential and parliamentary systems centers on the relationship between the executive and legislative branches. In presidential systems, the president, who serves as the head of government and state, is not selected by the legislature but rather by the electorate. In contrast, the legislature in parliamentary systems selects the prime minister and cabinet, who collectively comprise the government. Therefore, whereas parliamentary governments need the support of a majority in the legislature to stay in power, the president is free of such a requirement. Some countries have combined both forms of government, opting for a semi-presidential system in which executive duties are split between a popularly elected president and a prime minister.

What sort of institutional dynamics stem from this basic difference between presidential and parliamentary systems, and how are they likely to shape economic outcomes? First, checks and balances occur more frequently in presidential systems because there is more separation of powers between the executive and legislative branches than in parliamentary systems. The independence afforded to the president by virtue of being elected by the people and endowed with constitutional powers (such as legislative veto and unilateral executive authority) means that there will be more conflicts between the executive and legislature as each seeks to promote its institutional prerogatives. In cases of divided governments, when the president's political party does not control the legislature, inter-branch relations can become mired in partisan rivalry.

Advocates of presidential democracies point to several merits associated with separated powers. First, the presence of multiple veto players means that presidential systems are more effective in ensuring policy stability under the current government and reducing future policy uncertainty. Second, the direct election of presidents and legislators enhances their responsiveness to voters' interests and inclines both branches to appeal directly to the citizenry when they advocate competing policy ideas. Third, inter-branch competition inclines the executive and legislature to disclose information to the public about each other's intentions in hopes of influencing public opinion to their advantage. Whether the information stems from the legislature's oversight activities or reflects the president's frustration with the legislature's intransigent stance, as Gerring et al. (2009: 331) point out, "we can expect that the public will learn a good deal about policies and processes of government" in presidential democracies.

The fusion of power between the legislature and executive in parliamentary systems creates its own set of advantages. Parliament delegates legislative powers to the government when it is formed following legislative elections. Power is concentrated in the executive during the legislature's term as long as the prime minister and her cabinet maintain parliament's confidence. When single-party or coalition governments command a legislative majority, the two branches of government become practically unified insofar that the policy priorities of the party or parties in government find support among a majority of parliamentarians.

Proponents of the parliamentary system assert that the centralization of power enables the government to respond decisively to public demands for policy change. Whereas presidentialism is praised for its ability to avoid policy swings, parliamentarism is credited for having the capacity to be responsive to calls for policy adaptation. The concentration of power, as supporters of parliamentarism assert, also has the effect of enhancing, not curtailing, accountability. Voters' ability to reward or punish the government for its performance is made easier when the government commands a legislative majority. Further, because majority governments cannot evade accountability, the anticipation of being held responsible for policy results should induce them to exert as much of their efforts on voters' behalf.

Another institutional dynamic that distinguishes presidential and parliamentary systems relates to legislative cohesion. Diermeier and Feddersen (1998) have observed that the vote of confidence procedure in parliamentary democracies incentivizes legislators who are associated with the governing coalition to vote consistently together in favor of government bills. If the government links a piece of legislation to a confidence vote, it is asking legislators to vote on a bill as it is and connecting the bill's approval with the survival of the government. As they point out, the fear of losing agenda-setting authority due to a confidence defeat "creates an incentive for all those who profit from the current government [but who might object to some policy positions] to vote [nonetheless] for the government's proposals" (ibid: 611).

The situation can be quite different in presidential democracies. Because of the presence of multiple veto points—caused by the division of legislative powers between the president and the legislature, the possibility of a divided government, and involvement of legislative committees that exercise significant control over legislation (as in the United States)—unstable legislative coalitions are common and tend to form around issue domains rather than across them. Further, the absence of a confidence vote enhances the bargaining power of minority interests because they can leverage their participation in voting coalitions to extract side-payments. While this method of aggregating conflicting interests into public policy may help protect minority interests, it can also impede the coordination of efforts around the pursuit of collective gains (Gerring et al. 2009).

What sort of economic implications are likely to be associated with these institutional dynamics in presidential and parliamentary democracies? Scholars have argued that both power separation and lack of legislative cohesion tend to lead to smaller governments and the undersupply of collective goods such as education, pension, and unemployment insurance in presidential democracies (Persson et al., 2000; Persson and Tabellini 2004b). On the one hand, the electoral connections linking voters to both the president and legislators should lead politicians to contain public spending and tax collection. On the other hand, the presence of multiple institutional veto players with different and conflicting interests should lead to policies that target narrow geographic constituencies rather than the general public. Furthermore, these dynamics can impact macroeconomic performance. As Gerring et al. (2009: 354) point out, "when individuals or groups pursue their own agendas, the result is not what society as a whole would prefer." They and others (Knutsen 2011; McManus and Ozkan 2018) have suggested that institutional obstacles to the coordination of policymaking actions can adversely affect economic growth, unemployment, and inflation. The difficulty for individual incumbents to tune out particularistic interests, coupled with the diffusion of responsibility over economic performance, means that economic policies may not be as effective as they could be under institutional conditions that reward coordination and establish collective responsibility.

In parliamentary systems, both power concentration and legislative cohesion have a tendency to lead to larger governments, greater supply of collective goods, and better macroeconomic performance. As Persson and Tabellini (2004b: 92) explain, the government and its supporters favor higher taxes since the additional revenues can be channeled to programs that benefit the majority, while its cost can be distributed in a way that is partly absorbed by non-supporters. What is more, because the interest of majority (coalition) governments is more aligned with the general interest, they have an incentive to avoid economic policies that can injure the general economic welfare.

Electoral rules: plurality-majority and proportional representation

The research exploring the link between electoral systems and economic outcomes usually focuses on two classifications of electoral systems—namely, plurality-majority (P-M) and proportional representation (PR). They can be distinguished based on their electoral formula, district magnitude, and ballot structure.

The electoral formula determines how votes are converted to seats. In P-M systems, the person who obtains the most votes in a district, whether a plurality (the largest number of votes) or a majority (more than 50% of total votes), is elected. In PR systems, the allocation of seats is roughly equal to the share of votes obtained by a political party. District magnitude refers to the number of representatives elected in each electoral district. In P-M systems, single-member and multimember districts can exist, as illustrated in the U.S. House of Representatives and Senate, respectively. In PR systems, district magnitude can range from a minimum of two seats to one country-wide district from which all elected representatives in the national legislature are elected, as is the case in the Israeli Knesset. The ballot structure refers to how votes are cast. In P-M systems, voters cast ballots for individual candidates. In PR systems, the closed-list ballot enables voters to choose a list of candidates associated with a party (party list), while the open-list ballot lets voters select a party list plus rank candidates in order of preference (for more, see Lijphart 2012).

Electoral systems affect economic policies and outcomes by influencing the incentives of politicians and by shaping the party structure (Persson and Tabellini 2004a, 2004b). The incentives to cultivate a personal vote—the idea that candidates' election prospects are determined more by the services they provide to their own districts than by their association with a political party—tends to be stronger in settings where there are small districts with low district magnitudes and where elections are candidate-oriented (Cox and McCubbins 2001). In such a setting, individual incumbents calculate that it is easier for them to take credit for material improvements in their districts than it is for policy changes at the national level. Moreover, the direct election of representatives in single-member districts makes attribution of responsibility easier for voters. Accordingly, the more "pork barrel" projects incumbents bring to their districts—that is, locally targeted public goods like funds to improve the transportation infrastructure and health and education services—the better their chances of getting reelected. As a result, in single-member district plurality or majority systems, where the incumbent reaps all of the spoils of office, there should be more spending on geographically targeted programs than on universalistic ones. Pork barrel spending should also be higher in open-list PR systems like Japan, where the desire to be voters' first or second pick on a party list induces individual candidates to cultivate a personal base.

In contrast, incumbents face stronger incentives to supply collective goods in PR systems with large multi-member districts. There are four reasons for this. First, no individual representative in a multi-member district can claim that they alone should receive full credit for the improvements that occurred in a given electoral term. The personal payoffs of providing targeted benefits therefore are low. Second, because larger PR districts encompass a wider array of interests, elected representatives must ensure that the public goods they bring to their districts appeal sufficiently across disparate interests. Third, the higher voter turnout that PR engenders means that the share of lower-income voters in the electorate will be higher. Because of their preference for redistribution, incumbents seeking their vote have to commit to more social spending, a policy position that can also benefit middle-income voters (Iversen and Soskice 2006a; Tavits 2004). Finally, representatives are less swayed by particularistic pressures due to the weak constituency-incumbent link attributed to the closed-list ballot, and, therefore, have more latitude to exert their efforts on behalf of the general interest (Persson and Tabellini 2004b; Rogowski 1987).

It has been long established that electoral systems shape political party systems (Duverger 1964; Rae 1967). Single-member district plurality or majority systems tend to lead to two-party systems, while proportional representation leads to multi-party systems. In a P-M system, third party candidates struggle to cross the plurality or majority threshold. Seeing that third parties' winning probabilities are relatively low, voters generally coalesce around one of the two larger parties. The two-way contest is sustained by the "catch-all" nature of party politics, whereby the dominant parties position themselves in a way that appeals to as many voters as possible. In PR systems, smaller parties can gain a legislative foothold because seats are distributed among parties based on their vote share. This encourages the formation of smaller political parties who brand themselves as alternatives to mainstream parties.

The research on this topic has traced certain economic policy outcomes to particular dynamics between electoral and political party systems. With respect to P-M systems, Cox and McCubbins (2001), Persson and Tabellini (2004b), and Rogowski (1987) have observed that political parties are weaker and less capable of internalizing the benefits of providing collective goods. In an effort to cultivate a personal vote, individual incumbents seek to control the legislative process around issue areas that are central to their own electoral fortunes. At times, the legislative process is harnessed to serve the electoral needs of individual office holders rather than to advance the policy agenda of the ruling party. The result, as Cox and McCubbins (ibid: 39) point out, is that "one gets parties that cannot control legislative decision-making, cannot command the loyalty of their own members, and cannot avoid being torn apart by the competing and unaggregated demands" of their allies. Another contributing factor is that in SMD plurality systems, a party can secure a majority of legislative seats with less than a majority of the popular votes and go on to form a single-party majority government. Because of a government's non-majority voter base, it faces weaker incentives to promote universalistic spending programs.

The presence of strong parties and of multiparty governments is common in PR systems. Both features militate against efforts to cater to particularistic interests and incline parties in government to coordinate their efforts in pursuit of the general interest. On the one hand, party leaders' control of the party list—specifically, determining which candidates will appear on it—helps engender greater party loyalty among rank-and-file members. On the other hand, because the electoral reach of majority coalition governments encompasses a large portion of the electorate, the policy interests of governments overlaps with the general interest. As Crepaz (1996: 95) points out, since majority coalitions seek "to please all parties and their voters which are part of the coalition, the government has an even higher incentive to internalize the externalities of collective action than in the case of a bare majority single cabinet party." This incentive will lead majority coalitions to pursue policies that appeal across different groups of voters.

Empirical evidence of institutional effects

How do the hypothesized effects about forms of government and electoral systems square with the empirical data? Our first attempt at answering that question will be based on the sample of countries used throughout the book and rely on simple correlational evidence. In our second pass at that question, we will discuss the findings of pooled time-series studies.

Figure 3.1 looks at the relationship between type of government and economic outcomes between 1981 and 2010. Parliamentary governments are coded 1, semi-presidential governments as 1.5, and presidential governments as 2. Outlays or size of government refer to total spending by the central government as a percentage of GDP. Revenue is measured as total tax receipts by the central government as a percentage of GDP. Throughout this chapter, we only examine spending and revenue levels of the central government (as opposed to all governments) in keeping with the standard used by Perrson and Tabellini in their research. The misery index combines unemployment and inflation rates. In general, the correlational evidence shows that the size of government and tax revenues are larger in parliamentary governments than in nonparliamentary systems.

There is a fair amount of variation among parliamentary systems with respect to spending and revenue. The size of the fiscal regime in the Nordic countries is much larger than in the two Anglo countries (Australia and Canada). A pattern emerges if we array the nine parliamentary systems according to their level of executive dominance (incidence of single-party majority cabinets). Parliamentary systems with high levels of executive dominance such as Australia, Canada, and the United Kingdom have lower levels of outlays and revenues than parliamentary systems that have experienced more minority governments such as those often found in the Nordic countries and the Netherlands. In fact, the correlation between executive dominance and revenue is substantively and statistically high (−0.679 at a significance level of 0.001). Minority governments need to logroll and compromise with parties in the legislature in order to pass laws, a process that often leads to the expansion of government spending and revenue.

The patterns revealed in the scatterplots in figure 3.1 hold up well when other determinants of fiscal size are controlled for and the sample size is expanded. The multiple studies led by Persson and Tabellini consistently confirm that presidential systems have smaller governments (lower spending and revenue). Based on a sample of 17 industrialized democracies between 1988 and 1992, Persson et al. (2000) find that spending (measured as percentage of GDP) in presidential democracies is 10 percentage points lower than in parliamentary democracies

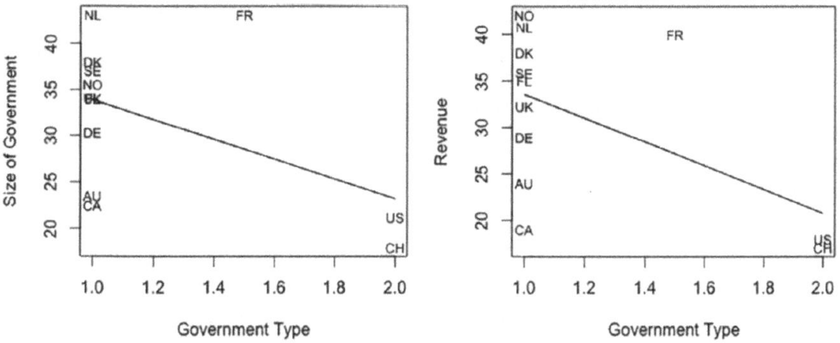

FIGURE 3.1 Types of government and economic outcomes, 1981–2010

Note: the correlations between government type and size of government and between government type and revenue are −0.505 and −0.533, respectively.

Sources: Cheibub (2007) for data on government type; Government Finance Statistics, IMF (multiple years) for data on size of government and revenue.

after controlling for per capita income, level of economic openness, level of ethnic heterogeneity, and share of population above 65 years of age. In another study which looks at 85 countries between 1990 and 1998, Persson and Tabellini (2004a) find that presidential systems reduced the size of government by roughly 5% of the GDP after controlling for various effects including the quality and age of the democracy. Further, they found weak support for the claim that parliamentary systems are conducive to universal programs; however, that claim gains more credence when the analysis focuses only on older and well-functioning democracies.

Various longitudinal multivariate studies report that parliamentary governments foster better economic conditions. In their study of 124 countries, Gerring et al. (2009) estimate that 50 years of parliamentary rule is associated with a per capita income that is 30% higher than in presidential systems. Focusing on 119 countries between 1950 and 2015, McManus and Ozkan (2018) find that inflation is about 4 percentage points higher, income inequality is 12% to 24% higher, and GDP growth is between 0.6 and 1.2 percentage points lower in presidential regimes relative to parliamentary systems. However, Knutsen's (2011: 87) study, based on over 100 countries using data going as far back as 1820, finds that the form of government "does not matter" for economic growth.

The correlational evidence reported in figure 3.2 suggests that economic outcomes vary across electoral systems. Proportional representation (coded as 2) is correlated with higher government spending, revenue, and social spending (not shown in figure 3.2). Of note, when Switzerland is left out, the individual correlations between electoral system and outlays, revenues, and social spending become much stronger. Among the countries with candidate-centered elections, Australia, Canada, and the United States have lower levels of spending and revenue than France and the United Kingdom. This cross-national variance in the size of government and revenue does not appear to be related to the type of electoral rule used in these five countries. For example, the fiscal sizes of central governments in Canada and the United States are smaller than that of the United Kingdom even though the three countries use single-member district plurality in national elections. Moreover, the differences in spending and revenue levels among PR countries do not seem to be associated with the type of PR list. There is a fair amount of spread among Denmark, Finland, Norway, and the Netherlands with respect to fiscal policy outcomes even though all use the open-PR list.

Several pooled time series studies have found evidence coinciding with the aforementioned results. Crepaz and Moser (2004), Iversen and Soskice (2006a), and Persson and Tabellini (2004a, 2004b) find that electoral systems have a large effect on government outlays. For example, Persson and Tabellini (2004a) estimate that transitioning from a PR to a plurality-majority system reduces the size of government by 6% of GDP after controlling for form of government, quality of governance, and duration of democracy. Using level of proportionality to distinguish between electoral systems—where lower/higher proportionality differentiates non-PR/PR systems, respectively—Crepaz and Moser (2004) find that higher proportionality boosts government spending by roughly 2% of GDP, after controlling for globalization, trade, macroeconomic performance, and number of veto points.

Focusing on the composition of public spending, Milesi-Ferretti et al. (2002), whose study is based on OECD countries starting in the early 1960s and Latin American countries in the first half of the 1990s, evaluate the claim that PR systems

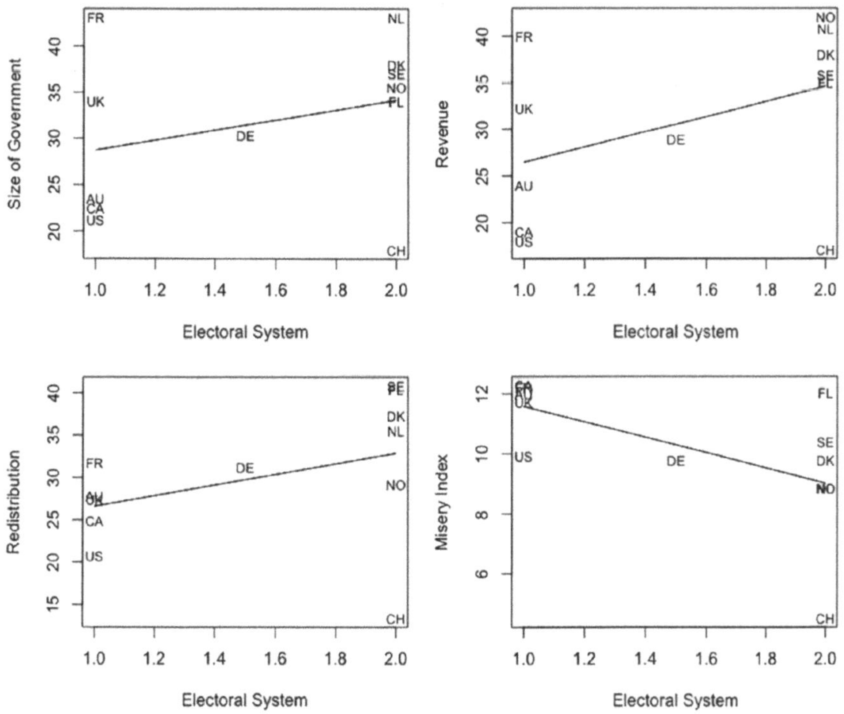

FIGURE 3.2 Electoral systems and economic outcomes, early 1980s to 2010
Sources: Lijphart (2012: 133) for classification of countries' electoral systems. Germany (DE) has a mixed system, coded as 1.5 on the electoral system scale. See figure 3.1 for outlays and revenue; table 2.5 for misery index; and table 7.1 for data on redistribution.

spend more on social transfers than P-M systems. They find that higher proportionality is associated with higher levels of social transfers in OECD countries but not in Latin America. Persson and Tabellini (2004a, 2004b) and Lizzeri and Persico (2001) also find evidence suggesting that incumbents in PR systems are less inclined to funnel public funds to pork-barrel projects, thus freeing up money to finance broad social programs. Persson and Tabellini (2004a) estimate that switching from PR to a P-M system would reduce social spending by roughly 2% to 3% of GDP.

PR countries tend to redistribute more relative to non-PR countries, as shown in figure 3.2. The correlation between electoral systems and redistribution—which is measured as the percent reduction in market income inequality caused by taxation and social transfers—increases from 0.390 to 0.800 and becomes highly statistically significant when Switzerland is omitted. Whereas the average redistribution in PR countries is 32.8% (or 36.6% without Switzerland), its average is 26.5% in non-PR countries. Further, PR is strongly associated with Left incumbency—the correlation between electoral systems and left-wing governments is 0.602 and is statistically significant at conventional levels. The average share of cabinet positions held by Left parties in PR and non-PR systems between the early 1980s and 2010 was 41.6% and 27.4%, respectively. This evidence corroborates Iversen and Soskice's (2006a) findings. Their multivariate study of 14 countries between the 1940s and late 1990s reveals that the average share of right-wing governments in non-PR countries is much higher than in PR systems, 75% versus 26%. They also find evidence that PR is strongly associated with higher redistribution after controlling for level of inequality, unemployment, per capita income, unionization, and number of veto points.

Figure 3.2 reveals some evidence of a relationship between electoral systems and macroeconomic performance. The negative correlation between electoral systems and misery index (−0.577, significant at conventional levels) suggests that PR systems on average perform better with respect to this performance measure. However, multivariate studies that use disaggregated measures arrive at mixed results. For example, McManus and Ozkan (2018) estimate that P-M systems are associated with inflation rates that are 6 to 9 percentage points lower than PR systems and with less inflation volatility. Further, while they find that GDP growth volatility is higher in PR systems, their study also uncovers suggestive evidence that economic growth is lower in P-M systems. The latter finding is corroborated in Knutsen's (2011) study, which estimates that annual GDP per capita growth is approximately 1 percentage point higher in PR systems after controlling for government form, religion, regional effects, colonial heritage, among other factors.

Configurations of political institutions

So far, we have assessed how individual political institutions shape economic outcomes by influencing distinctly the incentives of actors and ultimately their collective policy decisions. In this section, we broaden the scope of analysis to include research examining the economic effects of different configurations of political institutions. We will first review works that combine two types of political institutions and then proceed to studies that aggregate multiple institutions such as the research on majoritarian and consensus democracies and on veto players.

Varieties of dual institutions

There is a strong connection between proportional representation and multiparty systems. That insight figures large in Martin and Swank's (2012) historical account of why macrocorporatism, which we discussed in the previous chapter, emerged in some countries but not others. They argue that political party systems, in combination with the degree of state centralization that existed in the early 1900s, strongly affected the development of the organizational characteristics of producer groups. They uncover strong evidence of a "coevolution of political representation and economic organization" (ibid: 27). The logic is as follows. Political parties dedicated to representing business interests are more likely to emerge in multiparty systems. In unitary states, these parties develop centralized characteristics that enable them to aggregate business interests around common national objectives. In federal states, business parties tend to be more decentralized and allow for the expression of regional interests. On the other hand, business interests tend to be dispersed in two-party systems as the dominant catch-all parties vie to secure employers' support. The dispersion of employers across parties diminishes their collective political capacity, which is much weaker in federal systems.

A central point in Martin and Swank's analysis is that the choices of lawmakers, not just of employers, played an important role in shaping the divergent historical trajectories of business groups across today's affluent democracies. In multiparty systems, lawmakers representing business interests faced strong incentives to delegate policymaking authority to private channels. They turned to non-legislative channels because of the unlikelihood that they could gain full control of the government and because of their doubts about the ability of the parliamentary process to consistently produce favorable pro-business outcomes. Pro-business politicians strategically pushed for "society building," whereby they actively encouraged employers and labor to develop collective capabilities.

In their historical account, Martin and Swank observe that in multiparty-unitary systems like those in Denmark, Norway, and Sweden, labor and employers developed highly encompassing characteristics in the early decades of the 1900s. Moreover, in the postwar period, national lawmakers often elicited their cooperation in finding pragmatic solutions to the challenges of economic adjustment. In Germany, which has had a multiparty-federal system, labor and employers developed sectoral-level collective capacities. Throughout the twentieth century, the principle of Tarifautonomie, which prevents the state from interfering in collective bargaining, helped cement this type of coordination.

Figure 3.3 graphs the correlation between institutions of collective representation and level of macrocorporatism using averages for the period between the early 1980s and early 2010s. The correlation between electoral system and macrocorporatism is strong. Countries that use PR such as the Nordic countries generally have more encompassing producer groups than those that use P-M systems such as Canada, the United Kingdom, and the United States. The association between level of federalism and macrocorporatism is as predicted although weaker. Using a simple multivariate regression model, the combination of electoral system and federalism can account for 74% of the variance in macrocorporatism for the 12-country sample. This result suggests the coevolution of economic organizations and institutions of political

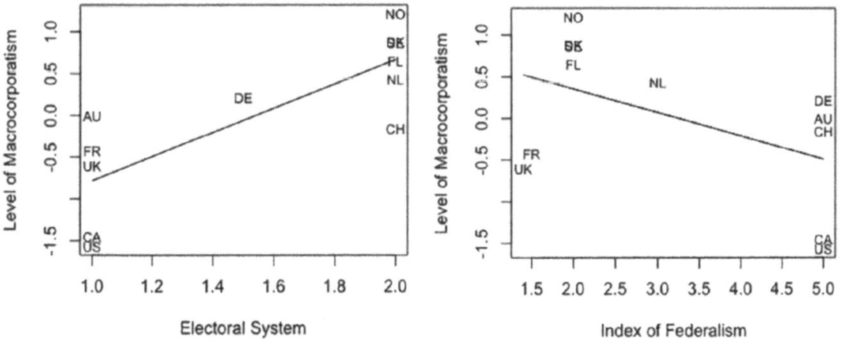

FIGURE 3.3 Political representation and macrocorporatism, early 1980s to early 2010s
Notes: r = 0.810, sig @ 0.001; r = −0.506, respectively.

Sources: See table 2.4 for data on macrocorporatism; figure 3.2 for electoral system classification; and Lijphart (2012: 306–307) for index of federalism.

representation, which Martin and Swank detected throughout the twentieth century, has held up throughout the last decades of that century and into the first one of the current century.

Is there a relationship between political institutions and trade? According to Rogowski (1987), certain democratic institutions are endogenous to trade. As he puts it, trade-dependent countries "will be impelled, more than their self-sufficient fellows, to adopt" parliamentary systems with large PR districts because they enhance the government's insulation, autonomy, and policy stability. In larger PR constituencies, which take in a wider array of interests, protectionist demands are unable to dominate thereby insulating representatives from such demands. Because PR systems tend to create parties that are more internally cohesive and centered around party leaders and lead to weaker constituency-representative links, parties are more autonomous from the pressure tactics that protectionist-oriented interest groups employ to promote their cause. Finally, the fusion of power between the legislative and executive branches means that agreements reached through bargaining among coalition leaders can be brought to bear more effectively on both branches thus fostering policy stability and predictability (see also Crepaz 1996; Powell 1982).

IN FOCUS BOX 3.1 TRADE OPENNESS AND POLITICAL INSTITUTIONS

Figure 3.4 reports data on level of openness—measured as imports plus exports as a percentage of GDP from the early 1980s to the early 2010s. The correlation between economic openness and electoral system is quite strong; in fact, the relationship is stronger during this time period than what Rogowski reported based on data from the 1960s to the 1970s. On average, non-PR countries have lower trade levels than countries with PR systems. Moreover, there is a negative relationship between trade and the number of districts, as Rogowski found. Less trade dependent countries tend to have more districts, such as France, Germany, and the United Kingdom while more trade reliant countries tend to have a smaller number of districts such as Denmark, the Netherlands, and Switzerland.

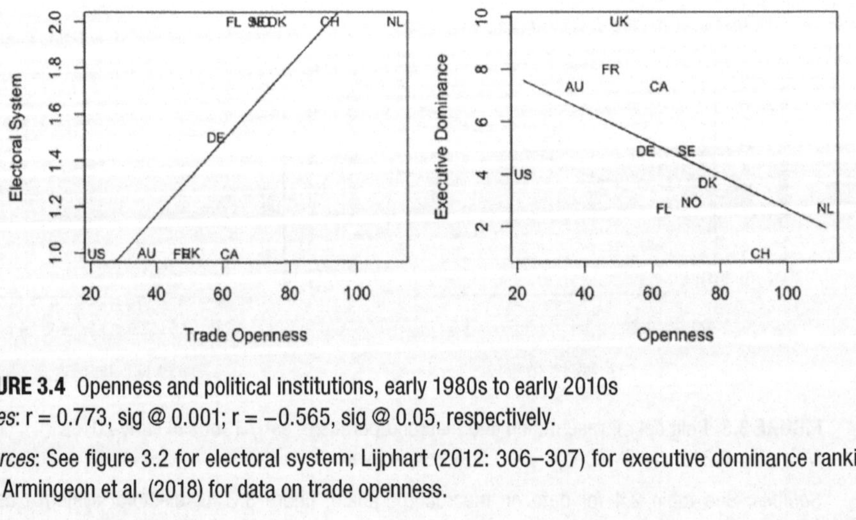

FIGURE 3.4 Openness and political institutions, early 1980s to early 2010s

Notes: r = 0.773, sig @ 0.001; r = –0.565, sig @ 0.05, respectively.

Sources: See figure 3.2 for electoral system; Lijphart (2012: 306–307) for executive dominance ranking; and Armingeon et al. (2018) for data on trade openness.

To capture the effect of parliamentarism on trade, figure 3.4 also looks at the relationship between openness and level of executive dominance. The logic here is that PR tends to lead to lower levels of executive dominance because it increases the likelihood of coalitions and minority governments. All Nordic countries plus Switzerland use PR and have lower levels of executive dominance. These parliamentary features elevate the importance of political bargains between the party or parties in government and opposition parties in the legislature. The imperative of consensus building in the policymaking process, as Rogowski and others have pointed out, militates against abrupt and major policy changes which trade-dependent countries prefer. As figure 3.4 shows, openness is negatively related with executive dominance, a relationship that is significant at conventional levels. The most open countries like Denmark, the Netherlands, and Switzerland tend to have lower levels of executive dominance due to the higher frequency of minority governments and coalitions, while less open economies like Australia, France, and the United Kingdom have higher incidences of single-party majority governments.

Crepaz (1996) argues that macroeconomic performance is better in PR-parliamentary systems than in alternative configurations of democratic institutions because these polities tend to lead to more encompassing governments. Given that governments in PR-parliamentary systems often represent a share of the electorate that exceeds a bare majority, not only are their policy interests more closely aligned to the general interest, they also face a "higher incentive to internalize the externalities" of their collective policy actions (ibid: 88–89). Further, since policymaking hinges on consensus building across different parties, economic policies are less vulnerable to be manipulated for electoral gains. Thus, the encompassing representation of coalition government coupled with the steadiness and predictability of economic policies, Crepaz argues, play instrumental roles in accounting for why these political systems in general tend to have lower inflation and unemployment.

Figure 3.5 reports data on the level of encompassment, which is measured as the percentage of popular support of parties in government. The average electoral support of cabinets in parliamentary-PR and parliamentary-P-M systems are 50% and 43%, respectively. These averages are lower than those reported by Crepaz, who used data from 1945 to 1987. This suggests that the macroeconomic effects which Crepaz observed may have eroded over time. Of note, in the parliamentary-PR cluster, Denmark, Norway, and Sweden have much lower levels of encompassment than Finland and the Netherlands. This is because the three Nordic countries were led by minority governments on a regular basis in the postwar period. The level of electoral support of governments is negatively correlated with the misery index; however, that effect virtually vanishes if Switzerland is omitted from the correlation. Crepaz's study, which covers 18 affluent OECD countries, estimates that a 1% increase in popular cabinet support cuts the misery index by 0.11 percent. The stylized evidence from the 1980s to 2010s suggests the link between macroeconomic performance and encompassment has weakened, calling into question the argument that governments backed by higher popular electoral support govern more responsibly.

Crepaz also finds that the level of encompassment is closely associated with the degree of consensus democracy, which we will discuss next. Remarkably, there has been little change in the position of the 12 countries from 1945 to the early 2010s.

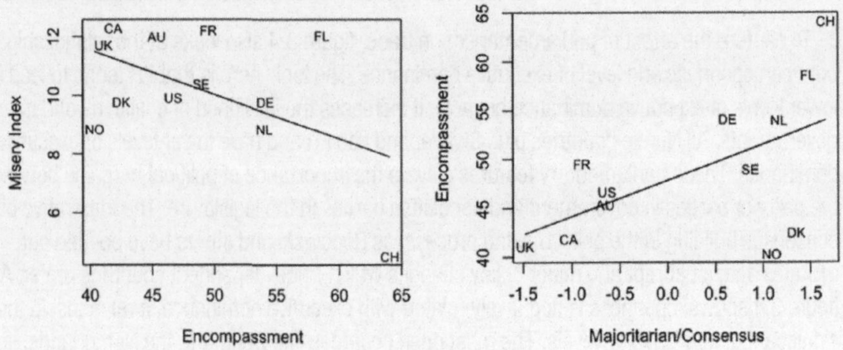

FIGURE 3.5 Encompassment and political-economic conditions, early 1980s to early 2010s
Notes: r = −0.514, sig @ 0.05; r = 0.563, sig @ 0.05, respectively.

Sources: see Cruz et al. (2016) for data on encompassment; table 2.5 for misery index; and Lijphart (2012: 305–306) for majoritarian/consensus ranking along the executives-parties dimension.

The correlation between these two measures from the early 1980s to early 2010s is close to the one in Crepaz's study.

Consensus and majoritarian democracies

Many scholars have traced cross-national differences in economic policy outcomes back to the type of democracy found in countries. The key difference between majoritarian and consensus democracies centers on "to whose interests should the government be responsive when the people are in disagreement and have divergent preferences," as Lijphart (2012: 2) points out. In majoritarian systems, the aim of governments is to be responsive to the majority of the people; in consensus systems, it is to be responsive to as many people as possible. Whereas majoritarian democracies are designed to concentrate public authority in the hands of a narrow majority, the institutional characteristics of consensus democracies disperse and restrain public authority, inducing power-sharing, bargaining, and compromise among competing interests. The result of these institutional dynamics in consensus democracies is that the size of the ruling majority is larger than in majoritarian democracies, meaning a wider range of interests is brought to bear on policymaking.

As Lijphart (2012) details in his work on patterns of democracy, the concentration of power in majoritarian democracies is facilitated by several institutional features: single-party majority cabinets, executive dominance of the executive-legislative relationship, two-party system, competitive and uncoordinated interest groups, unitary structure, unicameral legislature or asymmetric bicameralism where the lower chamber is more powerful, flexible constitution, absence of judicial review, and weak central bank independence. Within this institutional constellation, minority interests have few means of constraining the actions of the ruling majority. A small margin of victory in the electoral arena can translate into big changes in the policy arena.

On the other hand, the dispersion of authority in consensus democracies is owed to a different institutional arrangement: multiparty coalition cabinets, balanced executive-legislative relationship, multiparty system, corporatist-based interest groups, federal structure, balanced bicameralism, rigid constitution, judicial review, and strong central bank independence. In this institutional landscape, the policymaking arena is moderated by the power-sharing agreements that sustain coalition cabinets and by the institutional checks that minority interests wield.

Some scholars have observed that majoritarian and consensus democracies impact the size of government and macroeconomic performance differently. The imperatives of accommodating the demands of coalition partners and minority interests often lead to logrolling legislation which tends to drive up public spending and tax revenue (Crepaz and Moser 2004; Tavits 2004). Moreover, because governments in consensus democracies represent a larger share of the population, they are incentivized to internalize the costs of manipulating the economy for short-term political gains, which is expected to result in more consistent macroeconomic performance.

Figure 3.6 showcases some corroborating evidence for these arguments. Outlays and revenues positively correlate with the degree of consensus democracy. When Switzerland is omitted, both correlations become much stronger and statistically significant at conventional levels. Based on data from 1974 to 1995 on 22 countries (which exclude Switzerland), Tavits (2004) finds strong evidence suggesting that both outlays and revenues are higher in consensus democracies after controlling for other determinants of the size of government such as economic openness, federalism, and incidence of Left government. Tavits also finds that the fiscal effects of consensus democracy become stronger when Left governments are in power, a topic we take up in the next chapter.

The pooled time series analyses by Birchfield and Crepaz (1998), Crepaz (1996), Lijphart (2012), and others have found that consensus democracies perform better than majoritarian democracies. The last scatterplot in figure 3.6 provides preliminary and stylistic evidence, lending some support for this argument. Denmark, Germany, the Netherlands, Norway, and Sweden recorded better results than Australia, Canada, France, and the United Kingdom with respect to the misery index. Regardless of whether Switzerland is included or excluded, the correlation is always strong and remains significant at conventional levels. Crepaz (1996) and Lijphart (2012) also find corroborating evidence suggesting that consensus democracies have lower unemployment and inflation rates after controlling for various other factors. Further, because of their higher levels of income redistribution, consensus democracies tend to have lower levels of income inequality as reported by Birchfield and Crepaz (1998).

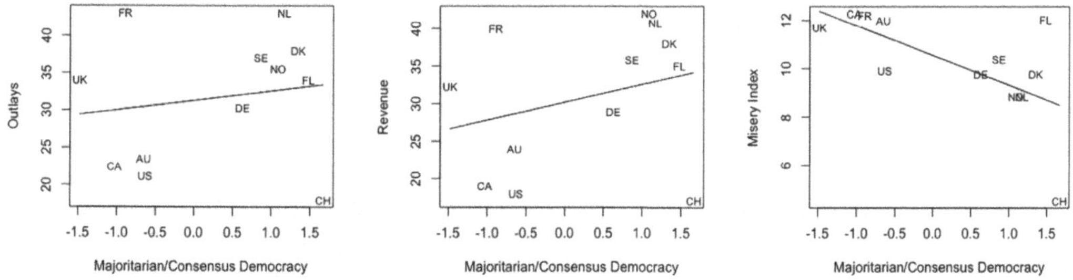

FIGURE 3.6 Patterns of democracy and economic outcomes, early 1980s to early 2010s
Sources: see figure 3.5 for majoritarian/consensus democracy ranking; and figure 3.2 for outlays, revenue, and misery index.

Several studies have explored the policy implications of these two types of democracy. Gourevitch and Shinn (2005) find a relationship between types of democracy and corporate governance arrangements. Their data on 39 countries, which together account for 99.5% of the total global equity markets by value, reveal the following patterns: majoritarian democracies such as Australia, Canada, and the United States tend to have diffused shareholding (a large number of small investors) and stronger minority shareholder protections (MSPs), while consensus democracies such as Denmark, Germany, and Switzerland tend to have more blockholding (a small number of large investors) and weaker MSPs.

IN FOCUS BOX 3.2 WHAT ARE MINORITY SHAREHOLDER PROTECTIONS (MSPs)?

MSPs protect small shareholders from potential abuses stemming from managerial authority. MSPs require companies to disclose information at regular intervals; mandate that firms align their financial reporting practices to internationally recognized accounting standards; require boards of directors to have some degree of independence from management as they perform their fiduciary duties on behalf of shareholders; provide voting rights to shareholders over important management decisions; and incentivize managers to maximize shareholder value through performance-based compensation. Where MSPs are weaker, insiders such as large blockholders and workers (who can be important stakeholders in some settings) can exercise direct oversight of managers. Gourevitch and Shinn find that MSPs tend to be inversely related to shareholding concentration—MSPs are strongest where shareholding is diffused.

For Gourevitch and Shinn, a key factor explaining cross-national variance in the degree of shareholding concentration is the feasibility of credible commitment. Because consensus democracy promotes greater policy stability and predictability, investors and other stakeholders are willing to invest in long-term arrangements, leading to stable and concentrated patterns of shareholding and greater reliance on insider control to monitor corporate management. In contrast, the possibility of swift and major policy changes in majoritarian democracies shortens investors' time horizons, and inclines them to diversify their portfolios and to focus on the short-term performance of their investments. In such a context, the system of shareholding is likely to be more diffused, have a high turnover rate, and feature stronger minority protections.

Cross-national differences in the level of taxation on capital can be attributed in part to the type of democracy found in countries. Based on data from 17 affluent OECD countries from 1965 to 1996, Hays (2003) finds that capital taxation is higher in majoritarian democracies than in consensus democracies (for a similar analysis, see Garrett 1998b). This pattern holds when we shorten the time span from 1980 to 1997 and use our 12-country sample. Using the same methodology employed by Hays to calculate capital and labor taxes, the average effective capital tax rate in majoritarian and consensus democracies is 42.6% and 37.9%, respectively. Further, as figure 3.7 reveals, labor-capital tax differential is positively correlated with the degree of consensus democracy. In general, majoritarian democracies tax capital income at a higher rate relative to labor income; the opposite is found among consensus

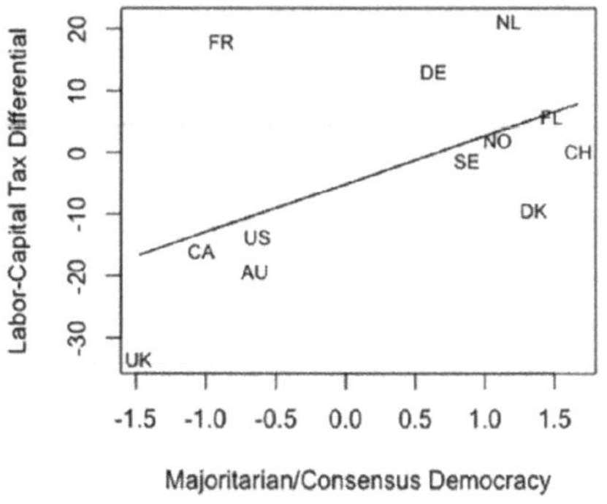

FIGURE 3.7 Type of democracy and labor-capital tax differential, 1980–1997
Note: r = 0.546, sig @ 0.05

Sources: See figure 3.5 for majoritarian/consensus democracy ranking; and Carey and Tchilinguirian (2000) for data on labor-capital tax differential.

democracies. The fact that Australia, Canada, the United Kingdom, and the United States impose higher taxes on capital income might surprise many given that these economies are modeled on market liberalism. Similarly, that Sweden, the Netherlands, and Norway, which have had social democratic corporatist economies, impose relatively low capital taxes seems to defy conventional wisdom. So, why have these cross-national patterns emerged?

The degree to which policymaking is responsive to the tax preferences of wage earners plays an important role in explaining this pattern of taxation across affluent OECD countries. Wage earners represent the majority of the electorate and seek the highest possible capital tax rate. The influence of wage earners on tax policy is expected to be lower in consensus democracies due to the constraints facing the political majority. Such constraints help safeguard business interests, enabling their parliamentary allies to block efforts to increase the capital tax burden. Thus, the dynamics of power-sharing and compromise, which are at the heart of consensus democracy, result in tax structures that are less punitive on capital, but that have more regressive features such as higher consumption and payroll taxes. In majoritarian democracies, where there is a lack of effective constraints on the political majority, tax policy is more responsive to demands for raising taxes on capital income relative to labor income. This has led to tax structures that rely more heavily on capital taxation and that depend less on regressive tax sources. Many majoritarian democracies have come to realize that their tax regimes are ill-suited to address the pressures arising from increased international capital mobility. As a result, capital tax rates have dropped more sharply in these countries than they have in consensus democracies in recent decades.

Veto points

A concept closely related to patterns of democracy is veto points. There are more veto players in consensus democracies than in majoritarian systems. Tsebelis (1995: 301) defines a veto player as "an individual or collective actor whose agreement (by majority rule for collective actors) is required for a change in policy." As the research on veto players points out, policy stability is enhanced as the number of veto players increases, as the level of ideological polarization among veto players increases, and as the similarity of positions among actors comprising a veto group increases. In short, as the quantity, polarization, and cohesion of veto players increase, policy shifts become harder to achieve.

There are two categories of veto players. Institutional veto players arise from the division of powers among independent institutions which have the constitutional means to check and balance each other. Constitutional designs such as bicameralism, federalism, judicial review, and presidentialism create competition among political actors that have veto powers. On the other hand, partisan veto players are political actors whose consent is needed to facilitate decision-making. Institutional settings that operate on the basis of collective leadership and shared responsibility, such as multi-party legislatures and coalition governments, bestow veto power on party officials to the extent that collective agency hinges on eliciting their support.

What effects do veto players have on the size of government? The logic behind the theory of veto player is that an increase in veto players should restrain public spending. Because political actors seek to defend their institutional interests and such interests often conflict with each other, agreeing on legislation that expands public outlays will be difficult to achieve. The first graph in figure 3.8 reports stylized evidence that lends some support for this claim. Countries with more institutional veto points such as Australia, Canada, Switzerland, and the United States have lower levels of outlays than countries with fewer veto players. Crepaz and Moser's multivariate analysis finds a similar result. Focusing on 15 OECD countries between 1960 and 1996, they find that institutional veto players reduce public expenditures, general government consumption of goods and services net of military spending, and social transfers, after controlling for other determinants of government size such as globalization, demographic factors, and proportionality of electoral system.

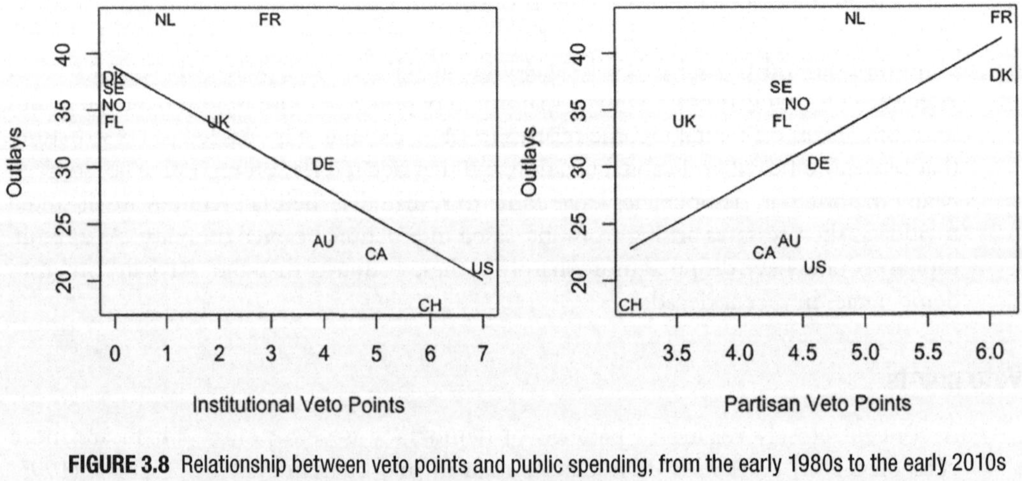

FIGURE 3.8 Relationship between veto points and public spending, from the early 1980s to the early 2010s
Notes: r = −0.796, sig @ 0.001; r = 0.626, sig @ 0.01, respectively.

Sources: Armingeon et al. (2018) for data on institutional veto points; Cruz et al. (2016) for data on partisan veto points.

However, as Crepaz and Moser (2004: 262) observe, the presence of veto players need not always produce such restraining effects. "Not all veto points are created equal and have equal effects," they note. Increasing the number of partisan veto players, Crepaz and Moser argue, enables rather than restrains the expansion of public spending. A key driver of this expansion is the dynamic of logrolling. In political settings such as government coalitions and multi-party legislatures, where party leaders wield significant veto power, as evidenced by their ability to withdraw their support of crucial political arrangements, policy agreements are often reached through logrolling. In such settings, political actors are encouraged to leverage the threat of withdrawal to promote their individual policy interests. Further, although all members of a coalition government might recognize the benefit of fiscal restraint, each is motivated to act otherwise if other members are floating their own spending proposals. In short, legislative logrolling will result in the growth of government.

The second graph in figure 3.8 shows a strong positive correlation between partisan veto players and size of government. Of note, all low institutional veto Nordic countries end up somewhere in the middle or higher end of the partisan veto player scale. France emerges as a high partisan veto point country largely because of the cohabitation periods it went through in the late 1980s, mid-1990s, and end of the 1990s and early 2000s. Switzerland, a high institutional veto country, had the lowest number of partisan veto players between the early 1980s and early 2010s. The results of the study by Crepaz and Moser (2004) and Swank (2002) corroborate what the aforementioned correlational evidence reveals. The impact of partisan veto points on the size of government is starkly different from the effect of institutional veto points. Public spending, government consumption, and social transfers tend to grow as the number of partisan veto players increases.

Conclusion

Certain types of democracies appear to be more successful than others at fostering favorable economic conditions. Furthermore, the size of government and public revenue seems to be larger in democracies with particular institutional characteristics. The patterns that have been detected between economic outcomes and political institutions hinge on how government officials generally react to the dynamics and incentives generated by their institutional environments.

The research on forms of government suggests that parliamentary systems foster better economic conditions than presidential systems in the long run. In addition, this line of research has found that parliamentary systems tend to have larger public outlays and revenue, and to allocate more funds toward broad-based social programs. Part of the explanation for these patterns is that parliamentary dynamics are more conducive to policy stability and legislative coordination. This is especially the case when parliamentarism is combined with proportional representation and a large number of partisan veto points.

The research on the economic effects of electoral systems suggests that public spending and revenue are lower in plurality-majority electoral systems. Moreover, this type of electoral system tends to be associated with inferior economic performance in the long run. These patterns are partly attributed to the fact that P-M, when combined with presidentialism, produces weaker incentives for government officials to internalize the effects of their policy actions and to coordinate their actions in the legislative process.

Key terms

Consensus democracy

Majoritarian democracy

Parliamentarism

Plurality-majority electoral system

Presidentialism

Proportional representation

Veto point

Discussion questions

- Some have argued that parliamentary systems perform better economically than presidential systems. Elaborate on the logic of this argument. Does the empirical evidence support that argument?
- Compare and contrast the effects of proportional representation and plurality-majority electoral systems on economic outcomes.
- Compare and contrast the effects of consensus and majoritarian democracy on taxation, government spending, and economic performance.
- Elaborate on the theory behind the relationship between veto points and the size of government. Explain why institutional and partisan veto points produce different effects on public spending.

Further reading

Haggard, Stephen, and Mathew McCubbins. 2001. *Presidents, Parliaments, and Policy*. Edited. Cambridge, UK: Cambridge University Press.

Explores the economic policy effects of different political institutional arrangements.

Lijphart, Arend. 2012. *Patterns of Democracy: Government Forms and Performance in Thirty-Six Countries*. 2nd edition. New Haven: Yale University Press.

Compares and contrasts majoritarian and consensus democracies.

McCarty, Noland, Keith T. Poole, and Howard Rosenthal. 2013. *Political Bubbles: Financial Crises and the Failure of American Democracy*. Princeton, NJ: Princeton University Press.

Contends that it is the combination of unresponsive political institutions, influence of special interest groups, and dominance of liberal market beliefs that set in motion a chain of events which culminated in the financial crisis of 2007–2009 in the United States.

Stasavage, David. 2011. *States of Credit: Size, Power, and the Development of European Politics*. Princeton, NJ: Princeton University Press.

Focusing on the early history of public debt (1250 to 1875), the book argues that the strong representative institutions found in European city-states gave them an advantage in accessing credit that in turn helped them achieve economic growth.

CHAPTER

4

Political cycles in economic policies and outcomes

How does the electoral calendar or the partisan composition of government impact growth, inflation, or unemployment? How do elections or government partisanship influence the direction, timing, and prioritization of economic policies? The fascination with these questions within the economics and political science disciplines has led to an extant literature exploring why, how, and when the electoral and partisan motives of politicians contribute to the cyclicality of economic policy instruments and macroeconomic outcomes in advanced capitalist democracies.

This chapter will explore these questions by drawing on various strands of research. The chapter is divided into two general sections. The first section reviews two models of electoral cycles—traditional and rational electoral models. It also addresses how the timing, size, and form of these cycles are conditioned by different contextual factors—an area of focus commonly referred to as context-dependent electoral cycles. The second section explores models of partisanship—namely, the traditional and rational partisan models. That is followed by a discussion of how partisan cycles are context-dependent.

Readers will find similarities between the scholarship on political cycles and economic voting, which we will cover in Chapter 5. This is the case because both areas of inquiry, first, study how the political choices made by voters and government officials are shaped by the interaction between these groups of actors and, second, make similar assumptions about the behavior of these actors in democratic settings. For example, if we assume that voters prefer lower unemployment and higher economic growth, then incumbents seeking reelection have an incentive to foster such economic conditions prior to elections, expecting that voters will reward them for doing so. Nevertheless, the main contrast between these two areas of study has to do with the focus of attention. The study of political cycles draws attention to the political control of the macroeconomy—specifically, how economic outcomes and policies are shaped by incumbents' objectives, whether it be to maximize votes or fulfill partisan goals. In contrast, economic voting focuses on the economy's effect on electoral outcomes—specifically, how economic conditions weigh on the minds of individuals and influence their vote choice. In short, the political cycles literature

DOI: 10.4324/9780429199462-4

explores how electoral-partisan politics impact the economy, whereas the economic voting literature examines how the economy impacts democratic politics.

Models of electoral cycles

Electoral cycle models hold that the handling of the economy by incumbents is influenced by the electoral calendar. These models assume that politicians are alike—they want to get reelected; they use the same economic policy tools to maximize votes, and they appeal to the same voters. These models also assume that voters have the same preferences over policy outcomes regarding growth, employment, and inflation and are "pocketbook" oriented, meaning that their political evaluations reflect their personal economic circumstances. In contrast, partisan models hold that incumbents distinctly manage the economy due to the fact that they represent different constituent groups with varying material interests. As agents of different voter groups, parties seek to promote the policies that favor their core supporters in the electorate.

The traditional electoral cycle model

The traditional electoral cycle model asserts that vote-maximizing politicians are inclined to manipulate the economy in the lead-up to elections to help them get reelected. It assumes that incumbents control monetary and fiscal policies, enabling them to exploit to their advantage the trade-off between level of unemployment and inflation. The model predicts that incumbent officials will stage a pre-election economic expansion—such as increase employment or income—by increasing public spending or lowering interest rates and taxes or combining some of these measures. Once reelected, they will shift to restrictive policies such as raising interest rates to stop the inflation caused by the pre-election, government-induced stimulus. Focusing on the unemployment rate, Nordhaus (1975: 184) points out that "immediately after an election the victor will raise unemployment to some relatively high level in order to combat inflation. As elections approach, the unemployment rate will be lowered until, on election eve, the unemployment rate will be lowered" to the level that yields the highest possible number of votes. Similarly, Tufte (1978) finds that office-seeking politicians are inclined to engineer pre-election boosts in real disposable income growth (income after taxes and transfers adjusted for inflation). As he puts it, "the quickest way to. . . [spur growth in] real disposable income is to mail more people larger checks; i.e., for transfer payments to increase." Tufte's work was among the first to suggest that electoral cycles can occur in economic policies, not just in economic outcomes.

If all voters are averse to inflation, then why do they reelect rather than oust incumbents who conduct economic policies that result in inflation? In the traditional electoral cycle model, it is assumed that voters form their expectations adaptively and evaluate incumbents retrospectively. Adaptive expectation means that voters' economic forecasts are based on past observations, not on a combination of what is likely to occur in the future and happened in the recent past. If inflation is relatively low in the six months before elections, then voters have reason to believe that it will be low in the future. In fact, because expansionary policies do not trigger inflation immediately (there is a lag effect), voters will not experience much (if any) inflation in the months leading up to election when incumbents are most likely to conduct stimulus policies. Further, voters are assumed to be myopic, that is they discount the distant past but rely on recent experiences to form their political judgment. Voters' myopia is what enables incumbents to escape electoral penalty for the high inflation voters experience at the beginning of an electoral term (Alt and Chrystal 1983).

To sum up, because incumbents are being evaluated based on what voters experience in the months prior to elections, they face a strong incentive to engineer favorable macroeconomic outcomes shortly before elections, an incentive reinforced by the fact that voters typically underestimate expected inflation. As Nordhaus (1975: 187) remarks,

> a perfect democracy with retrospective evaluation of parties will make decisions biased against future generations. Moreover, within an incumbent's term in office there is a predictable pattern of policy, starting with relative austerity in early years and ending with the potlatch right before elections.

Similarly, Tufte (1978: 143) concludes that "electoral-economic cycle breeds a lurching stop-and-go economy the world over [and] a bias toward policies with immediate, highly visible benefits and deferred, hidden costs—myopic policies for myopic voters."

This model has been widely challenged on empirical and theoretical grounds. Studies that have examined electoral cycles in macroeconomic outcomes find inconsistent and mixed evidence. Whereas Golden and Poterba (1980), Haynes and Stone (1989), Paldam (1991b), among others find supporting evidence, studies by Alesina et al. (1997), Beck (1982), Drazen (2000), Hibbs (1987), and others fail to detect electorally timed expansions. There has been, however, more consistent and corroborating evidence of electoral cycles in economic policies. Although economic outcomes might not fluctuate as predicted by this model, the same interactive dynamic between incumbents and voters can induce incumbents in the lead-up to elections to manipulate deficit spending—specifically, the distribution of money to organized groups in the electorate—as well as taxation and monetary instruments to improve their reelection prospects. Studies have found evidence of electorally induced cyclicality in veterans' benefits in the United States (Keech and Pak 1989), transfer payments in the United Kingdom (Schultz 1995), private credit growth in numerous countries (Aklin and Kern 2020), money supply in the United States and other industrial economies (Alesina et al. 1997; Beck 1987), and targeted and overall government spending in industrial and developing economies (Alesina et al. 1997; Drazen and Eslava 2010).

The rational electoral cycle model

Would electoral cycles exist if people were rationally foresighted? This model predicts that electorally timed expansions would still occur; however, they would be less frequent and smaller (Franzese 2002). The idea that incumbents vary in terms of their competence and that voters can only observe incumbent competency after a lag are key premises of this model. Although all incumbents are motivated by the desire to be reelected, some incumbents are more competent than others. Competency is generally understood as the ability of politicians "to solve problems and handle the economy efficiently," as Alesina et al. (1997) point out. For Rogoff and Sibert (1988) and Rogoff (1990), competency involves the ability to use less tax revenue to finance a fixed amount of government spending. In their model, Persson and Tabellini (1990: 80) conceive of competence as the ability "to cope with a shock to the price of oil, or to enact effective labor market legislation, or to negotiate with trade unions" or other policy problems in a way that maintains the noninflationary level of unemployment.

Competence is treated as private information. Incumbents know more about their competence than voters. This information advantage will be exploited by incumbents during the election year. They will engineer a pre-election expansion by manipulating the revenue and spending sides of fiscal policy in order to signal their competence and distinguish themselves from other contenders.

Voters elect officials they judge to be most capable of maximizing their future utility. Their expectations about the future economic performance are rationally formed by observing the competence of incumbents, which directs their attention to the state of the economy during the election year. Because it is assumed that competence persists over time, the information voters use to learn about incumbents' competence prior to elections also helps them to form predictions about what they are capable of doing after elections. One might wonder why rational voters "allow their expectations about postelection performance to be influenced by preelection budget antics," as Rogoff (1990: 21) points out. The reason is that voters cannot monitor incumbent competence directly. Voters observe tax and government expenditure levels, for example, and use that information to make inferences about the competence of incumbents. These inferences can only be verified sometime in the future when the effects of policy actions are fully revealed (Rogoff and Sibert 1988; Rogoff 1990). As Keech (2013: 68) notes, "this lag introduces a temporary information asymmetry that allows a government to deceive the voters about its competence."

The fact that electoral cycles tend to be small and irregular, lends some credence to the rational electoral cycle model. The model predicts that even though voters are foresighted and not easily fooled, the asymmetries of information between incumbents and voters about the effects of policy measures afford the former an advantage. Incumbents can exploit such information asymmetries to deceive voters about their competence. As Alesina et al. (1997: 31) point out,

> Suppose that in an election year the incumbent government raises certain transfers, claiming that no new taxes will be needed because a high expected growth rate will automatically increase revenue. Such a claim is quite hard for the average voter to check, certainly harder than observing inflation and unemployment in the election year.

In short, while the sophistication of voters acts as a constraint on government officials' pre-election economic manipulation, they are still able to feign competence due to the difficulty of verifying government claims at the time of their announcement.

Context-dependent election cycles

How might political and economic factors, at domestic and international levels, shape election cycles? The two models of electoral cycles we have just surveyed neglect for the most part how context can impact the occurrence, size, and form of such cycles. Below, we zero in on specific economic and political contextual factors and explore how they condition electoral cycles.

Economic context

Traditional and rational electoralist models assume that incumbents have control of monetary and fiscal policy levers. Both models also assume incumbents will use these levers to engineer a pre-election economic expansion in an attempt to improve their reelection prospects. In reality, the ability of incumbents to use both sets of policy levers is dependent on the economic context in which they maneuver. The literature examining the link between economic context and range of opportunistic maneuvering spotlights the intervening effects of central bank, capital mobility, and exchange rate regimes. As we will discuss next, the size of electoral cycles is conditional on the nature of these situational factors. These factors determine whether or not incumbents have control over monetary policy or fiscal policy or both and whether or not these policy tools are effective in achieving pre-election expansions (Clark 2005).

Monetary policy is typically managed by central bankers not elected politicians (for more on central banks, see Chapter 2). Furthermore, central bankers assign greater import than most elected politicians to price stability relative to growth stability. Therefore, if central bankers are independent of politicians, they will pursue a restrictive monetary policy in response to politicians' efforts to engineer pre-election growth. Monetary policy will counteract the effects of fiscal policy, foiling incumbents' electorally motivated efforts.

Since the 1980s, all OECD countries have liberalized capital mobility. There are two schools of thought regarding the effects of capital mobility on macroeconomic politics. One strand of literature argues that the globalization of production and finance restricts incumbent politicians' room of maneuver in the run-up to elections. Garrett (1998a: 793) best summarizes this line of thinking: "Governments are held to ransom by the markets, the price is high, and punishment for noncompliance is swift. If the policies and institutions of which the markets approve are not found in a country, money will hemorrhage until they are." From the viewpoint of firms and investors, electorally motivated interventions spell budget deficits in the short run and higher interest rates and taxes in the long run. Facing these potential costs, owners of capital will signal their readiness to exit, thus deterring politicians from attempting these maneuvers. In sum, this line of argument claims that globalization in general reduces the government's effective control of both monetary and fiscal policies. Leveraging them for political gains may lead to capital flight and consequently to non-electable conditions.

Another strand of literature holds that the impact of capital mobility on the effectiveness of macroeconomic policies depends on the type of exchange rate regime and type of central bank a country has (Clark 2005). Table 4.1 summarizes how different economic contexts shape the ability of incumbent politicians to use

TABLE 4.1 The expected macroeconomic policy effects in the run-up to elections under different situations

	Dependent Central Bank	Independent Central Bank
No capital mobility	*Fiscal Policy:* expansive *Monetary Policy*: expansive, if used	*Fiscal policy:* expansive *Monetary policy*: restrictive
Capital mobility with fixed exchange rate	*Fiscal policy*: expansive *Monetary policy*: none	*Fiscal policy*: expansive *Monetary policy*: none
Capital mobility with floating exchange rate	*Fiscal policy*: none *Monetary policy:* expansive	*Fiscal policy*: none *Monetary policy*: none

Source: Republished with permission of University of Michigan Press, from Clark (2005), *Capitalism, not Globalism: Capital Mobility, Central Bank Independence, and the Political Control of the Economy*, Ann Arbor: The University of Michigan Press (p. 28); permission conveyed through Copyright Clearance Center, Inc.

monetary and fiscal policies in order to bring about a pre-election expansion. When there is no capital mobility and the central bank lacks independence, incumbents are more likely to use fiscal policy (which is under their direct control) to foster re-electable conditions, unless they believe that a monetary expansion would be more effective in achieving such conditions. This was a scenario found in several OECD countries from the 1950s to 1970s, the period which earlier opportunistic electoral cycle models focused on. In a closed economy with an independent central bank, a situation that government officials in Germany and the United States faced from the 1950s to 1970s, electorally timed fiscal expansions are ineffective due to the neutralizing effects of restrictive monetary policies conducted by central bankers. This could account for the weak evidence of electoral cycles in the United States that Alesina et al. (1997) and others have found.

In situations where there is both capital mobility and a fixed exchange rate policy, monetary policy is ineffective regardless of whether or not the central bank is independent. Electorally induced fiscal expansions may occur, even when central bankers are independent. Focusing on the period from 1973 to the 1990s, a period in which countries liberalized capital mobility, Clark and Hallerberg (2000) and Clark (2005) find strong evidence that countries with fixed exchange rates witnessed electorally timed fiscal cycles but no monetary cycles.

Electorally timed monetary expansions are more likely to take place when the exchange rate is allowed to float and the central bank lacks independence. However, incumbent politicians are unable to orchestrate pre-election fiscal or monetary cycles in situations where there is a floating exchange rate and an independent central bank. Clark and Hallerberg (2000) and Clark (2005) find evidence suggesting that the occurrence of opportunistic monetary cycles is contingent on the degree of central bank independence and type of exchange rate regime as specified earlier. Further, their evidence confirms that fiscal cycles are absent when exchange rates float.

IN FOCUS BOX 4.1 HOW EXCHANGE RATE REGIMES AFFECT MACROECONOMIC POLICY

Under a fixed exchange rate

When a government adheres to a fixed exchange rate, capital mobility deters officials from using monetary policy but can induce them to use fiscal policy. Monetary expansion loses its effectiveness under a fixed exchange rate regime because the resulting drop in a country's interest rates forces monetary officials to intervene in exchange rate markets to counteract the effects of monetary expansion. A decrease in interest rates leads to capital outflow which in turn leads to a depreciation of the local currency relative to foreign currencies. To defend the currency peg, monetary officials must buy the local currency and sell foreign reserves. The consequence of such a move is that it decreases the money supply, raises interest rates, and slows output growth.

Fiscal policy, on the other hand, is more effective in fostering re-electable economic conditions. An increase in government spending and/or tax cut boosts domestic consumption but also raises real interest rates. This leads to an inflow of foreign capital causing the exchange rate to appreciate. To maintain the currency peg, monetary officials intervene in exchange rate markets however this time by selling the local currency and buying foreign currencies, in effect, increasing the money supply. In short, the electorally induced fiscal expansion triggers a monetary response that complements the fiscal measures of incumbent politicians.

Under a floating exchange rate

When the exchange rate is allowed to float, capital mobility augments the effectiveness of monetary expansion but foils the effectiveness of fiscal expansion (Clark 2005). As we established in the previous paragraphs, monetary expansion has the effect of decreasing a country's exchange rate due to the outflow of capital. In a situation where monetary officials do not need to protect currency pegs, currency depreciation ends up improving the price competitiveness of a country's exports. The resulting increase in the international demand for that country's products helps boost domestic output growth. On the other hand, fiscal expansion undermines a country's export performance by causing the local currency to appreciate relative to other currencies. The resulting decrease in export levels and in output growth counteracts the fiscal expansion.

Incentives to manipulate

Do incumbent politicians facing reelection always seek to engineer pre-election expansions as assumed in traditional and rational electoral models? Several scholars have questioned that assumption, arguing instead that the incentive to manipulate is conditioned by the political context. As Schultz (1995) notes, the idea that incumbent politicians always manipulate policies prior to elections is flawed given that the marginal benefits and reputational risks of taking such actions vary across elections. On the one hand, the marginal returns of policy manipulation depend on the level of electoral competitiveness. The marginal benefits of gaining extra votes by engineering election timed expansions are smaller for incumbents who anticipate winning reelection with a comfortable margin. However, for incumbents whose reelection prospects are uncertain, staging a pre-election expansion could help them avoid losing their seats.

On the other hand, leveraging policy instruments for political reasons can render incumbent politicians vulnerable to voter retribution. The inflation caused by policy manipulation not only exposes incumbents to accusations of being opportunistic and irresponsible, but also imposes future costs on voters as monetary authorities implement measures to wring out inflation. In short, Schultz observes that incumbents are unlikely to engineer electoral cycles if such cycles carry a high reputational cost and generate low marginal electoral returns.

The motive to manipulate the economy may be stronger among longer-term incumbent officials. Based on data from 19 OECD countries between 1972 and 1999, Clark et al. (2013) find that long-serving leaders, those in power for more than seven years, are more likely to engineer pre-election expansions and benefit electorally from such cycles. Several factors can explain why the motive to manipulate is stronger among longer-term leaders. Long-serving leaders are more vulnerable to the charge of "running out of ideas." Instead of responding to such a charge by freshening-up their parties' policy agenda, these leaders might find it easier to dodge it and instead strategically time an economic expansion before elections with the monetary or fiscal instruments at their disposal. Another factor is that a prolonged stay in power can instigate calls for a change of leadership. As Abramowitz notes, in the context of American politics, "the longer a party has been in power, the more likely the public is to feel that 'it's time for a change'" (Quoted in Clark et al. 2013: 565). Long-serving leaders may be able to delay the inevitable if they can create re-electable economic conditions. Finally, shorter-tenured leaders may face weaker incentives to manipulate the economy because of the timing factor. On the one hand, if these leaders are able to shift the responsibility for current economic difficulties onto their predecessors, they may feel less pressure to manipulate policies early in their tenure. On the other hand, because of the time lag between enacting expansionary policies and affecting short-term re-electable conditions, these leaders may not have enough time to reap the electoral benefits of policy manipulation.

Canes-Wrone and Park (2012) argue that the motives of private sector actors can be as impactful on pre-election economic conditions as the electoral motives of incumbents. Their reverse electoral business cycle argument holds that businesses and households may postpone fixed capital investments during a pre-election period if they are uncertain about the outcome of elections. They note that polarization between political parties and the competitiveness of elections foster policy uncertainty which, in turn, negatively affects the investment decisions of private sector actors. The higher the level of electoral uncertainty, the greater the incentive to delay investments, and, consequently, the more likely a pre-election economic slowdown will occur. Their study of ten OECD countries between 1975 and 2006 reveals that reverse election cycles occur in fixed capital investment activities (measured as a percentage of GDP) when there is above average polarization or electoral competitiveness. Of note, they find evidence of opportunistic cycles in GDP growth in the economic sectors that depend less on fixed capital investments. The fact that many studies have found inconsistent evidence of electoral cycles may be attributed to the differences in the average size of reverse election cycles across and within countries over time.

Models of partisan cycles

The traditional partisan model

Partisan models, in contrast to electoral models, assert that changes in macroeconomic policies and outcomes are influenced by changes in government partisanship. The transfer of political power from a right-wing government to a left-wing government, it is argued, leads to a reordering of economic policy priorities that reflect the distinct preferences of political parties. The differences in the policy preferences of political parties reflect the distinct material interests of their core supporters. At the center of the traditional partisan model, as Hibbs (1977: 1468) remarks, is the idea that "the macroeconomic policies pursued by left and right-wing governments are broadly in accordance with the objective economic interests and subjective preferences of their class-defined core political constituencies."

Hibbs argues that unemployment and inflation impact the main constituents of Left and Right parties differently. Left parties draw disproportionate support from lower-income, blue-collar individuals. They are particularly vulnerable to higher unemployment because their income is dependent on earnings from hourly labor and their jobs tend to be among the first to be terminated or scaled back during an economic slowdown. Therefore, policies that mitigate unemployment and foster income growth generate more benefits for downscale groups than upscale groups who are less exposed to the risk of unemployment. Thus, facing a trade-off between unemployment and inflation, Left parties prioritize policies aimed at achieving full employment, which is conducive to wage gains for lower-income groups, even though such a strategy may cause higher inflation.

Individuals in high-income, white-collar professional groups disproportionately lean toward Right parties. While upscale and downscale groups dislike inflation, Hibbs (1987) has argued that the distributional consequences of inflation are worse for affluent individuals. High-income groups are more likely to have internalized the belief that inflation poses a more serious problem than disinflation. Moreover, inflation may have a negative effect on financial assets, which are disproportionately held by high-income individuals (see also Franzese 2002). Thus, Right parties are expected to assign greater importance to promoting price stability even at the risk of causing more unemployment and slower output growth.

Hibbs and others have found evidence of partisan cycles in macroeconomic outcomes in the United States in the post-World War II period. Hibbs (1987: 225) estimates that unemployment was 2 percentage points lower and real GDP growth was 6% higher under Democratic than Republican administrations between 1948 and 1978. Analyzing a period from 1948 to 2014, Bartels (2018) has also found strong evidence of partisan influence on macroeconomic performance. His analysis shows that Democrats outperformed Republican administrations in terms of unemployment (nearly a full percentage point lower) and real per capita GDP growth (more than a full percentage point higher). The coincidence of Democratic incumbency and low unemployment in the United States, as Wright (2012) observes, has fostered the perception among voters that Democrats "own" unemployment—that is, they expect Democrats to be more effective in solving unemployment. The lower average unemployment rate under Democratic administrations did not translate to higher inflation. In fact, Bartels (2018: 53) finds that the average inflation rate was almost identical under Democratic and Republican administrations in the postwar period.

The evidence also points to partisan patterns of income distribution. For example, Hibbs (1987: 242) finds that roughly three-fifths of the reduction in the ratio of the share of post-tax income earned by the top 20% to the share received by the bottom 40% of the income distribution occurred during Democratic administrations between 1948 and 1978. Bartels (2008: 36) finds that the 80/20 income ratio (the ratio of family income at the 80th and 20th percentiles of the income distribution) dropped in four of the five Democratic presidents (with the exception of Jimmy Carter) but increased under all of the six Republican presidents between 1948 and 2005. He estimates that the 80/20 income ratio would have changed little from the late 1940s to the mid-2010s had there been continuous Democratic administrations during this period (Bartels 2018: 71). A key reason for these cycles in income distribution is that the average annual real income growth rate for families at the 20th percentile has been much higher under Democrats than Republicans (1.98% versus 0.20%). What is more, the impact of GDP growth has been more substantial on the incomes of lower- and middle-class families than on affluent families under Democratic administrations (ibid: 36, 56).

Partisan cycles in economic outcomes have also been found in other affluent political economies. Hibbs (1977) reports that inflation rates tend to be lower in countries where Right parties dominate, while employment situations tend to be better when Left parties regularly control the government. Alt's (1985) study of unemployment in 14 Western industrial countries between 1960 and 1983 confirms Hibbs's finding but adds that partisan patterns in unemployment are contingent on the institutional context, a point we will discuss later. In his study of 17 developed countries between 1948 and 1985, Paldam (1991b) finds that partisan cycles in unemployment are weak (though statistically significant), while the effects of partisanship on inflation are stronger.

The traditional partisan model also expects economic policies, not just outcomes, to be influenced by partisan politics. The material interests of the core constituencies of political parties are impacted differently by the economic policies of governments. As a result, Right and Left governments are expected to chart different courses of policy actions that, on the one hand, are inclusive enough to help them get reelected and, on the other, disproportionately benefit their core constituent groups. Cusack (2001) uncovers evidence that partisanship influences the fiscal stances of governments in the face of different labor market conditions. As figure 4.1 illustrates, Left

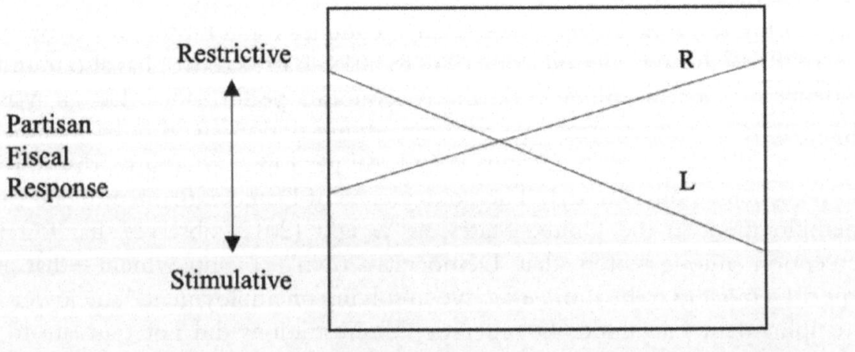

FIGURE 4.1 Partisan influenced fiscal responses to labor market conditions
Source: republished with permission of John Wiley & Sons—Books, from Cusack, Thomas R. 2001. "Partisanship in the setting and coordination of fiscal and monetary policies." *European Journal of Political Research* 40: 96; permission conveyed through Copyright Clearance Center, Inc.

governments increase public spending and/or lower taxes when unemployment is high, but follow a restrictive fiscal stance when the economy is at full employment. Right governments tend to be reluctant to open the fiscal spigot when unemployment is high under the assumption that market dynamics can correct the slack in aggregate demand. However, they are inclined to cut taxes without cutting back on government expenditures when the economy is performing well.

The counter-cyclical fiscal policies of Left governments tend to match the preferences of downscale groups. Fiscal stimulus during a recession lessens the personal cost of unemployment, for instance, by extending unemployment insurance. They also help spur labor market recovery by offering tax incentives to employers that hire new workers. The restrictive fiscal measures implemented after recoveries enable Left governments to reduce their budget deficits, thus minimizing the negative effects that a sustained imbalance would have on post-recession growth. The pro-cyclical posture of Right governments benefits employers to the extent that slack labor market conditions during periods of high unemployment militate against wage increases and drive down labor costs. During full employment conditions, tax cuts generally spur household consumption, resulting in higher corporate profits. If tax reductions disproportionately benefit the well-off, the Right can hedge against potentially alienating those who are left out by maintaining the current spending levels on broad based social programs (Cusack 2001).

Other studies have uncovered evidence of partisan influence on specific aspects of fiscal policies and other policies. In his study of tax expenditures in the United States, Faricy (2016) finds that Republican and Democratic parties distinctly use the tax code to distribute forgone federal tax revenue to their core supporters. The yearly level of tax deductions, which reduce the amount of income subject to taxation, tends to increase during Republican administrations as this type of tax expenditure advantages upscale voters. Democrats tend to expand tax credits, which reduce the amount of taxes owed to the government, because the income sensitive design of this tax expenditure tool enables poorer voters to claim more tax credits.

Focusing on the housing market, Broz (2013) and Ansell et al. (2018) find that home prices rise faster under right-wing governments and that this real estate condition is more likely to result in social spending cuts. Broz's study of OECD countries since the early 1970s and Ansell et al.'s study of 43 countries from the 1960s to 2011, find that housing bubbles occur more frequently under right-wing administrations, spurred by pro-market policies such as financial deregulation, capital market liberalization, tax cuts, and ownership promotion. These studies also find that right-wing governments are more responsive than left-leaning governments to calls for cutting redistributive social spending during housing booms.

The fact that capital flows tend to expand under right-wing governments, leading to asset booms, might be attributed in part to the pro-business policies that Right parties implement but also to changes in business perceptions about the security of property rights when these parties are in power. Weymouth and Broz (2013) argue that the property rights perceptions of firms improve when political power shifts from Left to Right parties. Specifically, a rightward shift of power reduces concerns about redistributive taxation, stronger regulations, and other forms of government actions which impinge on the protection of property rights. Their study, however, does not test for whether such improved confidence in the security of property rights following an electoral victory by the Right actually translates into better economic performance.

The effects of partisanship are not limited to the demand-side of the economy. Boix's (1997) study finds that partisan politics leave an imprint on supply-side policies, policies that impact the productivity of physical and human capital. Although left- and right-wing governments are equally focused on maximizing economic growth, they promote it using distinct supply-side strategies. With an eye on promoting both growth and equality, Left governments rely on public investment to upgrade fixed capital infrastructures such as transportation and information and communication networks. They also subsidize training and university education in order to improve the skills of the working age population. Funded largely by higher marginal tax rates, these public expenditures help raise the productivity of lower-skilled workers, and the workforce in general, as well as reduce low-income inequality. Alternatively, Right governments rely on the private sector to boost productivity and competitiveness. Their strategy hinges on the belief that more government intervention undermines market competition and interferes with the allocation of resources. Keeping taxes low, enforcing market-enhancing regulations, and maintaining a minimal government presence in the economy, Right governments calculate, create a market environment conducive to optimal physical and human capital investment decisions that ultimately lead to output and income growth.

The rational partisan model

The traditional partisan model expects party induced fluctuations in growth, unemployment, and inflation to be persistent throughout a party's term in government. In contrast, the rational partisan model asserts that such performance differences occur only when there is uncertainty about which party will win an election and, with the exception of inflation, are short-lived when they occur. The model assumes that nominal wage contracts are signed before elections and lapse sometime after elections. Because of fixed money wage rates, if inflation rises as a result of expansionary monetary and fiscal policy, real wages will decrease causing unemployment to drop and output to increase.

If wage and price setters were able to anticipate the likely winner of an upcoming election, they would adjust their price and wage contracts accordingly. For example, in anticipation of a Left party victory—an event that would signal future expansionary policies—economic actors would add an "inflation increment" into their contracts to protect their real wages and profit margins. The result is that unemployment would not drop below the natural rate while real GDP growth would not deviate above its potential level, conditions that could otherwise emerge if economic actors were unable to predict a left-wing victory. Similarly, an expected Right party victory would lead economic actors to adjust their contracts in anticipation of lower inflation in the future. As a result, unemployment would not drift above the natural rate nor would real GDP drop below potential GDP, conditions that could otherwise occur if voters were not able to forecast a right-wing victory.

Thus, when actors form expectations rationally, fluctuations in economic conditions can only occur when they cannot predict who the likely winning party will be. As Drazen (2000: 250) observes, "the driving force for fluctuations . . . is not partisan differences *per se*, but these differences combined with uncertainty about election outcomes." A surprise leftist or rightist victory would lead to partisan cycles, as sketched in the previous paragraph, until economic actors can rewrite wage and price contracts. Subsequently, real effects would fade, leaving only inflation permanently changed (Alesina et al. 1997). A key takeaway of the model is that partisan cycles are more likely to occur when elections are competitive enough to prevent economic actors from forming probabilities about election outcomes. Another takeaway is that for cycles to occur, the two dominant parties must offer to the electorate two distinct rightist and leftist policy alternatives.

Alesina et al. (1997) find empirical evidence based on the United States and several advanced capitalist democracies in support of the rational partisan model. Applied to the U.S. case, the model estimates that "a larger postelectoral boom (recession) [should occur] to the degree that the Democratic (Republican) surprise is greater" (ibid: 120–121). Looking at a period between the mid-1930s to early 1990s, their model estimates that a surprise Democratic victory led to a growth rate that was about 1.2% above normal in the first six quarters after an election and yielded an unemployment rate that was 1% lower than that of their Republican counterparts. These differences in macroeconomic performance, they note, were temporary and contingent on the degree of electoral surprise.

Using panel data from 18 OECD countries between 1960 and 1993, Alesina et al.'s statistical analysis reveals that the rate of GNP growth was about 1.1% above its normal value about 18 months after a transfer of power to a Left party. Partisan cycles in output, they find, have not diminished in size over time. Further, they estimate that the unemployment rate was roughly 1.3 percentage points above average about six quarters after a Right party assumed control of government. Their study, however, does not find a large difference in the inflation rate between Left and Right governments. In short, they find evidence of transient real economic effects, caused "only when there are unexpected policy shocks, in our case as a result of electoral surprises." They add, "there is no permanent gain in output or unemployment and the attempt to affect real output results only in a higher inflation rate" (ibid: 165–166). Alesina and colleagues observe that the rational partisan model has greater explanatory power in countries with a two-party system or where a shift of power from Right to Left and vice versa results in identifiable policy changes. On the other hand, the model provides little to no explanatory leverage in countries with a high incidence of coalition governments and frequent governmental changes.

Context-dependent partisan cycles

The ability of parties in power to affect partisan-motivated policy changes is conditioned by economic and political circumstances. The scholarship that has emerged since the introduction of the original models of Hibbs and Alesina and colleagues aims to capture these effects. Alt's (1984) study was one of the first comparative analyses that explored how political and economic factors at the domestic and international levels constrain partisan cycles. We address this area of inquiry selectively in this section. Specifically, we will examine the effects of labor market institutions, open economy, and changing social cleavages on partisan cycles.

Partisanship contingent on institutions

Alvarez et al. (1991), Beramendi and Cusack (2008), Cusack (2001), among others have explored how political economic institutions mediate the effects of partisanship on economic outcomes and policies. For instance, Alvarez and colleagues observe that in countries where labor is sufficiently encompassing—that is, has a high degree of density and centralization—Left governments are able to implement their preferred demand-side strategy and achieve economic growth and low unemployment and inflation simultaneously. Right governments can achieve similar outcomes using their preferred partisan strategy in countries with weak labor, as figure 4.2 illustrates. Less favorable macroeconomic outcomes occur when Left (Right) governments preside over economies with weak (strong) labor.

The two "coherent" configurations stem from the compatibility between labor's strategic capacity and a party's preferred economic management strategy. The underlying logic is as follows. The more encompassing unions are, the stronger the incentive to internalize the potential negative effects of wage militancy and the lower the risk of wage-push inflation. Against this backdrop, Left governments have a freer hand to pursue counter-cyclical policies to maintain low levels of unemployment. Further, Left governments compensate for labor's consent to wage restraint by maintaining high levels of social benefits, funded by a broader tax base. On the other hand, when unions lack the capacity to alter labor market conditions in their favor, neither Right governments nor employers are compelled to coordinate with labor. Accordingly, this affords rightist governments the latitude to pursue a pro-cyclical strategy which, by promoting the preferences of business during the ups and downs of a business cycle, leads to better overall macroeconomic performance.

Inferior performance is expected when the labor market-partisan match up is incompatible. In a rightist-strong union situation, mutual distrust between government and labor undermines the credibility of the commitments each makes

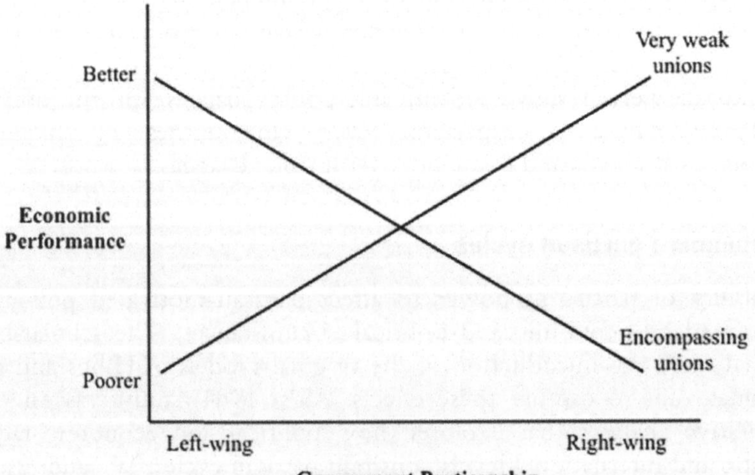

FIGURE 4.2 Conditional effects of government partisanship
Source: Alvarez, R. Michael, Geoffrey Garrett, and Peter Lange. 1991. "Government Partisanship, Labor Organization, and Macroeconomic Performance." *American Political Science Review* 85(2): 544. Reproduced with permission.

toward the other, resulting in poorer macroeconomic performance. In a leftist-weak union situation, the Left's pro-labor preference encourages wage militancy across various industries, leading employers to retaliate by threatening plant closures and announcing investment cutbacks, ultimately harming the economy.

Focusing on another organizational feature of labor markets, Beramendi and Cusack (2008) argue that the ability of Left governments to reduce wage inequality is contingent on the degree of coordination between capital and labor. Although governments can use minimum wage laws to promote wage equality, they argue that wage coordination between capital and labor creates an ideal environment for Left governments to achieve even greater reductions in earnings inequality without causing employment loss and impairing economic growth. That ability hinges on the compromise between capital and labor, one in which labor agrees to wage restraint while employers accept a more generous welfare state financed in part by higher labor taxes, of which employers shoulder a share. On the one hand, Left governments indirectly lower wage inequality by relying on solidaristic wage bargaining between labor and employers. On the other hand, they directly contribute to wage equality by raising labor taxes which helps suppress wage increases in the upper half of the income distribution and by increasing the generosity of social benefits which raises the reservation wage—the minimum market wage the unemployed are willing to accept.

The ability of political parties to use monetary policy to pursue partisan preferences is also contingent on the actions or expected actions of central bankers. Scholars have debated how exactly central banks constrain partisan cycles. One school of thought holds that partisan cycles flatten when inflation-averse central bankers are insulated from political influence. Such independence gives them the latitude to counteract partisan-motivated expansions by either Left or Right governments in order to maintain price stability. As Alesina and Summers (1993: 152) observe, "an independent central bank that is free from political pressure may behave more predictably, promoting economic stability and reducing risk premia in real interest rates . . . by reducing partisan shocks to policy following elections." It is the willingness and ability of central bankers to counter such political shocks that deter governments of any partisan stripes from orchestrating them.

Another line of argument holds that it is not so much the independence of central bankers but rather their ideological bias that ends up constraining cycles created by the policies of Left governments. Clark and Arel-Bundock (2013) and Cusack (2001) argue that central bankers are conditional inflation hawks; they tend to take a non-accommodative stance when Left parties are in power but do the opposite when governments are led by Right parties. Rather than being indifferent to who is in power, central bankers have an economic mindset that is more compatible with the policy vision of right-wing rather than left-wing parties, leading them to use monetary policy in a way that benefits Right governments. In their study of the Federal Reserve Bank, Clark and Arel-Bundock find that "the Fed lowers interest rates in response to declining growth . . . but is insensitive to inflationary expectations" when Republicans control the White House. Under Democratic presidents, "the Fed increases interest rates in response to increased inflationary expectation . . . but is insensitive [to slower growth]." Cusack's (2001) study of 14 OECD countries between 1961 and 1994, reveals that central bankers, regardless of their level of institutional independence, use monetary policy to offset the fiscal policies of Left governments.

Open economies

The much-referenced work by Alvarez and colleagues (1991) examined the effects of the interaction between government partisanship and labor organization in a closed economy. In the time period they investigated (1967–1984), internationalization was limited. In the current era of open economies, do partisan politics operate the same way as they did prior to the 1980s? Global economic integration has limited the ability of governments to use monetary and fiscal policies to advance their partisan preferences for the same reasons internationalization restricts electoral cycles. In integrated economies, expansionary monetary and fiscal policies can trigger capital flight, damage the price competitiveness of export sectors, and, as a result, potentially cause slower economic growth and employment loss. The growing prominence of market governance ideas in both the private and public sectors, it has been argued, has disproportionately impacted Left governments, forcing them to give up their preferred policies and move in the direction of Right parties. Boix (1997), Cusack (2001), and Garrett (1998b) find evidence suggesting that as national economies have become more integrated, Left governments are less inclined to use counter-cyclical policies in response to sluggish aggregate demand.

However, several scholars have argued that economic globalization leaves some room for Left governments to pursue other preferred policies. For example, Boix (1997) and Garrett (1998b) argue that there are no reasons why global markets would punish Left governments for pursuing their interventionist supply-side strategy. The benefits firms reap from public investment in education, training, and fixed capital projects—like improved productivity, innovation, and competitiveness—offset the cost of higher taxes that come with such a strategy. Further, contrary to popular beliefs, Cusack and Boix find that Left governments calibrate their discretionary spending plans in light of current and expected budget conditions. Public investment tends to increase when budget conditions permit. The fiscal prudence that guides Left governments' handling of supply-side investment helps alleviate concerns of higher, creeping taxes and thus reinforces business support for such a strategy.

Partisanship continues to leave an imprint on social welfare spending even in the current era of globalization. Social welfare plays an important role in sustaining public support for globalization by compensating workers who are adversely affected by global market forces. Because they draw more political support from these workers than Right governments, Left governments have been keen on bolstering the social safety net. Social welfare also plays an important role in maintaining a country's market competitiveness. Exposed sectors of an economy benefit when labor restrains its wage demand. When labor is sufficiently encompassing, Left governments can induce wage moderation by guaranteeing generous social benefits (Garrett 1998b; Swank 2002). It is for these reasons that globalization has not eliminated partisan differences with respect to social welfare redistribution.

New electoral cleavages

The alignment of partisanship with predictable policy differences has been disrupted in recent decades as a result of the rise of financial capitalism, transformation of occupational structure, greying of the population, among other developments commonly associated with postindustrialism. These structural changes have led to the emergence of new electoral cleavages such as insiders versus outsiders, sheltered versus exposed workers, skilled and professional versus unskilled workers, and elderly versus working-age people. These new electoral cleavages have transformed the traditional composition of the core constituents of left- and right-wing parties. Parties as a result have altered their policy strategies to better reflect the new constellation of constituency preferences. For example, the fact that Right governments draw support from a growing elderly population has forced them to move to the left on social welfare—it has made them more supportive of broad social programs like public pension and health care on which that segment of the population depend (Pierson 1996). Further, as Left parties rely increasingly on middle-class professionals, they have moved away from their "workerist image" and advocated greater market competition and postmaterialist policy views such as environmental protection (Esping-Andersen 1999).

Partisan politics in corporate governance and labor market policies have produced unexpected and surprising results. Cioffi and Höpner (2006) find that mainstream Left and Right parties have espoused opposite positions with regard to promoting pro-shareholder corporate governance reforms, positions that do not easily map onto traditional partisan lines of contention. Contrary to what traditional partisan arguments would predict, it is Left not Right governments that have called for stronger protections of shareholder rights. As they note, "the distributional consequences of [advocating shareholder rights reforms] would appear to conflict with traditional left-wing political commitment to working-class and low-income constituencies [because they have the effect of transferring] income and wealth from wage earners to shareholders . . . [and of diminishing] the power and influence of employees within the firm and economy at large" (ibid: 464).

Two key factors account for this unexpected coalition among leftist parties, workers, and shareholders. First, in an attempt to remain electorally viable in the face of a shrinking base of blue-collar workers, Left parties began promoting in the 1970s market reforms that appealed to middle-class voters as well as their core constituents. Corporate governance reforms had broad appeal among lower- and middle-class voters because they limited managerial autonomy, enhanced outsiders' voicing opportunities in managerial decisions, and held managers to account for financial and accounting scandals.

The other factor that has influenced the Left's decision to champion shareholder rights is that a growing share of citizens in rich OECD countries have become shareholders. Mass shareholding has emerged across countries in Europe and North America, albeit at varying speeds. In the United States, household investments in pension assets such as 401(k)s is widespread. This means that a wider segment of the population has a personal stake in the performance of securities markets. As a result, the distributional effects of rules on corporate reporting, oversight, and information sharing reach across a much broader segment of society, including important groups of voters from whom mainstream Left parties seek support.

The dualization of labor markets is another postindustrial development that has impacted the policy strategies of political parties. Dualization refers to the increasing differentiation of labor market experiences between "insiders" and "outsiders." A key distinction between the two labor groups relates to their level of employment stability. Insiders' full-time employment status makes them less exposed to the risk of job loss than outsiders who have jobs that offer little protection and employment rights. Contrary to the conventional view that workers' preferences over employment and social policies are the same, the dualization literature shows that insiders and outsiders express different levels of support for active labor market policies, employment protection regulations, and universalistic social benefits (Rueda 2006; Schwander 2019). Given their different labor market positions, insiders gain more from job protection laws and contributory-based social insurance benefits. Outsiders gain more from job promotion policies and general tax-funded, high replacement universal social policies such as unemployment and pension benefits. Insiders oppose job promotion policies because they expose insiders to more labor market competition from outsiders which can drive wages down. Their preference for contributory rather than redistributive universal programs reflects the fact that the cost of financing such programs falls disproportionately on them.

The unequal distribution of labor market risk between these two groups of workers has created what Lindvall and Rueda (2013) call an insider-outsider (I-O) dilemma for mainstream Left parties. If mainstream Left governments allocate more funds to job promotion programs and shore up universalistic social benefits to attract outsider support, they risk alienating insiders who may shift their support to a mainstream Right party. Alternatively, if Left governments aim to protect the prerogatives of insiders, that may lead outsiders to back radical Left parties or even support Right parties who advocate the deregulation of pro-insider protections.

The dilemma facing the Left can create opportunities for mainstream Right parties to lure insiders, as evidenced in Sweden's 2006 and 2010 parliamentary elections. Right parties have ways to appeal to insider preferences given their higher income status. Sweden's Social Democratic Party avoided the I-O dilemma in the first half of the 2000s because the Swedish economy performed well. However, in the face of rising unemployment in the second half of the decade, the Social Democrats chose to follow a pro-outsider labor market strategy instead of a pro-insider one as it did in the 1990s when unemployment numbers were also high. That choice turned out to be electorally costly for the party. In the run-up to the 2006 election, the Moderate Party, Sweden's mainstream Right party, campaigned on a message designed to appeal to insiders—cutting long-term unemployment benefits and income taxes. The Moderate Party's victories in that election and in 2010 were owed in part to its decision to seek out insiders' votes, which was made possible when Social Democrats switched to an outsider-oriented economic strategy.

Conclusion

Models of political cycles are based on the premise that elected officials are intrinsically motivated to intervene in the economy to reap political gains, whether it is to get reelected, promote partisan objectives, or a combination of both. Models of partisan cycles posit that economic policies and outcomes change when there is a shift in the partisan composition of government. A key takeaway of the literature we have reviewed in this chapter is that partisan cycles in macroeconomic performance are harder to achieve; however, partisan induced policy cycles are still noticeable even though parties on both sides of the ideological spectrum face common pressures and constraints. For instance, Left and Right parties are using different sets of policy tools to respond to the pressures of postindustrialism and globalization (Gingrich and Ansell 2015; Swank 2020), budget constraints (Adolph et al. 2020), and inequality (Huber et al. 2017).

Models of electoral cycles hold that an impending election incentivizes incumbent officials to manipulate the economy to their advantage. The research we covered in this chapter shed light on the political and economic circumstances that are more or less likely to trigger cycles in economic policies and outcomes. Staging electorally timed economic expansions is much harder to pull off nowadays since policymakers in advanced political economies have delegated monetary policy to independent central banks and have limited fiscal space within which to maneuver. Still, these constraints do not eliminate the incentives for incumbents to engineer short-term re-electable conditions. Recent scholarship has paid more attention to how elected officials seek to foster favorable or avoid unfavorable pre-election conditions even when they face monetary and fiscal constraints. For instance, the policymaking process can be manipulated to enact financial reforms that led to timely private credit growth (Aklin and Kern 2020) or to strategically delay the rollout of unpopular austerity reforms (Strobl et al. 2019).

Key terms

Counter-cyclical policies

Insider-outsider dilemma

Pro-cyclical policies

Rational electoral cycles

Rational partisan cycles

Reverse election cycles

Traditional electoral cycles

Traditional partisan cycles

Discussion questions

- Why do political cycles occur in democratic countries?
- What are the main differences between electoral and partisan cycles?
- Specify how political and economic conditions affect the occurrence, size, and form of electoral cycles.
- What economic policy positions have Left and Right parties traditionally taken? Do they match popular beliefs? In what ways have the positioning of Right and Left parties changed?

Further reading

Bartels, Larry. 2018. *Unequal Democracy: The Political Economy of the New Gilded Age*. 2nd edition. Princeton, NJ: Princeton University Press.

Argues that distributional outcomes are strikingly different when power shifts from the Republicans to Democrats in the United States.

Boix, Carles. 1998. *Political Parties, Growth and Equality: Conservative and Social Democratic Economic Strategies in the World Economy*. New York: Cambridge University Press.

Left- and right-wing parties respond to increased economic openness by using different supply-side economic strategies.

Clark, William Roberts. 2005. *Capitalism, not Globalism: Capital Mobility, Central Bank Independence, and the Political Control of the Economy*. Ann Arbor: The University of Michigan Press.

Contends that government manipulation of economic policies is more consistent with the theoretical expectations of the context-dependent electoral cycle approach.

Rueda, David. 2007. *Social Democracy Inside Out: Partisanship & Labor Market Policy in Industrialized Democracies*. New York: Oxford University Press.

Torn between promoting the interests of labor market outsiders versus insiders, social democratic parties often align themselves with the latter group.

PART

II

The effects of the economy and society on domestic politics

CHAPTER

5 Economic voting

In the final days of his campaign for the presidency in 1980, Ronald Reagan offered voters a few words of advice to help them decide between him and incumbent President Jimmy Carter: "Next Tuesday all of you will go to the polls . . . and make a decision. I think when you make that decision, it might be well if you would ask yourself, are you better off than you were four years ago?" What Reagan wanted voters to do was to evaluate Carter based on his administration's economic performance. He and many other politicians operate under the belief that election prospects are shaped by the economy. To what degree does the economy influence vote choice? That is the focus of this chapter.

The objective of this chapter is to investigate economic voting—the claim that the economy influences election outcomes. After a brief look at the empirical link between the economy and incumbent party support, the first section of the chapter elaborates on the two main theoretical approaches to economic voting—the reward-punishment and selection approaches. The second section surveys empirical studies—starting with scholarship focused on the United States then moving to comparative studies of OECD countries. That section concludes by investigating economic voting during the Great Recession of 2007–2009. The third section looks at key controversies regarding different aspects of the link between the economy and vote intention.

"Yes, there's a link, no there isn't"

Let's begin by looking at the data on the relationship between economic performance and election results. Using the results of legislative elections in nine OECD countries from the mid-1970s to the 2010s, figure 5.1 plots changes in incumbent party vote against real GDP growth. Real GDP growth is measured as the change in the level of real GDP in the 12 months leading up to an election. The incumbent party is the largest party in government—it holds the most cabinet-level positions as well as the position of head of government. The change in vote share is

DOI: 10.4324/9780429199462-5

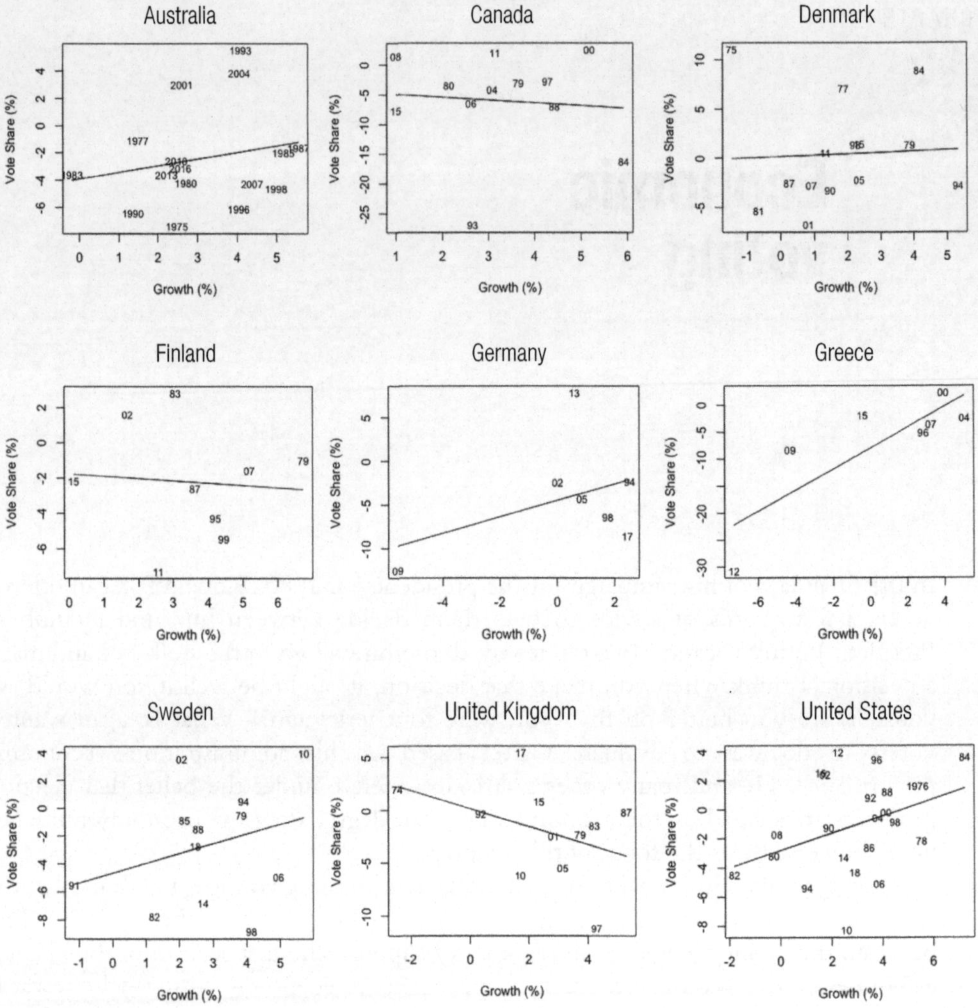

FIGURE 5.1 Incumbent party vote change and GDP growth rate

Sources: Armingeon et al. (2018); Cruz et al. (2016).

measured by comparing the share of the popular vote of an incumbent party in the latest election in the lower legislative chamber to its vote share in the last election. For example, the Conservative Party in Canada had been in the government for many years in the lead-up to the 2015 parliamentary election. In that election, the incumbent party received 31.9% of the popular vote compared to 39.6% it had received in the previous election held in 2011. Thus, the incumbent party's vote share dropped by 7.7 percentage points.

The logic of economic voting tells us that the vote share of an incumbent party will increase when growth increases or will decrease when growth slows or turns negative. The fact that a positive relationship is found in six of the nine countries might be taken as confirmation that economic voting is prevalent. However, some further excavation of the correlation results reveals bits of information that should give us pause.

First, the magnitude of the economic vote varies considerably among the six countries in which the economic vote is detected. Second, there are many election observations in each country panel that are scattered around the best-fit line. These first two points tell us that growth accounts for a very small portion of the variance in vote share change. Finally, in Canada, Finland, and the United Kingdom the vote share of an incumbent party seems to drop as growth increases! In short, the economy-vote link operates inconsistently across countries and across time within countries.

What should we make of these results? Can they be interpreted as a rejection of the economic vote claim? The answer is not really. The economy-vote connection does not operate in a straightforward way, as illustrated in figure 5.3. For economic events to have a bearing on election outcomes, they must be perceived by voters, evaluated based on some benchmark, and weigh sufficiently on voters' minds such that they become a key driver of voter behavior. Individual-level surveys shed light on important questions concerning the complex processes linking the economy to election outcome: Do voters focus on past economic performance (retrospective voting) or on expected economic outlook (prospective voting)? Is voting behavior a reflection of personal economic situation (egocentric) or collective economic situation (sociotropic)? Are voter perceptions consistent with the objective economy? How does the level of individual sophistication affect the orientation (retrospective versus prospective) and target (egocentric versus sociotropic) of voting as well as the strength of the economic vote? Is attribution of responsibility tied to economic performance or to random events—floods, shark attacks—that are beyond officeholders' control?

The complexity of the economy-vote link is also owed to contextual factors which affect clarity of responsibility and clarity of available alternatives. There has been much attention paid recently to how political and economic contexts enhance or obfuscate voters' ability to assign responsibility. If the presence of certain political institutions and economic openness interfere with attribution allocation, then it should not surprise researchers when they come across results suggesting that incumbent parties are unscathed by worsening economic performance. Note that the absence of economic voting may not be due to voters' misperceptions or biases but rather to institutional obstacles. Context contingency explanations shed light on several other important questions relating to the economy-vote link: What political institutions magnify or dull assignment of credit or blame? Are voters more or less likely to punish incumbents for poor performance in the face of globalization? What institutional conditions make it possible or impossible for officeholders to manipulate the economy-vote link in ways that work to their advantage? Finally, if the electorate seeks alternatives to an incumbent party because it has performed poorly, what institutional features enhance or dull the clarity of available alternatives?

Theoretical foundations

The literature has usually addressed the question of how the economy impacts voting choice from two general theoretical perspectives. Whereas the reward-punishment approach asserts that voters evaluate incumbents based on how well they have handled the economy in the recent past, the selection approach holds that the electorate selects leaders who they judge are the most competent in handling the economy. The key difference between the two perspectives turns on the decision rule voters use when casting a vote. Vote choice might be a reflection of the public's penchant to hold incumbents accountable for their economic performance—reward them when conditions are good, punish them when they are not. The expectation that voters are motivated by this norm urges incumbents to be effective economic managers. Alternatively, vote choice can be indicative of the electorate's desire to select political leaders who are economically competent and expected to deliver the kind of performance that voters want.

The scholarship relating to these two perspectives share some similarities. First, studies on economic voting usually assume that voters are rational in the sense that they use elections instrumentally to make decisions aimed at advancing their individual or collective material interests. In his pioneering investigation of how economic voting works, Kramer (1971: 140) noted that "one might picture the voter as a rational, information-processing individual who proceeds by collecting information of various kinds. . . [and] analyzes this information in light of his own self-interest." Whether rationality is the main psychological operative linking the economy and vote choice has been the subject of debate in the recent literature on economic voting, a debate we will explore later in the chapter.

Another similarity is that both perspectives recognize that contextual factors shape the magnitude of economic voting and, accordingly, account for a lot of the cross-national inconsistency in the extent of economic voting. Certain political institutions obstruct clarity of responsibility—the ability of voters to assign credit or blame—or hinder the ability of voters to discern politicians' competencies (Duch and Stevenson 2008; Powell and Whitten 1993). What is more, structural economic factors such as the level economic openness and of economic development have been found to also condition the economy-vote link (Hellwig 2001; Singer and Carlin 2013).

Finally, the scholarship informed by insights from either perspective has relied increasingly on individual-level election surveys to study the economy-vote link in an effort to address the problem of ecological fallacy. Ecological fallacy refers to the mistake of drawing conclusions about individual voting behavior from national-level aggregate data (Kramer 1983: 92). In other words, scholars cannot infer that voters take account of economic conditions simply because a connection appears to exist between the macroeconomy and national election outcomes. Survey-based studies have been effective in unpacking the economy-vote link by investigating, first, the connection between the objective national economy and individual economic perceptions of the macroeconomy and, second, the connection between individual economic perceptions and national election outcomes. Table 5.1 summarizes the differences between the two models with respect to key factors which we elaborate below.

TABLE 5.1 Summary of economic voting models

	Reward-Punishment Approach	Selection Approach
Problem facing voters relative to officeholders	Moral hazard	Adverse selection
Role of elections	Mechanism of accountability	Mechanism to select competent leaders
Time horizon of voting	Retrospective	Prospective
Policymaking implication	Pre-election policy manipulation	Commitment to a policy agenda
Voting behavior	Voting on performance of incumbents	Voting over differences between incumbents and challengers

The reward-punishment approach

The reward-punishment (R-P) approach is based on a particular understanding of the relationship between citizens and elected officials in a democratic system. On the one hand, the inexperience of voters renders popular control of government untenable (Achen and Bartels 2017; Converse 1964). On the other hand, entrusting a small group of elected officials with governing responsibilities risks encouraging moral hazard behavior—that is, the inclination to pursue their private interests at the neglect of the public interest (Ferejohn 1986). The two imperatives facing modern democracies therefore have been, first, to regulate how the public influences the operation of government and, second, to ensure that officials act in the public interest.

Retrospective accountability serves as a mechanism to address both imperatives. The role of voters, as depicted in the R-P approach, is to cast judgment periodically on the recent performance of incumbent officials. This characterization of the electorate is vividly captured in an often quoted passage from V.O. Key's (1966: 61) pathbreaking work on retrospective voting: elections showcase

> the electorate in its great, and perhaps principal, role as an appraiser of past events, past performance and past actions. It judges retrospectively; it commands prospectively only insofar as it expresses either approval or disapproval of that which has happened before.

The fact that voters lack detailed knowledge about recent government actions or demonstrate poor command of economic facts does not diminish the efficacy of their role as appraisers. As Fiorina (1981: 5) observes, retrospective voters

> need not know the precise economic or foreign policies of the incumbent administration in order to see or feel the results of those policies. . . . In order to ascertain whether the incumbents have performed poorly or well, citizens need only calculate the changes in their own welfare. If jobs have been lost in a recession, something is wrong. If sons have died in foreign rice paddies, something is wrong. If thugs make neighborhoods unsafe, something is wrong. If polluters foul foods, water, or air, something is wrong.

Thus, the rationality assumption that informs the R-P approach holds that voters' decisions to either credit or blame incumbent leaders are instrumentally based on their assessment of whether their material well-being has improved in the recent past.

Retrospective accountability also holds the answer to the question of how to motivate incumbents to act on voters' behalf. When analyzed from a principal-agent perspective, the question can be reformulated as follows: given that principals (voters) cannot monitor how agents (elected representatives) use their delegated authority, how can they be incentivized to focus consistently on the public interest? Ferejohn (1986) notes that office-seeking incumbents can be induced to act on behalf of the electorate if elections are instrumentalized as sanctioning devices. Because voters cannot monitor the policy actions of incumbents, they must settle on a standard of performance that is demanding enough to exert the fullest attention and efforts of incumbents. As Ferejohn (1986: 13) notes, such a standard "will induce the incumbent to pay attention to the requirements of retaining office." However, if the standard for reelection is set too high, then incumbents will realize that their prospects of reelection are low no matter what they do. As a result, they will be less inclined to act on voters' behalf during their term in office. Thus, two features must exist to induce officeholders to be attentive to voters' preferences. First, voters must develop a performance standard that aims to maximize their utility, yet is feasible in light of recent conditions. Second, voters must convey to incumbents that if the efforts they exert during their term satisfy that standard, they are certain to be reelected.

A key takeaway of the R-P approach is that democratic elections are not an exercise in comparing and contrasting incumbent officials and challengers based on some combination of their promises, qualities, and competencies. Instead, elections are stock-taking exercises. The electorate decides between voting approvingly or disapprovingly for incumbents based on whether recent economic conditions are good or bad. As Lippmann (quoted in Achen and Bartels 2017: 90) pointed out, "to support the Ins when things are going well; to support the Outs when they seem to be going badly, this . . . is the essence of popular government." Viewed in this light, officeholders need not pander to the electorate's preferences. Rather, they are afforded latitude to carry out whatever policies they judge will satisfy voters' performance expectations. As Achen and Bartels (2017: 108) remark, "One of the most attractive features of theories of retrospective accountability is that they free elected officials from subservience to the policy preferences of ordinary citizens—preferences that are often likely to be vague, uninformed, or incoherent." This conclusion is also echoed by Fiorina (1981: 201): retrospective voting "lays no policy constraint on the governing administration; rather, the government is free to innovate, knowing that it will be judged on the results of its actions rather than their specifics."

The selection approach

As discussed earlier, the R-P approach understands elections as a stock-taking exercise. In the voting booth, voters evaluate officeholders based on how the outcomes of policy actions impact their material well-being; voters do not sort among candidates based on their policy preferences, competence, ideology, or some combination of these and other factors. They are content with dispensing "contingent renewal" accountability—incumbents retain office so long as they perform well (Manin et al. 1999a: 10). However, what if someone conceived of elections as opportunities to select leaders who will serve the public interest competently and diligently? As Fearon (1999: 60) puts it, this understanding of elections "is arguably much closer to the popular understanding in the United States (and probably other democracies as well) than is the understanding that thinks of future elections as a sanctioning device."

The selection approach defines the relationship between voters and office-seekers differently than what the R-P approach sketches. The problem that voters confront vis-à-vis incumbents is adverse selection, not moral hazard (Fearon 1999). Voters must discern among competing parties the one which has the highest probability of delivering good economic performance in the future. That view of voting was first elaborated by Downs (1957: 39): "When a man votes, he is helping to select the government which will govern him during the coming election period." Making such a political decision is not simple. After all, officeholders can mislead the electorate into thinking they are competent by engineering short-term economic boosts in the lead-up to elections. A naïve voter would simply make extrapolations of the future from recent economic conditions unaware that what they are observing might be the product of cyclical manipulation.

Borrowing insights from rational expectations theory, the selection approach contends that voters are sophisticated and farsighted enough to grasp the future effects of current economic policies. According to the "sophisticated voter" model, voters understand—based on their experience—that inflation, unemployment, and growth are interrelated. Voters know that if the unemployment rate is forced below its natural rate, undesirable outcomes consistent with the long-run Phillips curve will arise (Chappell and Keech 1985). Because of voters' ability to forecast, the only way they can be surprised is if unexpected shocks to the economy occur. Here again, voters' knowledge and discernment help them to figure out whether a shock is attributed to factors beyond officeholders' control (exogenous shocks) or owed to the competent leadership of incumbents (competency shock) (Duch and Stevenson 2008: 14).

Although voters are forward looking, they nonetheless engage in some form of retrospective evaluation (Downs 1957; Kramer 1971). The general idea informing selection voting models is that an instrumentally rational electorate, first, discerns the competence of incumbents by evaluating the economic conditions they experienced during their term and, second, uses that information to guide their vote decision (Duch and Stevenson 2008: 14). To the extent that opposition candidates are unable to signal their competence because they do not have a performance record, voters will have to imagine how the economy would have performed had they been in office, use that and other sources of information to weigh the relative competence of all candidates, and then vote over those differences (Downs 1957: 40). In short, competence is signaled by way of the experiences that voters recall under different officeholders but also by way of making informed guesses when voters lack evidence.

Recent selection models posit that voters can extract competency signals from historical patterns in macroeconomic fluctuations under different parties. As Achens and Bartels (2017: 99) note, "a rational voter's assessment of the incumbent's competence will take into account performance in every relevant period, not just in the current period." From this retrospective exercise, voters can develop rational expectations about how future performance will vary based on which party is in power, which in turn can become a basis "for more or less durable partisan preferences" (ibid). The idea that voters recognize differences in the competence of parties is central to the issue-priority model. The model asserts that unemployment and inflation affect Left and Right parties differently due to issue-ownership and competency effects (Clarke and Elliot 1989). When applied to the United States, voters expect Democrats to prioritize unemployment and implement effective measures to combat joblessness and expect Republicans to care more about inflation and be more competent in controlling it. A key takeaway is that voters discern a comparative partisan advantage in the handling of different economic conditions based on the historical track record of parties. They leverage this knowledge to generate rational expectations about the future performance of different parties under different macroeconomic conditions.

The selection approach yields an important implication about the nature of economic voting. Elections are opportunities for voters to select leaders whose qualities reassure voters that they will act competently on behalf of the public's interest in the years to come. This implies that voters look for candidates who have similar policy preferences, pay attention to the campaign promises of candidates, and infer the competencies of candidates from their prior experiences. In essence, it is the demand for responsiveness, not accountability solely, that figures prominently in elections according to the selection approach. The difference is not trivial. If elections are mechanisms to mete out sanctions on officeholders, then they become a referendum on what they have achieved. What officeholders promised prior to their elections and whether they pursued a policy agenda with discipline and consistency does not matter much to voters according to this view (Fearon 1999: 62). On the other hand, if elections are mechanisms to enhance the responsiveness of officeholders, then voters will use elections to choose leaders who can commit credibly over the next several years to executing a policy agenda that is aligned with voters' preferences (Mansbridge 2009).

Empirical studies

U.S.-based studies

One of the first studies to test the retrospective voting argument was produced by Kramer (1971). His analysis of elections in the U.S. House of Representatives between 1896 and 1964 (31 elections in total) showed that election outcomes were influenced by economic fluctuations. Among the independent economic variables assessed—income, prices, and unemployment, all expressed as change from the previous year—income (specifically, per capita personal income) was the only variable found to have a significant independent effect on congressional elections. In particular, Kramer's analysis estimated that a 10% drop in personal income contributed to a 4 to 5% loss in the vote for the congressional incumbent party. His work was one of the first rigorous studies to weigh in on the debate about whether voters engage in retrospective or prospective voting. Finding evidence for the former, he concluded that election results "are not 'irrational,' or random, or solely the product of past loyalties and habits, or of campaign rhetoric and merchandising" (Kramer 1971: 140).

Stigler's (1973) rebuttal of Kramer's (1971) findings triggered a lively debate about how the economy-vote link actually worked. Not only did Stigler's study fail to detect electoral effects of changes in real income, he cast doubt on the notion of retrospective voting. He argued instead that the behavior of voters seemed more aligned with what the competency approach claims—the electorate engages in prospective voting. As he put it, if

> per capita income falls over a year or two—should the voter abandon or punish the party in power? Such a reaction seems premature. In appraising the macroeconomic policies of political parties, the voter should ask which party is on average more likely to maintain a high and steady rate of growth of income.
>
> (Stigler 1973: 164–165)

In seeking to "narrow the disagreements" that had emerged among scholars about how economic voting worked, Fair (1978) used what had been learned about voting behavior in the United States to estimate how economic factors affected the presidential vote. In particular, his study shed light on two empirical questions: (1) Do voters focus on the level of or change in the unemployment rate, real GNP per capita, and GNP deflator? (2) Do voters have a high or low discount rate? Fair found that the presidential vote was sensitive to changes in real per capita GNP and the unemployment rate. Furthermore, not only did voters highly discount the past performance of the incumbent president, they did not take account of the past performance of the opposition party. To sum up, the behavior of voters seemed to corroborate the claim that elections function as accountability mechanisms for the recent actions of incumbents.

Cross-national analyses

Lewis-Beck's (1986) work represents the first comparative micro-level study investigating economic voting. He compared the economic vote in Britain, France, Germany, and Italy using data from Euro-Barometer surveys conducted in 1983. His study sought to estimate how different economic considerations impacted voters' likelihood of voting for an incumbent party. Specifically, how much weight did voters assign to personal versus sociotropic economic conditions? Did voters believe the government had a positive or negative effect on their personal financial situation and general economic situation? Finally, did voters think the policies of the government would improve and worsen the national economy in the near future?

Lewis-Beck found that voters' judgments about their financial situation and of their country's economic situation in the year leading up to an election had little effect on their vote choices. However, voters who believed that government policies had hurt their financial well-being were more likely to vote against the incumbent party. Moreover, voters who were of the view that government economic policies had damaged or would damage the national economy were more inclined to reject the incumbent party. Vote choice was found to be also affected by voter anger over government actions. With these results, Lewis-Beck concluded that "a strictly retrospective theory of economic voting is inadequate. . . , excluding affective and prospective variables will inevitably underestimate the influence of economic conditions" (Lewis-Beck 1986: 329–330). Although the economic vote took on a similar form across the four countries, Lewis-Beck (1986: 340) observed that the strength of the economic vote weakened "from Britain to Germany, then to France, and finally to Italy." Similar to other works reviewed in these pages, he attributed this pattern to the fact that the clarity of government responsibility varied across these countries, mediating the relationship between economic perceptions and vote choices.

The field of economic voting witnessed a wave of cross-national macro-level studies beginning in the early 1990s with the publication of works by Lewis-Beck and Mitchell (1990), Paldam (1991a), Remmer (1991), among others. In their study of 27 elections held between 1967 and 1987 in France, Germany, Italy, Spain, and the United Kingdom, Lewis-Beck and Mitchell (1990) found that inflation and unemployment had modest effects on the vote for incumbent parties while growth had little influence on election outcomes. The results of Paldam's (1991a) analysis of 197 elections held in 17 OECD countries between 1948 and 1985 differed somewhat from Lewis-Beck and Mitchell's findings. The effects of key macroeconomic indicators (unemployment, inflation, and GDP growth) on changes in the vote share of the incumbent party were either indistinguishable from zero or had weak effects.

Focusing on Latin America, Remmer's (1991) analysis of 21 competitive presidential elections between 1982 and 1990 showed that the electoral prospects of incumbent parties in new democracies were sensitive to adverse changes in short-term economic performance, but not more so than in older democracies. Moreover, the inflation rate (in the quarter prior to election), the exchange rate (in the quarter prior to election), and party structure (whether or not a two-party system existed) had substantively important effects on election outcomes. However, GDP growth (in the quarter prior to election) had little effect. Remmer observed that two-party democracies experienced less economic-induced electoral volatility than fragmented party systems. Moreover, her study called into question the claim that economic downturns cause more political instability in emerging democracies than in mature ones, and, worse, threaten the consolidation of new democracies. On that point, Remmer (1991: 85) remarks that "newly established democracies do not appear to function according to a separate set of rules" than the one applying to older democracies.

Pacek's (1994) study of the economic vote in the early 1990s in East Central Europe (Bulgaria, former Czechoslovakia, and Poland) arrived at results comparable to Remmer. Unemployment's effect on incumbent support in the three countries was statistically significant and in the expected negative direction. The economic hardship brought on by the market reform agendas of incumbent parties led voters to withdraw their support for them and to back mainstream and radical challengers. Based on ten parliamentary elections held between 1990 and 1996 in a sample of post-Communist countries (Czech Republic, Hungary, Poland, Russia, and Slovakia), Tucker (2001) reached a similar conclusion as Pacek (1994). Of note, because these polities at the time witnessed ever-changing political party landscapes and multiparty ruling coalitions, the task of establishing responsibility for economic conditions was not a simple one. Tucker (2001: 327) finds that the economic vote had a greater effect on the parties in a ruling coalition that exerted the most influence on the direction of government policy. "Just because a party joins a coalition that may be instituting painful economic reforms, that does not mean that party will be as affected by economic conditions as the Primary Incumbent party," he concluded.

Alongside the burgeoning regional and cross-national research produced in the 1990s and 2000s was an ongoing effort to explain the lack of consistency in the results on economic voting. Paldam (1991a: 26) summed up the problem as follows: economic voting was "statistically highly significant for some countries and time periods," but there was "great instability as [the economic vote] disappear[ed] in some other countries and time period." Many aggregate cross-national studies up to that time had not fully accounted for the fact that not only were there cross-national differences in the strength of the economic vote, but that such differences changed over time because of within-country changes in how the economy moved voting behavior. Such "instability dilemma" therefore required scholars carrying out pooled analysis to model systematically cross-country and cross-temporal differences (Nannestad and Paldam 1994).

Much of the scholarship that has emerged since the early 1990s has in some form or another tackled the "instability dilemma." Modeling cross-national political institutional differences has become common in this endeavor. Moreover, scholars have turned to individual-level analysis in hopes of gaining greater analytical leverage on why the strength of the economic vote varies.

Political context matters

Powell and Whitten's (1993) study was among the first to elaborate systematically how political context affected economic voting. They first sought to replicate Paldam's (1991a) work against a smaller data set comprising about 102 national elections held between 1969 and 1988 in 19 developed democracies. Their baseline model generated results consistent with Paldam's findings. They modified their baseline model by classifying polities based on clarity of political responsibility—the presence of institutional arrangements that facilitate or hinder assigning government responsibility for economic conditions. Their key finding was that economic voting is conditioned by institutional context. The election effects of GDP growth, unemployment, and inflation are weak in political systems with strong bicameralism, minority coalitions, and weak party cohesion for example. On the other hand, economic conditions have a stronger effect on election outcomes in polities with single-party governments, strong party cohesion, and other features that sharpen lines of responsibility.

Three important contextual studies using comparative survey data came out in the early 2000s. Anderson (2000), Hellwig (2001), and Nadeau et al. (2002) investigated more systematically than previous contributions how context interacted with economic perceptions to shape voting intentions. Anderson's (2000) comparative individual-level analysis relied on 1994 Eurobarometer survey results from the then 12 European Union countries plus Norway. The dependent variables in his study were vote intention for governing parties and for the prime minister's party. The key independent variables were retrospective egocentric economic evaluations, retrospective sociotropic economic evaluations, the Powell-Whitten index, governing party target size, and clarity of available alternatives.

Anderson's statistical results revealed that the effects of the Powell-Whitten index on vote choice originally observed using aggregate data held true with individual-level data. He also found that the economic vote is strengthened when a governing party's command of legislative seats and cabinet posts is relatively large and when the effective number of parties is small. As Anderson (2000: 168) noted, "taken together, these findings suggest that voters' ability to express discontent with economic performance is enhanced when accountability is simple"—in other words, when voters can easily identify the party that bears the most responsibility for economic conditions and when they have a clear alternative to choose when they are dissatisfied with the incumbent party. In contrast to Anderson's findings, Chappell and Viega's (2000: 194) time-series study of 13 Western European countries did not find evidence to corroborate the "conjecture that variations in political responsibility can account for the instability of vote function parameter estimates across countries."

Nadeau et al.'s (2002) study is based on survey results from 165,000 respondents in eight European countries between 1976 and 1992. They created a more dynamic model of clarity of responsibility—one that tracked "variations in clarity simultaneously across time and across countries" (Nadeau et al. 2002: 418). To achieve this, they developed an expanded clarity index consisting of the Powell-Whitten index, size of largest government party, number of parties in parliament, time in office, and ideological cohesion. Consistent with previous studies, Nadeau et al. found that voting intentions are influenced by national sociotropic evaluations and that such an effect is stronger (weaker) in polities with higher (lower) clarity of responsibility.

The novelty of their model stems from its ability to estimate the effects of within-country change on the economic vote. A key takeaway is that the differences in the strength of the economic vote between high-clarity and low-clarity polities can become blurry at different time points. "When clarity is high in the usually low-clarity countries, the impact of a given shift in [the general economic situation] is as large as when clarity is low in the usually high-clarity countries," Nadeau et al. (2002: 417) noted. Because clarity and economic evaluations change "considerably over time, as well as across countries, it is easy to see how researchers could reach different conclusions about the impact of economic evaluations on the vote."

Since the publication of Powell and Whitten (1993), most contextual studies have focused on how domestic political institutions mediate democratic accountability. However, few have considered how the global economy can affect the economic vote. Hellwig's (2001) study investigated whether economic openness affects the association between economic perceptions and vote intention. Using Comparative Study of Electoral Systems data generated from surveys conducted in nine countries between 1996 and 1998, Hellwig found that the interactive effect of retrospective sociotropic evaluation and trade openness dampens the economic vote. Is this effect evenly seen throughout the population? His findings suggested that the more educated a person is, the more aware they are that some of the recent domestic economic conditions are not of the incumbent party's own doing. As a result, their vote is likely to be less influenced by their economic perceptions. Hellwig's study confirmed the predicted effects of the clarity of responsibility variables developed by Powell and Whitten (1993) and Anderson (2000).

To date, Duch and Stevenson (2008) are credited for completing the most comprehensive micro-level time-series-cross-sectional study. To estimate the economic vote, they analyzed the behavior of slightly over 200,000 voters who voted in 163 elections in 18 countries between 1979 and 2001. They found that economic voting "is [sizable] and pervasive in the advanced democracies" and concluded that the preponderance of evidence "should put an end to any speculation about the importance of cross-national economic voting" (Duch and Stevenson 2008: 62–63). Cross-national variance in the magnitude of the economic vote, their evidence showed, can be accounted for by three contextual factors: degree of political control of the economy, distribution of policymaking responsibility among parties, and pattern of contestation among parties. As economic openness increases, incumbents' control over macroeconomic outcomes decreases, resulting in lower economic voting. Political arrangements that concentrate administrative responsibilities—for example, presidential systems under unified governments and parliamentary systems under single-party majority cabinets—augment the economic vote. Finally, when the prospects for replacing incumbent parties by opposition parties are high and when opposition parties represent viable alternative cabinets, the economy-incumbent connection is stronger.

Economic voting during the Great Recession

How did the Great Recession affect the economic vote? Received wisdom tells us that in the face of economic adversity an avenging electorate will be especially harsh on incumbent officeholders. Table 5.2 reports information about the fates of incumbent

TABLE 5.2 Electoral fates of incumbent parties in OECD countries, 2008–2009

Country	Election Date	Incumbent Party	Incumbent Ideology	GDP Growth	Vote Gain/ Loss	Defeated	Direction
Austria	28-Sept-09	SPÖ	Center	−0.8	−14.4	No	→R
Bulgaria	05-Jul-09	BSP	Left	−3.6	−16.3	Yes	L→R
Canada	14-Oct-08	CON	Right	1.0	1.4	No	→R
Chile	13-Dec-09	CPD	Left	−0.8	−7.4	Yes	L→R
Germany	27-Sep-09	CDU/SPD	Center	−6.2	−12.6	No	→R
Greece	04-Oct-09	ND	Right	−3.5	−8.4	Yes	R→L
Iceland	25-Apr-09	SSF	Right	−5.4	−12.9	Yes	R→L
Italy	14-Apr-08	PD	Left	0.2	−7.9	Yes	L→R
Israel	10-Feb-09	Kadima/Lab	Center/Left	1.6	−4.7	Yes	L→R
Japan	30-Aug-09	LDP	Right	−6.5	−11.5	Yes	→C
Lithuania	12-Oct-08	LSDP	Left	2.6	−8.9	Yes	L→R
Luxembourg	07-Jun-09	CSV	Center	−2.9	1.9	No	NCD
New Zealand	8-Nov-08	Labour	Left	−0.6	−7.1	Yes	L→R
Norway	14-Sep-09	DNA	Left	−2.3	2.7	No	NCD
Portugal	27-Sep-09	PS	Left	−3.5	−8.5	No	→R
Romania	30-Nov-08	PNL	Right	−7.1	−13.2	Yes	NCD
Slovenia	21-Sep-08	SDS	Right	4.9	−0.6	Yes	R→L
Spain	09-Mar-08	PSOE	Left	3.1	0.6	No	NCD
United States	04-Nov-08	Rep	Right	−0.6	−1.7	Yes	R→L

Sources: Bartels (2014:189–90); LeDuc and Pammett (2013: 496); and authors calculations.

parties that faced elections between March 2008 and December 2009 in OECD countries, GDP growth the year leading up to national elections, and whether elections resulted in a partisan shift. Governing parties in 15 of the 19 countries that held elections during this period lost voter support, and the vote loss resulted in the defeat of 12 incumbent parties. On average, incumbent parties lost 6.8% of the popular vote.

IN FOCUS BOX 5.1 THE ELECTORAL CONSEQUENCES OF THE GREAT RECESSION

Figure 5.2 shows a strong positive association between GDP growth and incumbent vote. Incumbent parties faced major electoral losses in hard hit economies; those losses were milder in economies that were not as buffeted by the Great Recession. Interestingly, although economic growth in Italy, Israel, Lithuania, and Slovenia remained positive in the lead-up to elections, the electorate in these countries took little comfort in such performance and ended up voting out their governing parties. The opposite occurred in Luxembourg and Norway—negative growth did not translate to electoral setbacks. As it has become abundantly clear from the literature we have reviewed so far, aggregate-level analysis can take us only so far in exploring the economic vote. Taking into account individual and contextual factors can shed light on observed inconsistencies like the ones involving the economic vote in these six countries.

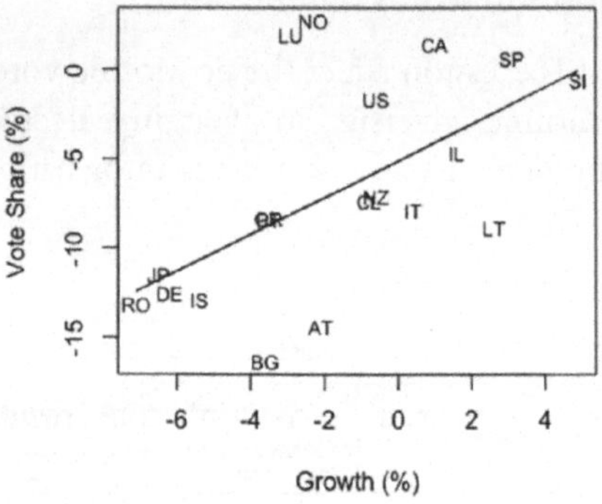

FIGURE 5.2 Vote share and growth, 2008–2009
Note: r = 0.58, sig @ 0.001

Source: Table 5.2.

LeDuc and Pammett (2013) do just that. Their analysis of European elections held between June 2008 and June 2010 finds that prospective evaluations had a greater effect on economic voting than retrospective evaluations. "It is the perception that the economy is likely to worsen in the next year that is more important than past evaluations of its condition," LeDuc and Pammett (2013: 497) remark. Their results also confirm that the loss of incumbent support was greater in political environments that eased blame attribution.

The fact that voting behavior during the Great Recession was influenced by what voters perceived would happen to their economies in the months to come rather than what had recently happened, can account in part for why recent growth was not a good predictor of vote share in many countries. As Lithuanians were preparing to vote in the October 2008 election, arguably what weighed on their minds was the general feeling that the country's overheated economy could not last much longer. Those hunches proved correct—the economy contracted sharply by the end of 2009 after experiencing double-digit growth two years before. In Great Britain, which held elections in May 2010, the specter of a double-dip recession coupled with an expected increase in national insurance contributions the following year brought punishing results for the single-party majority government led by the Labour Party. The data tracking economic opinions in Great Britain showed the economic mood of voters was trending downward in the months leading to the national election.

Anderson and Hecht (2014) show that macroeconomic conditions figured larger on the minds of European voters during the Great Recession than in earlier years. As they put it, "results do appear to show that European publics generally became more responsive to macroeconomic conditions after the onset of the crisis than they had been earlier" (ibid: 53). The negative association between changes in economic opinion and changes in unemployment and inflation were substantively and statistically more significant from the outset of the crisis to 2011 than in the period from 2004 to the outset of the crisis. What is more, they find that the size of the welfare state had an important intervening effect on the economy-opinion nexus. During the Great Recession, voters' economic moods were hardly affected in the face of short-term changes in unemployment and economic growth in countries with large welfare states.

In effect, by supporting people who are experiencing economic hardship, social safety nets helped shore up economic moods—particularly, perceptions of personal well-being. In Germany, for example, the combination of generous social benefits and fiscal stimulus helped sustain positive egocentric economic evaluations even though voters expressed negative opinions about the overall economy. Between 2008 and 2010, the share of Germans who reported that their personal economic situations were bad averaged 13% (never rising above 15%); those who reported that the national economic situation was bad peaked at around 47% in March 2009 and stood around 37% on the eve of the September 2009 national election (Anderson and Hecht 2012: 9).

Did the victories of right-wing parties during the Great Recession signify an ideological shift in political behavior? Table 5.2 shows that out of the 12 countries in which incumbent parties were defeated, six resulted in a shift of power from left- to right-wing parties. Did this signal that voters viewed these parties as more competent than their left-wing counterparts in nursing economies back to health? Not necessarily. Greece, Iceland, Slovenia, and the United States witnessed Right to Left shifts during that period. Further, Bartels's (2014) cross-national analysis of elections in 42 OECD countries between 2007 and 2011 shows that election results are more consistent with the punish-reward approach than the selection approach to economic voting. On average, the electoral fortunes of right-wing parties were better than those of left-wing counterparts. However, when significant outlier elections are removed, Bartels notes that the differences in the electoral fates of Right and Left governments were small.

Lindvall's (2014) pooled time-series analysis contributes another important empirical observation about the ideological impact of the economic crisis. In comparing the economic vote during the Great Depression (1929–1939) and Great Recession, he finds that right-wing parties are advantaged in the early phases of a crisis while left-wing parties face better election prospects in later phases. Lindvall, along with other scholars studying the topic (see Anderson and Hecht 2014), uses the "luxury goods" argument to account for this pattern. The argument holds that the public is less willing to support high levels of public spending during economic downturns. As Lindvall notes, this view is likely to be conditioned by the gravity of a crisis. The pressure to cut social spending comes from middle- and upper-income groups who are usually less affected in the early stages of a recession. However, as economic hardship reaches the well-off segments of society, their social policy preferences become more aligned with those of lower-income groups. This creates a political environment conducive to the formation of a center-left electoral alliance. Although results of cross-national aggregate studies lend credence to the "luxury goods" argument, the micro-foundations of this argument remain underexplored.

Key controversies

A key takeaway of the extant literature on the economic vote is that it is highly contingent on both individual and institutional factors at the domestic and international levels. Accordingly, the challenge facing scholars has been to identify those factors, determine their relative importance, and figure out their interactive effects. Unless progress is made on those fronts, economic voting models risk lacking explanatory and predictive power, and, more importantly, doubts about "the efficacy of elections as mechanisms for selecting and sanctioning political leaders" cannot be put to rest (Achen and Bartels 2017: 115; see also Anderson 2007; Cheibub and Przeworski 1999).

The vast literature on economic voting, some of which was summarized in the previous section, has raised a number of controversies regarding different aspects of the link between the economy and vote intention. This section covers a number of them; in doing so, it will sketch what the disagreements are about and report the progress that has been made to address them. As figure 5.3 illustrates, a host of factors intervene at different junctures along the link between the real economy and vote intention. Some controversies have emerged concerning how economic perceptions derive from economic reality; others relate to how economic perceptions translate to vote intention.

Retrospective versus prospective voting

What decisional rule do voters use to form economic opinions? Do voters engage in a retrospective or prospective evaluation of the economy? The difference between the reward-punishment and selection approaches we reviewed earlier hinges on the decisional standard voters use. To describe voters as retrospective evaluators means that they judge officeholders based on their well-being in light of past economic performance. On the other hand, prospective voters evaluate candidates based on the expected state of their utility in light of probable future economic outcomes.

Prospective voters—at least those depicted in rational expectations-informed models—are farsighted and sophisticated. They have the capacity to discern the consequences of anticipated events, a more demanding task then simply extrapolating from past conditions. Additionally, voters are aware of the "feasibility constraints"

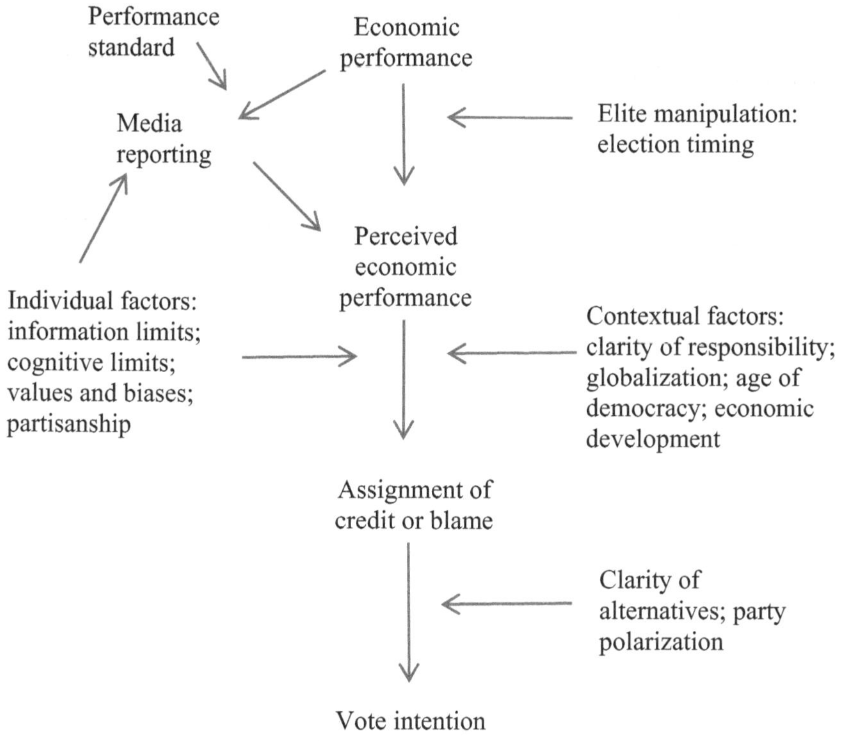

FIGURE 5.3 The complexity of economic voting
Source: adapted from Kayser, Mark Andreas. 2014. "The Elusive Economic Vote." In Lawrence LeDuc, Richard Niemi, and Pippa Norris, eds., *Comparing Democracies: Elections and Voting in a Changing World*, fourth edition. Used with permission of SAGE Publications.

that candidates are facing in light of current conditions, and will modulate their expectations about the future accordingly (Chappell and Keech 1985: 13). For example, if the unemployment rate is reaching its natural rate, prospective voters would not demand lower unemployment for fear of future inflation and would not support a candidate promising to lower joblessness. If one were to relax the rational expectations assumption, it is also possible for prospective voters to be less sophisticated and even engage in some retrospection. They can make simple projections about what is likely to happen over the next year or so based on what they currently or recently experienced. Moreover, they can rely on partisan reputational cues to help them estimate their future utilities (see Downs 1957; Fiorina 1981; Kramer 1971).

Alternatively, retrospective voters are usually myopic and naïve. Voters are myopic in that they assign disproportionate value to conditions that have transpired over the past year. They are naïve to the extent that they usually do not take account of the fact that inflation, unemployment, and growth are interrelated, and that such macroeconomic conditions are subject to political manipulation. The implication is that retrospective voters develop a general sense of recent national economic trends while discounting the far past and future. As Norpoth (1996: 777) remarks, "the requirements for that kind of behavior are far more modest regarding both the average citizen's capabilities and motivation to follow politics . . . [and are] consistent with a limited form of rational behavior." However, as some scholars have noted (see Chappell and Viega 2000; Duch and Stevenson 2008), retrospective voters can form their economic opinions using more refined and demanding standards. For example, they can compare the performance of their country relative to other countries, or interpret recent economic events from the viewpoint of what is sustainable in light of macroeconomic constraints, or distinguish between macroeconomic fluctuations attributed to the actions of domestic officeholders and to exogenous forces.

In their comprehensive review essay of economic voting, Lewis-Beck and Stegmaier (2013: 370) acknowledge that "most researchers seem to opt for the retrospective, rather than the prospective, specification . . . indicat[ing] that retrospective evaluations dominate." However, in a narrower survey of the literature, Lewis-Beck and Paldam (2000: 114, 118) remark that "retrospective variables work better" than prospective ones, "but the difference is small." Their conditional nod to retrospective voting stems from the fact that instances of prospective voting "keep popping up" in single-country and cross-national studies. Prospective behavior has been exhibited among voters in Canada (Bélanger and Gélineau 2010), in the United States (MacKuen et al. 1992), in the United Kingdom (Sanders 2000), in France (Lewis-Beck and Stegmaier 2013), and in Denmark (Nannestad and Paldam 2000). Further, in their analysis of 212 surveys conducted in 18 Latin American countries between 1995 and 2009, Singer and Carlin (2013) find that prospective voting is more likely to emerge when voters face new incumbents who have yet to develop an economic track record.

Although the prospective versus retrospective controversy might be settled for the most part, what remains open to question is the retrospective standard used by typical voters. There is consensus in the field on two patterns: first, that voters discount past events exceeding one year; and, second, that voters are usually more sensitive to changes in rather than levels of growth, inflation, and unemployment. But beyond that, there is less agreement. For example, whereas Chappell and Viega (2000) and Powell and Whitten (1993) find evidence suggesting that voters use the economic performance of neighboring countries as a benchmark to evaluate their national performance, a study by Bartels (2014) fails to corroborate that finding. While Chappell and Keech (1985) observe that the retrospective behavior of American voters "is consistent with a sophisticated standard of evaluation,"—which includes an awareness of the logic underpinning the long-run Phillips curve—Achen and Bartels (2017) find little evidence of such sophistication. Instead, their evidence points to "blind" retrospection among American voters—random events like shark attacks influencing citizens' vote choices.

The question of which economic indicators figure large on voters' minds and affect retrospective voting the most also remains open, particularly if one focuses on recent cross-national studies. Chappell and Viega (2000) observe that neither unemployment nor growth has any reliable election impact, a finding contradicted by Kayser (2014), Powell and Whitten (1993), and Anderson and Hecht (2014). What is more, notwithstanding Chappell and Viega's finding (2000), the electoral significance of growth appears to have increased over time. In their 1994 survey of the economic voting literature, Nannestad and Paldam labeled inflation and unemployment as the "big two" macro variables. In contrast, in their 2013 literature survey, Lewis-Beck and Stegmaier remarked "that now the 'big two' are unemployment and growth." Recent studies (Anderson and Hecht 2012; Dassonneville and Lewis-Beck 2014, 2019) have found that voters pay closer attention to the change in and level of economic growth.

Pocketbook versus sociotropic voting

When voters form economic opinions about the state of their national economy, which matters most politically—personal economic experience or national economic conditions? Whereas pocketbook voters form political judgments based on their recent personal fortunes, sociotropic voters evaluate politicians based on recent trends in business and macroeconomic conditions. As the two leading scholars on this topic have put it, "Pocketbook voting reflects the circumstances and predicaments of personal economic life; sociotropic voting reflects the circumstances and predicaments of national economic life" (Kinder and Kiewiet 1981: 132; see also Kinder and Kiewiet 1979).

According to the pocketbook voter argument, it is voters' self-interests rather than other-regarding interests that shape their political preferences. If their financial situation has worsened or is expected to worsen, perhaps because they face or expect to face job insecurity, they will be inclined to blame the incumbent for their woes. The pocketbook argument—and its self-interest maximizing assumption—was woven into early economic voting models. Its earliest elaboration was made by Downs (1957: 42) who remarked that voters "are not interested in policies *per se* but in their own utility incomes. If their present utility incomes are very low in their own eyes . . . it is rational for them to vote against the incumbents." What is more, earlier works on the economic vote presumed that the prevalence of pocketbook voting in society had to do with its low information cost (Kinder and Kiewiet 1981). Pocketbook voters did not have to read up on economic news; what they experienced as ordinary consumers spoke volumes about their own state of material comfort.

Contrary to this view, Gomez and Wilson (2006) have observed that the cognitive process guiding pocketbook voting actually reflects a high level of political sophistication. Their investigation of voters in Canada, Hungary, Mexico, and Taiwan reveals that "high sophisticates are more likely than their less sophisticated counterparts to understand the political-economic linkage (e.g., political-business cycles, partisan differences in tax and spending priorities, etc.) and how changes in a government's economic policies might affect their personal financial situation" (Gomez and Wilson 2006: 132). The policy implication of pocketbook voting is that incumbents seeking to retain their offices will want to implement targeted policies such as tax expenditures or more generous social transfers to constituents who are dissatisfied with their personal economic situations.

How does the pocketbook vote argument stack up against empirical findings? It turns out that sociotropic voting trumps egotropic politics under many circumstances (Lewis-Beck and Stegmaier 2013; Kayser 2014). In general, voters' economic perceptions are more influenced by the state of national economic affairs. What matters politically is their perceptions of how consumer and business confidence, unemployment, inflation, and growth are trending, or of how the government has handled the national economy, or some combination of both. In both small- and large-N survey analyses, sociotropic effects have been found to be more important than pocketbook ones even when accounting for different contextual configurations (Anderson 2000; Lewis-Beck 1986; Nadeau et al. 2002). Singer and Carlin (2013) suggest that the strength of sociotropic effect can also be conditioned by the level of economic development. Their study of voters in Latin America finds that pocketbook and sociotropic effects are about the same in poor countries such as Nicaragua and Honduras; however, the importance of sociotropic evaluations grows as countries prosper.

Although a consensus has emerged about the dominance of sociotropic politics, there is disagreement about whether sociotropic voters are or are not guided by other-regarding motives. As Kinder and Kiewiet (1981: 132) observe, "The motives that underlie sociotropic voting . . . are not so transparent." It "may proceed out of altruistic concern" for the collective well-being of society or it "may be totally self-interested." The fact that public interest considerations figure on the minds of voters need not block out self-interested considerations. After all, as Lewis-Beck and Stegmaier (2013: 371) note, a voter can "use national economic performance as a proxy for their personal economic circumstances. . . [,] they understand intuitively that when the country prospers they are more likely to prosper." As esoteric as this debate may seem to some, what is clear is the policy implication of sociotropic politics. To the extent that collective economic evaluations is at the heart of economic voting, incumbents have an incentive to harness economic policies in order to smooth out business cycles and to cultivate an environment conducive to business investment and job creation (Hellwig 2010).

IN FOCUS BOX 5.2 BREXIT AND SOCIOTROPIC VOTING

On June 23, 2016, 51.9% of the voters who participated in the Brexit referendum chose the Leave option. What influenced the Brexit vote? Colantone and Stanig (2018) argue that the Leave vote was higher in regions of the country that experienced significant job losses in manufacturing. Global competition, particularly from China, has been a key factor behind the deindustrialization of these regions. The regions hit hardest by the globalization shock have witnessed the largest decreases in GDP per capita. Colantone and Stanig find that these regions were more likely to support U.K.'s exit from the European Union. Further, they find strong evidence of a sociotropic reaction to the globalization shock. Brexit supporters tended to be more influenced by the overall economic situation of the regions they lived in than by their personal economic situations.

Elite manipulation

Politicians have an incentive to shape how voters perceive the economy and how economic opinions are converted to vote choice. As we have discussed previously, incumbents might engineer electorally timed economic expansions to improve their reelection prospects. If the option of triggering an opportunistic business cycle is not available to elected officeholders—because of fiscal constraints or delegation of monetary policy to an independent central bank or both—they might be able to use other tools in their reelection efforts. We will focus on three elite manipulation techniques—blame avoidance, gimmickry, and election surfing.

The literature exploring how globalization impacts electoral accountability has shed light on how incumbents might be able to dodge responsibility for negative economic outcomes. The globalization of national economies has meant that more domestic economic policies are aligned with international standards and rules such as those embodied in the World Trade Organization and other global economic institutions. While the harmonization of national policies facilitates global trade and investment, it can also limit national leaders' domestic policy autonomy. What would appear as a liability for incumbents can instead be exploited to escape electoral punishment. Incumbents can strategically divert responsibility for recent domestic economic conditions by persuading voters that globalization is the main culprit whether it is in fact the case. As Hellwig and Samuels (2007: 298) note, "Strategic politicians may use economic openness as a scapegoat for poor performance outcomes—even if those outcomes can be traced back to their own competence as economic managers." The fact that several studies have found that the election effect of economic performance is attenuated as economic liberalization levels rise, suggests that voters can be swayed by elected leaders to believe that "globalization ties their hands as policymakers" (Hellwig 2010). In sum, the higher the level of economic openness, the greater the incentive for incumbents to shift responsibility and the weaker the economic vote.

Further, opportunistic politicians might be able to improve their reelection chances by concealing or spinning factual information that is damaging to their reputations. A government might want to misreport the actual financial losses the public has incurred because of poorly administered public infrastructure projects or subsidy programs. If this information were revealed to the public, it might signal government incompetence and affect voters' economic evaluations. Alt et al. (2014) show evidence that fiscal gimmickry—fudging public finance statistics to make them look better than they actually are—by elected officials is more likely to occur when there is a lack of budget transparency, elections are approaching, and they face demanding supranational fiscal rules such as those embodied in the EU's Stability and Growth Pact.

A third form of elite manipulation that can affect the economic vote concerns the strategic timing of elections. In polities that do not have fixed elections—parliamentary and semi-presidential systems for the most part—incumbents might be able to stage elections right when propitious economic conditions prevail. The extant literature on election surfing has investigated two questions: Under what conditions are early elections called? Does election surfing help incumbents get reelected? Riera's (2015) study of elections in 21 OECD countries from 1945 to 2010 reveals that the likelihood of early elections increases when an economy grows and inflation rate drops (see also Hellwig 2010; Kayser 2014). Under such economic circumstances, single-party minority governments, more than other cabinet types, are likely to resort to opportunistic election timing. Palmer and Whitten (2000: 422) find that "minority governments are typically 25.7 to 33.9 percentage points more likely to call an early election than majority governments." Interestingly, their study detected a partisan effect on election surfing. The probability of a right-wing government calling early elections increases as inflation decreases; for left-wing governments, it increases when unemployment decreases.

According to this strand of scholarship, incumbents take advantage of endogenous elections, calling snap elections when recent and current economic conditions are favorable. In contrast, Smith (2003) contends that early elections foreshadow an expected economic downturn. According to this interpretation of election surfing, incumbents stage elections now to avoid the electoral losses governments usually suffer when elections occur in the middle of an economic recession.

If election timing is endogenous to recent and current economic performance, then one should expect such opportunistic behavior to pay off at the ballot box. However, if early elections stir up voter suspicion about the state of the economy in the near future, as Smith (2003) contends, electoral punishment should result from election surfing. The extant scholarship has found more evidence supporting the former claim. Strategic timing of elections, as Hellwig (2010) reports, can generate a modest boost to the incumbent vote share of roughly 3.7% or a significant boost (7.5 percentage points) as Schleiter and Tavits (2016) find. Further, although voters appear to have negative impressions of opportunistic election timing, they "assign significantly higher importance to economic performance than to election timing in their vote choice," as Schleiter and Tavits (2018: 1194) observe.

Knowledge, biases, and media

Can voters accurately perceive actual economic conditions? Do they have the motivation or cognitive capacity to translate their economic evaluations into vote intentions? What is the role of the media in shaping economic opinions? Formal models of economic voting usually answer the first two questions in the affirmative and tend to depict mass media as a transmitter of unbiased economic news. These assertions are based on the premise that voters are sophisticated. The sophistication of average voters enables them to decode and interpret the objective economy with the aid of credible information and link their evaluation of the economy to their vote choice. Moreover, whatever idiosyncratic influences are expressed at the individual level will be cancelled out at the aggregate level.

Voters, according to Chappell and Keech (1985) and MacKuen et al. (1992), have the cognitive capacity to generate informed opinions of the recent and future economy. Given the "common sense" of the average voter, a voter would "accept recessions only as a means of reducing inflation" and not "demand economic expansion when most of the economy is working at capacity," as Chappell and Keech (1985: 13) observe. The media figures large in shaping what is economic common sense. As MacKuen et al. (1992: 604) remark, "without trying, the public is exposed to the best information . . . about the past and the present but also about future" economic performance by listening to "the experts who translate the economic numbers into good times and bad times." It is the sophistication of voters that enables them to discern the credibility of "politically relevant information," adapt their prior beliefs in light of new information, and bring their updated beliefs to bear on their vote preferences (Alt et al., 2016: 330). That disposition on the part of average voters, as Anderson and Hecht (2014: 42) observe, leads to "significant congruence between objective economic conditions and subjective economic opinions." Importantly, these voters have the capacity to effectively assign attribution of responsibility insofar as holding officeholders accountable for events that are under their control. Random lapses in voter judgments—that is, those rare instances when voters behave irrationally—are offset by the collective rationality of the electorate. "The net perception of the economy, neither biased nor ignorant, is . . . right on the mark" as Stimson (2004: 165) remarks.

These assertions have come under scrutiny. In fact, scholars have suspected for some time that it might be less, not more, politically sophisticated voters who are inclined to display political behavior as depicted in electoral accountability models. Drawing on insights from Campbell et al. (1960) and Converse (1964), recent studies have contended that less informed voters are less ideological and more willing to internalize new information. In short, less informed voters possess the kind of temperament ideal for dispensing electoral accountability (see Kayser 2014).

A number of factors can hinder a person's ability to accurately perceive the real economy and bring it to bear on one's political choice (Anderson 2007). Cognitive limits can prevent a person from accurately decoding and interpreting economic data, let alone distinguish reliable from unreliable information sources. People filter incoming information through personal biases such as preconceived ideas and heuristics which can oversimplify reality. Emotions, passions, and delusions might cloud one's political judgment to the extent that any one of these mental states can impair sensible causal reasoning. Personal experiences and situations can incline voters to perceive the economy differently. Short-time horizons cause voters to overlook important long-term trends. Insofar as voters' economic perceptions are heavily shaped by media reporting, such perceptions are vulnerable to the media's tendency to emphasize negative economic events and are limited by the media's bias toward retrospective evaluation. As Nadeau et al. (1999: 120) observe, "the media's emphasis on changing conditions includes an emphasis on how we got where we are but much less on where we are going."

There is also evidence suggesting that economic evaluations are rationalizations of partisan beliefs. The endogeneity of economic perception argument holds that voters' judgments of the economy are merely "superficial masks for partisan identification" or other personal values (Kinder and Kiewiet 1981: 150). For example, I may have a positive view of the economy because I identify with the incumbent party, but my younger sibling might have a negative view because she is against the ruling party. Because voters see the economy through partisan lens, vote intentions are unlikely to be closely connected with economic reality (Wlezien et al. 1997; for a different view see Nadeau et al. 2012). Recently, scholars have examined how partisan retrenchment witnessed in advanced democracies has impacted the economic vote. Kayser and Wlezien (2011) argue that the decline in partisan affiliation in Europe may have contributed to a stronger economic vote at both the individual and aggregate levels. However, Dassonneville and Lewis-Beck (2019: 94) "find no indication that the importance of [partisan anchoring] is weakening over time" and leading to an "over-time change in the economic vote."

These individual-level constraints on the economic vote are so pervasive that some have called into question the methodological claim that the aforementioned individual factors are simply random and do not matter in the aggregate (MacKuen et al., 1992). In their extensive research on American political behavior, Achen and Bartels (2017: 41 and 128) conclude that "voters *consistently* and *systematically* punish incumbents for . . . misfortunes that are clearly beyond the leaders' control. When thousands or millions of voters misconstrue the same relevant fact . . . no amount of aggregation will produce the requisite miracle" of aggregation—the notion that "the electorate as a whole may be much wiser than any individual voter" (italics original).

Conclusion

A key takeaway of the literature reviewed in this section is that scholars should be careful when making inferences about a national-level economy-vote link from individual patterns of political behavior—a type of fallacy of inference referred to as micrological fallacy (Dassonneville and Lewis-Beck 2014). Ever since Kramer (1983) alerted us to this issue, discrepancies have been found between the research investigating the voting effects of individuals' subjective perceptions (micro-subjective results) and the research exploring the election effects of aggregate economic conditions (macro-objective studies). The conflicting evidence is owed in part to the fact that survey results pick up the effects of individual partisan biases and other idiosyncratic factors. Some other sources of the discrepancy are that survey participants may not accurately represent the electorate and that most surveys report respondents' vote intentions rather than who they voted for. Some progress has been made to address these methodological and empirical problems. One promising approach found in recent studies is the creation of instrumental variable controls for respondents' partisan ideologies (see Nadeau et al. 2012; Dassonneville and Lewis-Beck 2019).

Key terms

Clarity of responsibility

Ecological fallacy

Economic voting

Endogenous election

Pocketbook voting

Prospective voting

Retrospective voting

Sociotropic voting

Discussion questions

- Compare and contrast the reward-punishment and selection approaches to economic voting. Which one do you think is more insightful and why?
- How did the Great Recession affect economic voting?
- The link between the economy and vote is not straightforward. Explain why.
- Describe how the economy affects how you vote. Do you vote prospectively or retrospectively? As a voter, which economic performance indicator concerns you the most? Why?

Further reading

Achen, Christopher H., and Larry M. Bartels. 2016. *Democracy for Realists: Why Elections Do Not Produce Responsive Government*. Princeton, NJ: Princeton University Press

Challenges the conventional thinking that voters are rational and exhibit behavior that is consistent with electoral accountability.

Duch, Raymond M., and Randolph T. Stevenson. 2008. *The Economic Vote: How Political and Economic Institutions Condition Election Results*. New York: Cambridge University Press.

Argues that the ability of voters to select competent government officials is conditioned by economic and political institutions.

Hellwig, Timothy. 2014. *Globalization and Mass Politics: Retaining the Room to Maneuver*. New York: Cambridge University Press.

Explores how the internationalization of trade, finance, and production affects electoral accountability.

Hellwig, Timothy, Yesola Kweon, and Jack Vowles. 2020. *Democracy Under Siege? Parties, Voters, and Elections After the Great Recession*. New York: Oxford University Press.

Analyzes the long-term effects of the Great Recession on citizens' perceptions of political elites.

CHAPTER

6

Inequality

Consider these comparative facts about economic inequality in the United States and France. In 2014, the richest 10% of the population in the United States—which amounted to roughly 23.4 million adults—earned 47% of the total national income. The income share of the bottom 50% of the population—representing 117.2 million adults—stood at 12.5%. In France, the top 10% of the population—roughly 5.2 million adults—commanded 32.7% of total national income while the bottom 50%—some 25.9 million adults—controlled 22.5% of national income (Garbinti et al. 2018; Piketty et al. 2016).

What's the takeaway? Although the richest 10% in both countries claim an oversized share of total income, top income inequality is much higher in the United States. Moreover, while the bottom 50% in both countries command a disproportionately small share of total income, bottom income inequality is less severe in France.

This highly skewed distribution of national income in the United States relative to France is the result of divergent income growth trends across different income groups. Between 1946 and 1980, total accumulated income growth for the top 10% and bottom 50% was 79% and 102%, respectively. In France, during roughly the same period, income growth for the top 10% and bottom 50% was 157% and 236%, respectively. During this period, the bottom half of the population in both countries was able to achieve significant income gains relative to the richest 10%, especially in France.

Between 1980 and 2014, income grew by 121% for the richest 10% and by just 1% for the poorest half of the population in the United States. In France, the top 10% saw their income grow by 49% while adults in the lower half of the income distribution experienced a 31% increase in income during this period (Garbinti et al. 2018; Piketty et al. 2016).

Clearly, the rich have been getting richer faster in the United States in recent decades. And, while income growth for poorer citizens has slowed in both countries, the prospects of income gains for poorer Americans have been especially abysmal since the 1980s.

DOI: 10.4324/9780429199462-6

The main objective of this chapter is to analyze income inequality across countries and over time. This chapter will focus on the distribution of income before taxes and social transfers. The chapter is divided into several sections. The first section elaborates on the tools used to measure inequality. The second section discusses why income inequality matters from social, economic, and political perspectives. The third section investigates various economic and political determinants of earnings inequality. The final section explores the rise of top income inequality in the United States from a comparative perspective. It draws on scholarship in economics, management, and political science to shed light on the sources of the emergence of the "winner-take-all" economy in the United States.

How to measure inequality

In this chapter we are interested in identifying factors that influence the distribution of income. Before we do that, let's be clear about the meaning of concepts commonly used to measure inequality.

Market income represents earnings from employment, investments, property, and savings before paying direct taxes and receiving income transfers from the government. Gross income (or money income) equals market income plus receipt of cash and near-cash transfers such as housing allowances and food stamps. Disposable income represents gross-income net of direct (income and payroll) taxes. Finally, full income equals disposable income minus indirect (sales, excise, and property) taxes plus in-kind benefits such as public education, health services, childcare, and elderly care (see Garfinkel et al. 2006).

As a general rule of thumb, the degree of inequality should decrease from market income to gross income to disposable income to full income. This is due to the fact that taxes and government transfers have the effect of reducing the dispersion in income distribution. In this chapter we will focus on market income—specifically, identifying the determinants of inequality in the distribution of market income.

We can measure the distribution of income with respect to different reference units—person, household, and family. In this chapter, we will focus on the earnings of individuals. The OECD's employment database enables researchers to gather earnings data of full-time dependent employees for either women or men or both; however, it leaves out individuals who are self-employed or are working part-time. Because table 6.1 draws on such data, readers should bear in mind that it does not provide a complete picture of wage inequality, for it excludes wages of non-dependent and part-time individuals. As such, the data underreport the extent of wage inequality.

There are several measures of inequality one can use to gauge differences in the degree of income dispersion. In this chapter, we will use three ratios (90–10, 90–50, and 50–10) and gini coefficient. The 90–10 ratio measures the income difference of someone representing the 90th percentile of a country's income distribution (the bottom of the top 10%) and someone occupying the 10th percentile (the top of the bottom 10%). A higher or lower 90–10 ratio means that high-income earners are pulling further away from or moving closer to low-income earners, respectively. Whereas the 90–50 ratio measures the difference between the income of the 90th percentile and the median of the income distribution, the 50–10 ratio measures the income gap between the median and 10th percentile.

In 2017, the 90–10, 90–50, and 50–10 ratios for female and male Canadians with full-time employment were 3.61, 1.91, and 1.89, respectively. What do these numbers mean? A Canadian representing the median earned 1.89 times as much as someone at the 10th percentile. Another way of looking at it, a worker at the 10th percentile earned a little more than half (52.9%) as much as the median earner [1 ÷ 1.89]. Similarly, a worker at the 90th percentile earned 191% of the Canadian median or the median earned a little over half (52.3%) of what the 90th percentile earned. Note that once you have both ratios, you can calculate the 90–10 ratio if not provided: 1.91 ÷ 0.529 = 3.61.

The advantage of using the 90–50 and 50–10 ratios is that they enable us to compare and contrast the degree of dispersion or compression of income in the upper and lower halves of the income distribution. As we investigate various determinants of income distribution later in the chapter, it will become evident that certain factors impact one half of the wage hierarchy more than the other. The gini coefficient is another measure of inequality. It ranges from zero (perfect equality) to one (perfect inequality).

IN FOCUS BOX 6.1 GINI COEFFICIENT

To calculate the gini coefficient, one has to determine the income share of each quintile as illustrated on the left side of figure 6.1. American households are grouped into quintiles (each representing 20% of the total population) and arranged from lowest to highest in terms of their share of total income. For example, whereas the percentage of total income going to the lowest quintile in 2017 was 3.1%, the highest quintile commanded 51.5% of total income. These data are then used to plot the income Lorenz curve as seen on the right side of figure 6.1.

Households			Income	
	Quintiles	Cumulative percentage	Percentage	Cumulative percentage
A	Lowest	20	3.1	3.1
B	Second	40	8.2	11.3
C	Third	60	14.3	25.6
D	Fourth	80	23.0	48.6
E	Highest	100	51.5	100.0

Note and Source: The data represent money income in the U.S.—market income plus cash payments to households from the government such as social security, supplemental security income, welfare payments from state and local welfare offices, unemployment insurance, survivor and disability benefits, workers' compensation, in addition to cash payments in the form of child support and alimony. Money income does not reflect payment of taxes and does not include noncash benefits. The data are from the U.S. Census Bureau. See Fontenot et al. (2018)

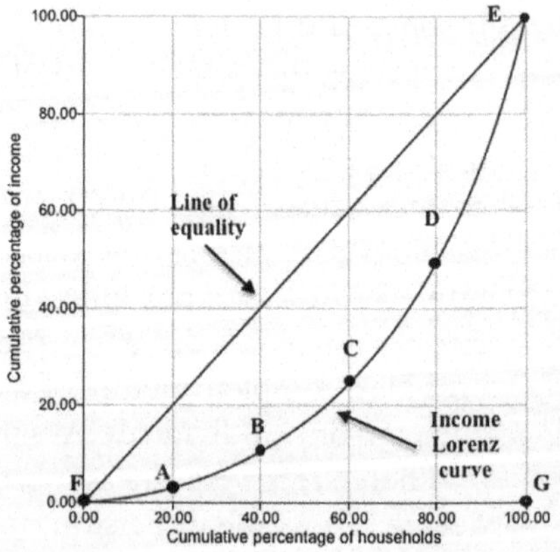

FIGURE 6.1 Income Lorenz curve, 2017

Note that the Lorenz curve lies below the line of equality. Upon closer observation, the line of equality reveals that the income share of each quintile is the same; therefore, if the Lorenz curve rested exactly on top of it the gini coefficient would be zero. To figure out the gini coefficient one needs, first, to calculate the space between the equality line and Lorenz curve (which equals to 0.2228) and then divide the result by the triangle FGE (which equals to 0.5). Thus, the gini coefficient of American household income in 2017 was 0.4456, placing the United States in the category of OECD countries with relatively high levels of economic inequality.

Why inequality matters

Why should societies be concerned about rising economic inequality? Studies point to a number of reasons.

Fairness

Rising inequality affects perceptions of fairness. Consider the income inequality between a married couple in their upper 50s who have both held professional jobs for 35 years and a newly married couple in their mid-20s fresh out of university and about to enter the workforce. For many, the inequality between the two couples seems justified and fair. Justified because where you are along the cycle of life matters in terms of determining your income status relative to others. In contrast to the older couple, the younger couple is about to begin their working careers, earning entry-level salaries in their professions. Incomes generally rise with age, job tenure, and degree of professionalized skills. The inequality between the two couples is also fair because many would assume that there is no reason why the younger couple cannot reach or exceed the income level of the older couple with time.

However, the run-up of income at the top casts increasing doubts about how economic rewards are dispensed. Are we to believe that those in the top 10% work harder and are better educated than everyone else? The perception that those at the top are there due to luck and family background rather than merit tends to be more prevalent in countries that have witnessed accelerated inequality levels. A comparison of the responses of Americans and Norwegians to the question of "how important is coming from a wealthy family to get ahead in life" illustrates this point well. According to a 1999 International Social Survey Programme survey, 46% of American and 50% of Norwegian respondents stated that being raised in a wealthy family was important in getting ahead. In a similar 2009 ISSP survey, 63% of Americans and 49% of Norwegians believed it was important. As top income inequality has risen in the United States, more and more Americans are of the view that meritorious factors—such as hard work, educational attainment, and work experience—matter less to achieve upward mobility. The concentration of income at the top is eroding the belief that equality of opportunity exists for all.

Economic growth

Rising inequality can also undermine economic growth. Okun (1975: 4) contended that a trade-off existed between equality and efficiency. As he put it, "the market creates inequality and efficiency jointly, . . . we can't have our cake of market efficiency and share it equally." Okun's trade-off argument rested on an important distinction between equality of rewards and equality of opportunity. Inequality of rewards, Okun argued, was necessary to motivate people to work harder, innovate, and skill-up. Under a situation of equality of rewards, would anyone exert themselves if it amounted to the same economic payoff as someone who opted for the path of least effort? On the other hand, to achieve efficient allocation of resources—what fuels growth—equality of opportunity was central. However, the ability to allocate your talent to those activities that need them the most would also bring about inequality because some talents are prized more than others (Pontusson 2005).

Freeman (2012) revises the logic underpinning Okun's trade-off, arguing instead that there is an inverted-U relationship between output and inequality. In egalitarian countries (as represented by A in figure 6.2), an increase in inequality results in higher output; in less egalitarian countries (as depicted by C), output drops as inequality rises. The logic goes as follows. The individual incentive to be productive rises as the prospects of higher returns on efforts also rise—a dynamic captured as we follow the inverted-U curve up until it crests at point B where "output-maximizing level of inequality" is reached (Freeman 2012: 69).

In countries that exceed the optimal inequality level, individuals are disinclined to work harder, to invest in education, and to be as entrepreneurial as they can be because rewards are few and out of reach for most. Suppose the organizers of the annual marathon in Burlington, Vermont, announce that they will give a single prize to the male and female runner who crosses the finishing line in first place. The other

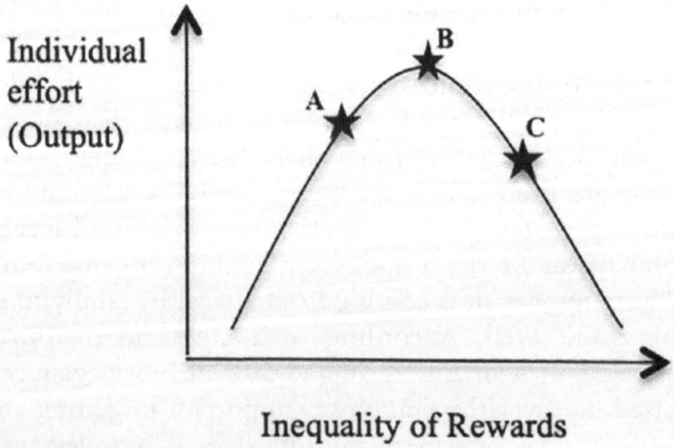

FIGURE 6.2 Okun's trade-off

Source: republished with permission of Stanford University Press, from Freeman, Richard B. 2012. "(Some) Inequality is Good for You." In David Grusky and Tamar Krichell-Katz, eds., *The New Gilded Age: The Critical Inequality Debate of Our Time*. Stanford: Stanford University Press, (p. 69); permission conveyed through Copyright Clearance Center, Inc.

top-ranking finishers and everyone else walk away empty handed—no participation medal, no event T-shirt. Given the winner-take-all reward, the marathon would draw far fewer runners and, among the elite runners, only those with a high chance of winning would bother to participate. This explains why organizers of marathons spread concession prizes across the top three to ten finishers and usually award all other runners a finishing medal or an event T-shirt.

Recent empirical studies corroborate the logic behind the inverted-U curve. According to a 2017 OECD report, rising inequality fuels average per capita real GDP growth in countries that have gini coefficients of disposable income of less than 0.27. Inequality has increasingly negative effects on growth in countries with higher gini levels (Grigoli and Robles 2017).

Health and social well-being

Another reason for worrying about rising inequality is that it undermines health and social well-being. Research by Pickett and Wilkinson (2015) finds that higher levels of inequality are associated with less healthier societies and higher crime levels. They develop a composite index of health and social problems that includes data on distrust, educational attainment, homicides, imprisonment, infant mortality, life expectancy, mental illness, obesity, social mobility, and teenage births. Among OECD countries, they find a strong positive relationship between income inequality and index ranking: more egalitarian countries have healthier societies, better educational performance, and lower crime rates; less egalitarian countries are plagued by poorer health conditions and have more prevalent social problems. Moreover, inequality is linked to violent crimes as well as property crimes according to Metz and Burdina (2016). They find that as inequality increases between poorer and richer neighborhood blocks, property crime levels in the well-off blocks rise.

Why is inequality linked to various health and social problems? For Pickett and Wilkinson, widening income gaps accentuate social status differentiation which in turn is linked to such psychosocial factors as stress, status anxiety, envy, and anger. Other studies, especially those focusing on the inequality-crime link, point to material incentives and frustration. If low-income individuals have dim views of their socioeconomic prospects because they feel they have little opportunity of achieving upward mobility, their frustration and material deprivation can lead to criminal behavior such as theft and engaging in illegal income-generating activities (Freeman 2012; Kenworthy 2008). Importantly, the social effects of inequality can be ameliorated by government policies. In particular, policies that seek to equalize funding of public services across regions and that ensure broad access to them, can reduce the negative effects of income inequality on health and social well-being (Kenworthy 2008).

Household debt and financial crisis

Inequality has been linked to household debt and financial crisis. The conventional account used to explain rising household debt holds that borrowing increases when interest rates are low and credit is easily accessible. Such macroeconomic conditions fuel consumption of big-ticket items, especially homes. A growing demand for houses pushes up home prices thus forcing prospective buyers to borrow more. According to this account, this cycle is sustainable as long as household purchasing power continues to rise. However, Lebarz (2015) observes that in OECD countries debt load has been more onerous for lower- than higher-income households and has become more unbalanced as inequality rises. A determining factor according to Paul (2018) is that wages for lower- and middle-income households have risen much slower relative to those at the top of the income distribution. In an effort to preserve their relative standard of living (and purchasing power), lower- and middle-class households have been forced to borrow more.

Focusing on the United States, Rajan (2010) exposes the political dimension connecting inequality, household debt, and the financial crisis of 2007–2009. From the viewpoint of elected officials, the rising inequality prior to the crisis could have become a political liability had consumption not been shored up. As Rajan (2010: 8–9) puts it "if somehow the consumption of middle-class householders keeps up, if they can afford a new car every few years and the occasional exotic holiday, perhaps they will pay less attention to their stagnant monthly paychecks." The political solution was to ease credit access: "Easy credit has large, positive, immediate, and widely distributed benefits, whereas the costs all lie in the future" (Rajan 2010: 31, see also Piketty 2013: 297–298). This political decision, coupled with laxed financial regulations, reckless risk management practices by several financial institutions, and other factors set in motion market dynamics that ultimately culminated in the financial crisis.

Political consequences

We need to also consider the political effects of economic inequality. To the extent that income and wealth can be leveraged to obtain political power, the more concentrated are income and wealth at the top of the distribution ladder, the more likely will representation, responsiveness, and policy outcomes be biased in favor of affluent individuals. As Dahl (1971: 82) noted several decades ago, "inequalities in the distribution of such key values as income, wealth, knowledge . . . are equivalent to . . . inequalities in political resources." In echoing this point, Anderson and Beramendi (2008: 278) have more recently observed that "economic inequality leads to inferior democratic outcomes because it concentrates power among a smaller group of people and increases politicians' responsiveness to an ever-smaller group of advantaged citizens." This matters enormously because income, wealth, and status are important determinants of preferences and drivers of collective behavior. The affluent and less affluent voters have divergent views on redistribution, economic openness, and, more broadly, the role of government in the economy. The more unequally distributed resources are, the more politics resembles a zero-sum game: a government that is more responsive to the preferences of the rich, is a government that increasingly overlooks the needs and interests of less affluent citizens.

To show why economic inequality matters politically in a democracy, it is important to distinguish between descriptive and substantive representation (Pitkin 1972). Descriptive representation focuses on the extent to which the diversity in society is reflected in the composition of elected representatives. In a situation of perfect descriptive representation, the demographic composition of representatives (in terms of occupational status, income, educational credentials, race, and gender for example) mirrors the demographics of the voting population.

Substantive representation relates to the extent to which the actions of lawmakers match the interests of citizens. There are two dimensions of substantive representation. Ideological congruence concerns how closely the policy positions of representatives reflect what citizens want at a given point in time. Perfect congruence means that the current actions of lawmakers are aligned with the public interest. Responsiveness, the other dimension, relates to the degree to which representatives adapt their actions to shifts in citizens' interests over time. Equality of responsiveness implies that lawmakers are responsive to the preference changes of all income groups, thus ensuring that congruence is maintained over time. Economic inequality impacts both forms of political representation.

Income inequality can result in the descriptive underrepresentation of poorer voters for two reasons. First, the propensity to vote is shaped by one's relative income. As Andersen and Beramendi (2008: 291) note, "individuals whose income falls below the median are less likely to turn out to vote [whereas] citizens above the median income are less likely to abstain." A higher voter turnout among upscale voters means that a larger share of elected representatives will have profiles that resemble this group of voters. The other reason economic inequality can cause affluent citizens to be descriptively overrepresented in legislatures is that they have more resources (connections, money, time) to deploy in order to improve the election prospects of their preferred candidates. To be sure, the advantaged position of the affluent is not the only determinant of this outcome. For example, Wüest and Pontusson (2018) observe that Swiss voters across all income groups are biased against low-income candidates. Specifically, they find that low- and middle-income voters prefer middle-class and upper middle-class candidates.

There is also evidence suggesting that income inequality adversely affects substantive representation. A study by McCarty et al. (2016) reveals that the polarization of the American party system and income inequality have co-evolved as shown in figure 6.3. In the context of American politics, polarization means "a separation of politics into liberal and conservative camps" (ibid: 4). The fact that the income share of the top 1% and polarization have increased in an almost lock-step fashion since the late 1970s is not a coincidence according to McCarty and colleagues. On the one hand, the increase in income at the top has pushed the Republican party (the preferred party of affluent voters) further to the right while pushing the Democrats slightly to the left. On the other hand, the increasingly anti-redistributive Republican agenda has undermined programs that could help dampen income inequality (Hacker and Pierson 2011). What is more, equipped with minority-protecting veto devices such as the filibuster, Senate Republicans have been able to block Democrats' legislative measures designed to combat inequality (McCarty et al. 2016: 12–15).

It is not just ideological congruence that has been undermined as a result of inequality; there is also evidence that it has eroded policy responsiveness. In the context of American politics, Gilens and Page (2014) find that Congress and the policies it promotes are more responsive to the interests of the rich than the poor. "The preferences of economic elites . . . have far more independent impact upon policy change than the preferences of average citizens," they remark. Insofar as

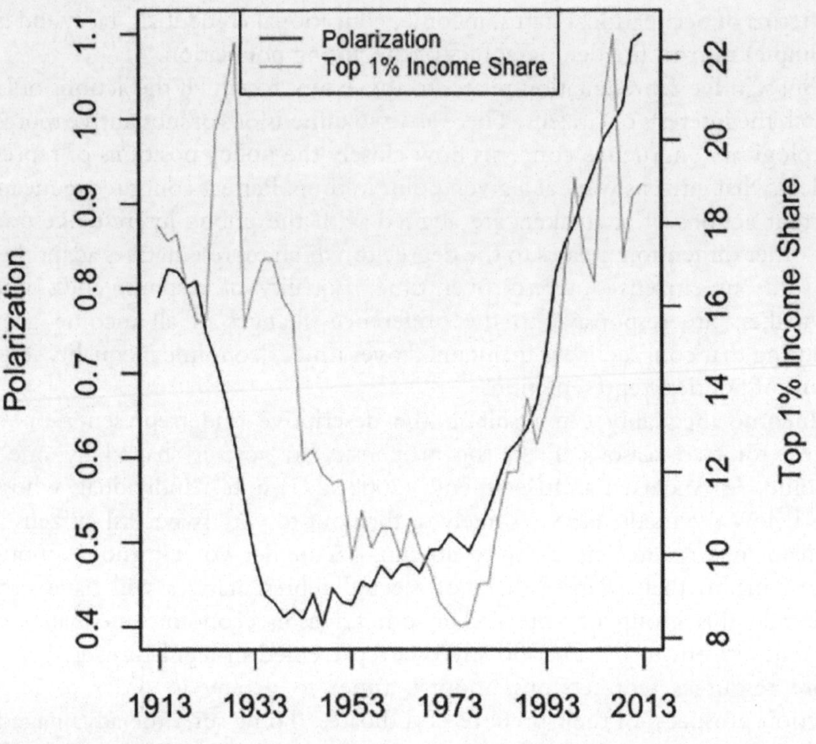

FIGURE 6.3 Polarization and top 1% income share
Source: adapted from McCarty, Noland, Keith T. Poole, and Howard Rosenthal, *Polarized America: The Dance of Ideology and Unequal Riches*, second edition, Figure. 1.2, © 2016 Massachusetts Institute of Technology, by permission of The MIT Press.

poorer citizens do obtain the policies they desire, it is primarily because "those policies happen also to be preferred by the economically-elite citizens who wield the actual influence" (ibid: 576). Bartels's (2017) research also discovers suggestive evidence of unequal responsiveness across rich OECD countries. In his study of 15 countries between the mid-1990s and mid-2000s, Bartels finds a persistent disjuncture between public preferences for higher social spending and actual spending levels, an outcome he attributes largely to the unequal influence of affluent voters on lawmakers.

Aside from the disproportionate political power of affluent voters, there are other factors that can account for the erosion of policy responsiveness. That lawmakers are usually more affluent than ordinary citizens, might lead them to hold personal interests more aligned with those of rich private citizens. Also, substantive misrepresentation can arise due to the influence of organized interests, a topic we will discuss in greater detail later in the chapter.

Political and economic determinants of wage inequality

This section will explore various factors that have been found to influence the shape of wage distribution. Wage or earnings (terms which will be used interchangeably) refers to the monetary reward individuals receive in exchange for the labor they provide. The wage data we will use represent gross cash earnings by full-time employees—that is, these figures omit other sources of income obtained from self-employment, capital gains, property rental, and government transfers, and these figures also omit taxation on income. Thus, the distribution of wage earnings will be different from the distribution of household market incomes because the former only considers labor-generated earnings and leaves out individuals not engaged in full-time employment. Still, because cash earnings represent a sizable share of total household market income, changes in the dispersion of wage earnings tend to be closely associated with changes in the distribution of market income (Gottschalk and Smeeding 1997; Wallerstein 1999).

Table 6.1 provides cross-national data on wage inequality, measured using the 90–10 ratio, for 12 OECD countries from 1980 to 2014. This time span has been segmented into seven five-year periods to yield a more granular view of how the distribution of earnings of full-time employees has evolved in recent decades. With the exception of Canada and France, wage inequality has increased by as little as 2.8% in Finland to as high as 29.7% in the United States. Important differences are revealed when comparing and contrasting liberal market economies (LMEs) and coordinated market economies (CMEs), but also countries within each cluster. Unlike other countries, the Nordic CMEs have managed not only to keep earnings dispersion more compressed during each time period but also to temper its upward trend. Moreover, wage inequality in Germany has been trending more or less the same way it has in Australia. Among the LMEs, it is only in the United States that runaway inequality has occurred. Further, despite their divergent starting points, wage inequality trends in Australia, Canada, and the United Kingdom have recently converged.

Studies on inequality have identified several political institutional factors as potential determinants of the distribution of labor earnings. This section will focus primarily on union density, wage centralization, and Left party governance.

Union density

Union density can shape the results of wage negotiations by bolstering the bargaining power of workers relative to employers (for more on union density, see Chapter 2).

TABLE 6.1 A cross-national view of wage inequality (90–10 ratio), early 1980s to mid-2010s

Waves	AU	CA	DK	FL	FR	DE	NL	NO	SE	CH	UK	US
1	2.88	4.01	2.16	2.48	3.23	2.69	2.51	2.08	1.94	—	3.10	3.91
2	2.83	4.43	2.20	2.50	3.14	2.54	2.49	2.15	2.01	—	3.32	4.23
3	2.83	4.27	2.17	2.41	3.25	3.10	2.58	1.98	2.11	2.71	3.41	4.40
4	2.94	3.55	2.47	2.38	3.08	2.92	2.82	1.94	2.23	2.55	3.47	4.57
5	3.08	3.65	2.37	2.43	3.04	3.04	2.79	2.07	2.30	2.63	3.52	4.66
6	3.27	3.74	2.42	2.53	2.97	3.25	2.82	2.21	2.29	2.73	3.62	4.89
7	3.39	3.71	2.53	2.55	3.00	3.37	3.02	2.36	2.27	2.77	3.57	5.07

Note: Waves 1 = 1980–1984; 2 = 1985–1989; 3 = 1990–1994; 4 = 1995–1999; 5 = 2000–2004; 6 = 2005–2009; 7 = 2010–2014.

Source: OECD, *Employment Outlook* (multiple years).

Specifically, Freeman (1980) and Pontusson et al. (2002) have elaborated two dynamics to account for the egalitarian effects of unionism. First, because of unions' aversion to inequality, wage dispersion in unionized workplaces and industries are expected to be less than in non-unionized workplaces and industries. One way unions have sought wage compression is by calling for wage standardization, which in practice limits managerial discretion over wage-setting. Another way is by preventing the median union wage from losing ground relative to the average wage. Second, unionism reduces wage dispersion by bestowing on union members a wage premium relative to non-unionized workers. Because unionization in OECD countries tends to be higher in the bottom half of the wage distribution, wage premium pushes up the earnings of low-wage workers relative to higher-wage earners. In short, union density should be negatively related with wage inequality.

Figures 6.4 and 6.5 plot levels of union density against wage inequality (measured in terms of 90–10 ratio) in the early 1980s and in the early 2010s, respectively. The expected negative relationship is borne out by the data. The high union density Nordic countries have lower wage inequality than low union density countries such as Canada, France, and the United States. However, a comparison of both scatterplots and corresponding statistical results reveals that the estimated effect of union density on inequality has declined over time.

To gain a deeper understanding of the impact of union density on inequality, one should observe the relationship not only in its static form but also dynamic form. Figure 6.6 focuses on the change in union density and in inequality, which is measured as the percent change between the early 1980s and mid-2010s. In general, as union density decreases, inequality rises. It is the countries that witnessed large declines in union density (Australia, Germany, the Netherlands, and the United States) that saw some of the larger increases in inequality. However, Denmark,

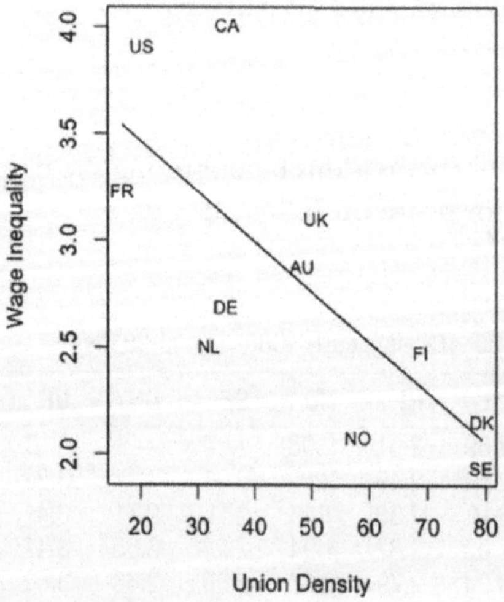

FIGURE 6.4 Wage inequality and union density, early 1980s

Note: r = −0.741, sig @ 0.001

Sources: Tables 2.1 and 6.1.

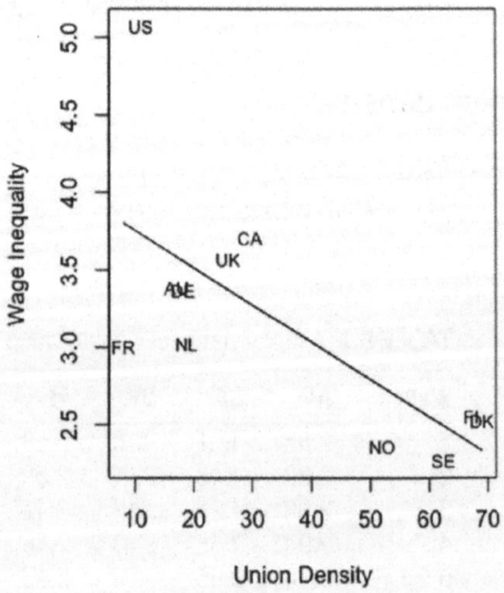

FIGURE 6.5 Wage inequality and union density, early 2010s

Note: r = −0.703, sig @ 0.01

Sources: Tables 2.1 and 6.1.

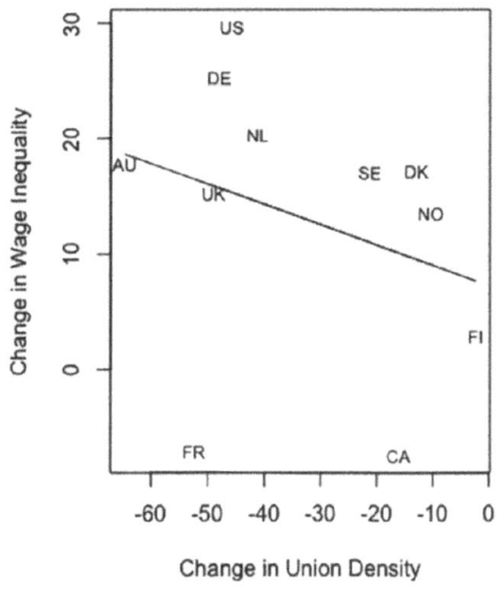

FIGURE 6.6 Change in union density and inequality, early 1980s to early 2010s
Notes: r = −0.303; change in union density is lagged by one year.

Sources: Tables 2.1 and 6.1.

Norway, and Sweden also experienced sizable increases in inequality during this period even though they faced much smaller declines in union density. It should be noted that these Nordic countries had low levels of inequality to begin with; therefore, the relatively large percent changes in their 90–10 ratios have not made them look more like LMEs.

The fact that there are many countries scattered about the best-fit line suggests that changes in union density is a weak predictor of change in inequality (see Pontusson 2013). Further, this bivariate analysis overlooks the effects of other variables on inequality and does not ascertain the direction of, let alone prove, the existence of a causal relationship (Pontusson 2013; Scheve and Stasavage 2009).

Several pooled time series analyses have assessed the egalitarian effects of union density. In Wallerstein's (1999) study of wage inequality in 16 countries from 1980 to 1992, union density is negatively associated with the 90–10 ratio, but it is not statistically significant, and its effect is small compared to coverage of union contracts and wage centralization. Other studies based on a longer time series, however, find strong evidence of the inequality-constraining effect of labor unions. In their comparative analyses of affluent democracies from the early 1970s to early 2000s, Rueda and Pontusson (2000) and Beramendi and Cusack (2009) discover suggestive evidence that strong and encompassing unions are highly conducive to lower levels of wage inequality.

The extant research on union density shows that high union density helps push up the wages of low-paid workers relative to the median income. Using a similar dataset as Rueda and Pontusson (2000), Pontusson et al. (2002) find that the long-term effect of an increase in unionization "is more than twice as large in the lower half of the wage hierarchy" as in the upper half. Looking at a longer time period from the 1960s to 2013, Huber et al.'s (2020: 249) study reveals that the egalitarian effect of union density is roughly the same on the overall income distribution (90–10 ratio) as on the bottom half distribution (50–10 ratio). As they put it, "strong unions keep the bottom from falling too far below the median and the top from rising too far above the bottom."

Despite its weakening association over time, cross-national evidence shows that, on average, countries with higher levels of unionization tend to have lower levels of inequality. Furthermore, multivariate studies based on longer time periods confirm a robust and strong negative correlation between union density and wage inequality. However, we cannot infer from the studies reviewed earlier that the decline in union density has directly and independently caused wage inequality to rise. That pattern is not borne out in Canada and France. Moreover, among the countries that experienced similar changes in wage inequality, we find significant differences in the extent of unionization loss.

Clearly, there is more to rising wage inequality than the erosion of union density. In fact, evidence gleaned from single-country studies, which are better suited for exploring the relationship between unions and inequality up close, suggests that the relationship may be two-directional. In other words, rising inequality may lead to lower unionization, not just the other way around. In their study on wage inequality in the United States, Western and Rosenfeld (2011) find that wage disparities undermine the mobilizational capacity of unions by eroding social and material connections among workers. In their weakened state, unions not only lack the political leverage to counter wage inequality, they also cease to be effective rallying agents in labor markets where economic interests are increasingly polarized.

Wage centralization

Wage centralization is another labor market institution that has been shown to impact wage inequality. The egalitarian effect of wage centralization stems from its role in reducing wage differentials across firms and across industries. The potential for wage compression is higher when wage bargaining occurs at the confederal level.

However, as several studies have pointed out, it is not centralization alone that guarantees wage compression. Instead, it is the collective policies that accompany collective bargaining—policies that have usually empowered low-wage unions relative to higher-wage unions—that can account for more egalitarian pay outcomes. For example, the practice of "solidaristic pay"—which we discussed in Chapter 2—became a central component of centralized bargaining in Sweden and Norway starting in the 1950s. In these and in some other continental countries, peak-level collective bargaining governed wage-setting for white-collar and blue-collar workers with an eye on reducing pay disparities between the two groups. These policies raised the earnings of low-wage workers at a faster rate than those of higher-wage workers. In the Nordic CMEs, where national level wage-setting was common from the 1950s to the 1980s, employers "provided critical support" for such arrangements. This practice facilitated the coordination and moderation of wage increases across industries (a crucial factor behind the success of the region's export sector) and helped avoid the kinds of industrial conflicts that had gripped their economies in the past (Moene and Wallerstein 2008c: 459; see also Scheve and Stasavage 2009).

Figure 6.7 displays the relationship between the level of wage centralization and wage inequality (measured in terms of the 90–10 ratio). Wage centralization is measured using an indicator that gauges the level of union authority and union concentration, thus it combines wage coordination and bargaining level, as described

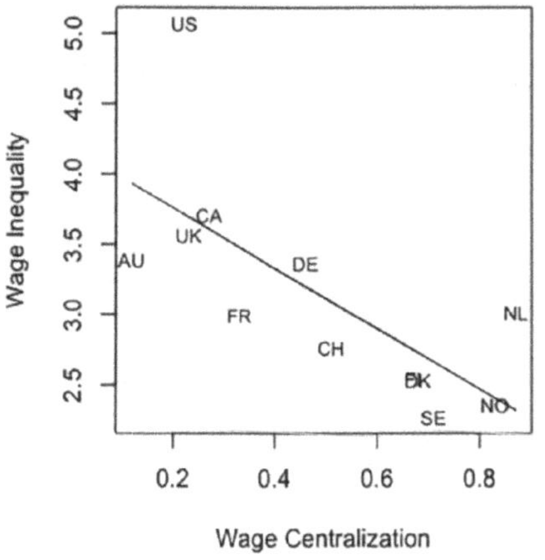

FIGURE 6.7 Earnings inequality and wage centralization, early 2010s

Note: r = −0.713, sig @ 0.001

Sources: Table 6.1; Brady et al. (2020).

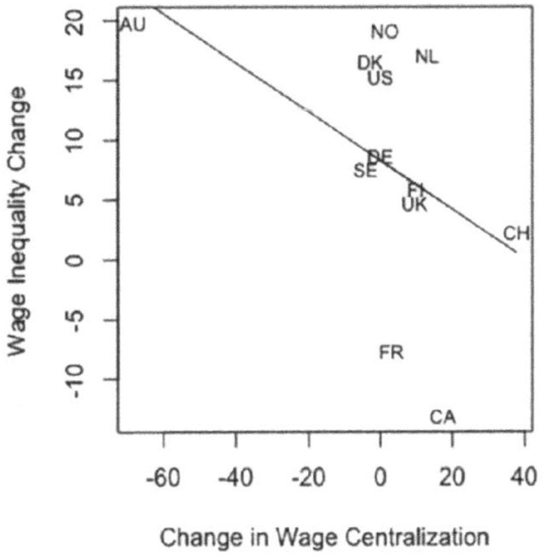

FIGURE 6.8 Percent changes in wage centralization and inequality, early 1990s to early 2010s

Note: r = −0.483; change in wage centralization is lagged by one year.

Sources: Table 6.1; Brady et al. (2020).

in Chapter 2. Even though centralized bargaining reached its apex in the Nordic CMEs in the 1970s, they still maintained relatively high levels of centralization in the 2010s. New Zealand and Australia stand out among LMEs because both countries centralized wage-setting starting in the 1980s until the early 1990s when this institutional practice was abandoned. Although there is some scattering along the best-fit line on the left side of figure 6.7, high wage centralization countries in the Nordic region and the Netherlands have lower 90–10 ratios. Overall, the correlation is both substantively and statistically significant.

Figure 6.8 plots the change in wage centralization against changes in 90–10 ratio from the early 1990s to early 2010s. It reveals that the large decrease in wage centralization in Australia coincides with a significant increase in wage inequality. On the opposite end, the decrease in wage inequality in Canada and France, occurred when wage centralization increased. However, we should be cautious about inferring causation from this correlational evidence. There is significant cross-national variation in wage inequality change among the countries that witnessed little changes in wage centralization.

Several multivariate studies find evidence corroborating the assertion that centralized wage-setting is linked to lower inequality. According to Wallerstein (1999), the estimated long-run impact of changes in wage centralization is large and statistically robust. For example, the decentralization of Sweden's wage-setting system in the early 1980s down to the industry-level was predicted to increase wage differential by 50% in the long run. Further, if Canada's wage-setting system had shifted from firm- to industry-level wage bargaining, inequality was predicted to drop by 30%. Although wage centralization increased in Canada in the 1990s, in practice wage bargaining has occurred predominantly at the firm level. In their reanalysis of Wallerstein's (1999) data, Golden and Londregan (2006: 212) observe that wage centralization "has a much more attenuated impact" on wage inequality than what Wallerstein estimated; however, the relationship remains statistically significant.

Pontusson et al. (2002) and Rueda (2008) also reach similar results about wage centralization's effect on wage inequality. In analyzing the impact of wage centralization in the lower and upper halves of the earnings distribution between 1973 and 1995, the former study finds that centralization's egalitarian effect is "considerably larger" on the 50–10 ratio. This finding corroborates the argument that centralized wage-setting helps push up the earnings of low-wage workers.

Perhaps the strongest challenge to the claim that wage centralization is conducive to lower wage inequality comes from Scheve and Stasavage (2009) who look at inequality from 1919 to 2000. They find no evidence that the centralization of wage bargaining, which the Nordic countries adopted in the 1930s, independently produced "a downward break in inequality." In fact, they conclude that inequality was declining prior to the establishment of centralized collective bargaining, and that inequality's downward trend did not accelerate once this practice was in place. Scheve and Stasavage's (2009: 250) findings raise the possibility that wage centralization and inequality are causally unrelated and are outcomes that have "evolved over time in response to an underlying political and economic process."

Left government

Wage inequality can be influenced by the policies instituted by Left governments which, in general, are more committed to equitable growth than right-wing governments. One version of this argument is that left-wing parties promote egalitarianism by increasing the wage floor. Measures like raising the minimum wage or increasing unemployment insurance generosity—a measure that forces employers to increase low-pay wages as a way to entice the unemployed back to work—help raise the wages of low-income workers. Another version holds that Left governments lower inequality by raising marginal taxes on top-income earners, a policy that moderates increases in top incomes (Beramendi and Cusack 2009). Thus, we would expect the wage floor path to achieve wage compression by pushing up the earnings of low-wage workers while the marginal income path would do so by containing the earnings of high-wage workers (Pontusson et al. 2002).

Figure 6.9 plots the average frequency of Left governments from the early 1990s to mid-2010s against average wage inequality (using the 90–10 ratio) between late 2000s and mid-2010s. It reveals that longer periods of Left governments are associated with lower wage inequality. However, there is a lot of cross-national variation in wage inequality among countries with shorter periods of Left governments. This is not surprising given that the egalitarian effects of partisanship is conditioned by the policies left-wing parties promote when in government. For example, if Left governments promote market deregulation and social welfare retrenchment—as they have in Australia, Germany, and the United Kingdom—then we should expect inequality to rise over time under either Left or Right governments.

The egalitarian effects of Left governments are revealed more clearly when we shift emphasis to left-wing policies. Figure 6.10 plots the average top marginal tax rate against average wage inequality from the early 2000s to early 2010s. The negative correlation is strong and statistically significant. High top marginal tax rate countries such as Denmark, Finland, the Netherlands, and Sweden have lower earnings inequality than low top marginal tax rate countries like the United Kingdom and the

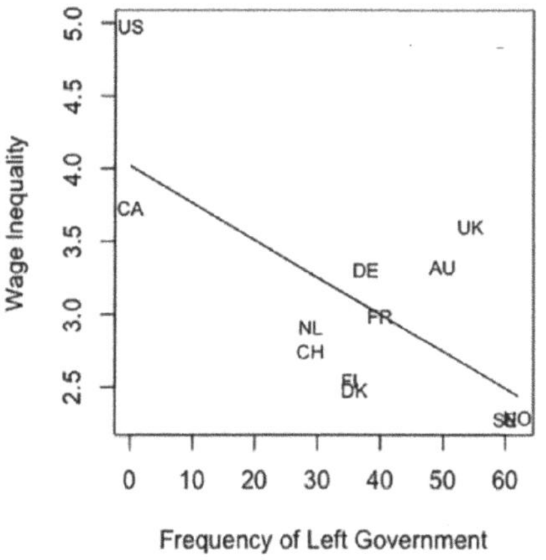

FIGURE 6.9 Left government and average inequality, late 1990s to mid-2010s
Note: r = −0.671, sig @ 0.01

Sources: Armingeon et al. (2018); and table 6.1.

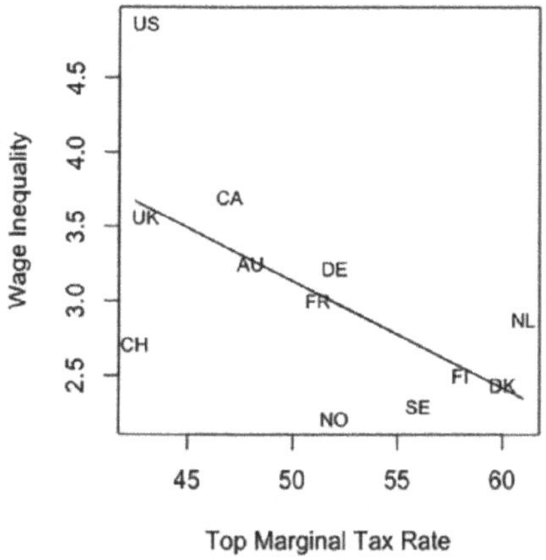

FIGURE 6.10 Inequality and top marginal income tax, early 2000s to early 2010s
Note: r = −0.633, sig @ 0.01

Sources: Table 6.1; and OECD, Tax Database, Table 1.7.

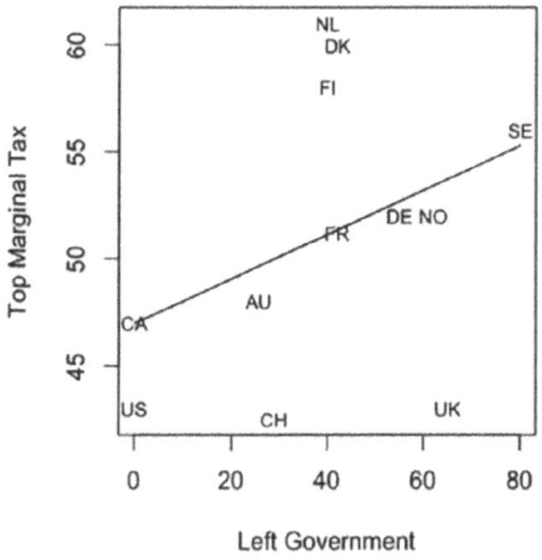

FIGURE 6.11 Left government and top marginal income tax, early 2000s to early 2010s
Note: r = 0.380

Sources: Figure 6.10; and Armingeon et al. (2018).

United States. A weaker association between inequality and top marginal tax exists when earnings inequality is measured using the 90–50 ratio, a result also found in Pontusson et al.'s (2002) multivariate analysis. Moreover, a positive relationship exists between Left government and top marginal income tax (see figure 6.11), but is much weaker than what Pontusson et al. report in their study covering a period from 1973 to 1995. While Left governments have led Finland, France, and the Netherlands for a similar period of time, these countries have very different top marginal tax rates.

In figure 6.12, average unemployment income replacement rates (a tool used to raise the wage floor) is plotted against average earnings inequality from the early

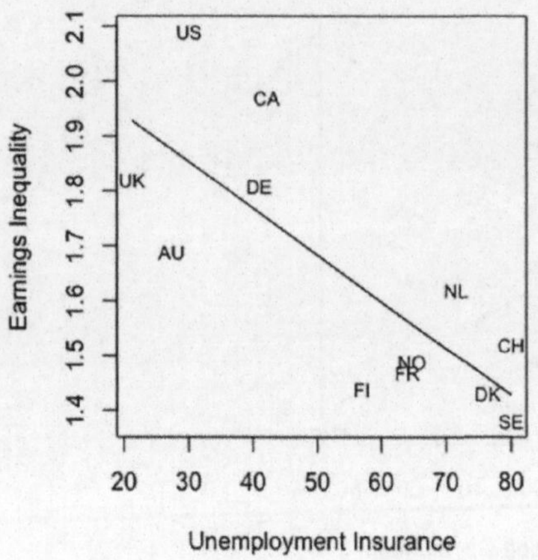

FIGURE 6.12 Earnings inequality and unemployment replacement level, early 2000s to early 2010s

Note: r = −0.749, sig @ 0.001

Sources: Brady et al. (2020); and table 6.1.

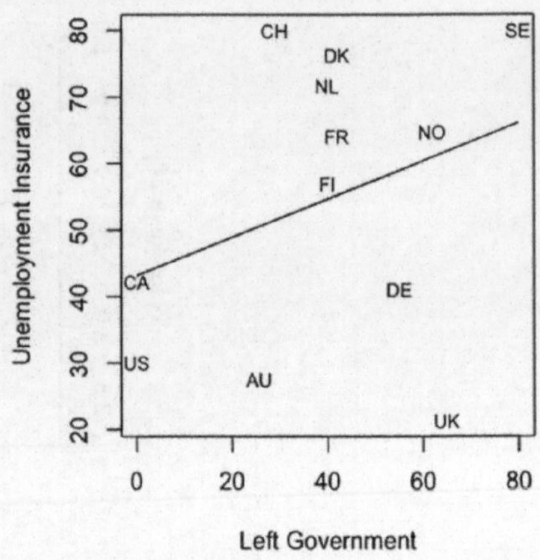

FIGURE 6.13 Left government and unemployment replacement level, early 2000s to early 2010s

Note: r = 0.324

Sources: Figures 6.11 and 6.12.

2000s to early 2010s. The scatterplot reveals a strong negative association. Where unemployment replacement rates are relatively high, wage inequality tends to be relatively low. When the 90–10 ratio is replaced with the 50–10 ratio, the correlation increases, suggesting that this labor market policy tool significantly helps reduce the earnings inequality in the bottom half of the income distribution.

In general, higher unemployment replacement rates are found in countries that have been led by Left governments for a longer period of time, as figure 6.13 illustrates. However, the association is weak because the unemployment replacement rate is high in several continental political economies even though they have had shorter periods of Left government. As we will discuss in Chapter 7, it is the legacy of the welfare state regime in these countries, in addition to government partisanship, that accounts for the varying levels of unemployment insurance.

Although the evidence from the correlation analysis and from the research by Pontusson et al. (2002) and Huber et al. (2020) point to a direct link between partisanship and inequality, other studies suggest that the impact of partisanship is conditioned by the institutional context. Beramendi and Cusack (2009) observe that the effects of Left governments on earnings inequality is stronger when wage bargaining coordination is high. Coordination between employers and workers, they argue, creates the policy space for governing Left parties to "use the tools at their disposal to reduce wage inequality without incurring negative economic externalities" (Beramendi and Cusack 2009: 263). In contrast, Rueda (2008) argues that the effects of Left governments on policies are muted when corporatism—a set of labor market institutions that facilitates centralization and coordination between labor and employers—is high. Because corporatism enables unions and employers to negotiate wage floors, they can " 'take care' of wage compression" without the involvement of the government as Rueda (2008: 176, 188) notes.

A New Gilded Age in the United States: a comparative look

Anyone who finds the widening income disparity between someone at the 90th percentile and at the 10th percentile disconcerting is likely to be even more so when they examine the distribution of income within the top 10% in the United States. The World Inequality Database (WID), which is based on the pioneering research of Thomas Piketty and Emmanuel Saez on top income, has enabled scholars to track changes in the income shares of the superrich—top 1%, 0.01%, and 0.001%—in the United States and a few other advanced capitalist democracies since the early 1900s. An examination of the historical data on the top 1% from a comparative perspective reveals a central puzzle: Why has the income share of the superrich in the United States returned to early 1900s levels while it has not in other countries?

Figure 6.14 tracks the national income share of the top 1% in the United States. Income concentration reached an all-time high in 1928 when the richest 1% earned 23.9% of total national income. High levels of income concentration were seen even earlier in the mid- to late 1910s in France, Germany, Sweden, and the United Kingdom, as illustrated in figure 6.15. Remarkably, a significant and abrupt deconcentration of income occurred in the 1930s and 1940s. And for many of these countries, further though slower reductions in top income shares occurred from the 1950s to the 1970s. In the United States, for example, after dropping to 13% in 1950, the top income share continued to decline, eventually reaching a low of 8.2% in 1976. Of note, around that time, Canada, France, Germany, Japan, and Switzerland had top incomes higher than that of the United States; other countries were not that far below the United States. In looking at the general trajectory of the top income shares of these countries from the 1940s to mid-1970s, one would be hard pressed to find a noticeable difference between LMEs and CMEs. A different picture, however, emerges when one looks at the next 40 years.

There has been a reconcentration of top incomes in the United States since the 1970s unlike what we have seen in other countries. By 2015, the income share of the richest 1% stood at 22%, an upward trajectory that seems to have been counteracted only temporarily by the Dot-com market crash in 2000 and the Great Recession of 2007–2009. A New Gilded Age has reemerged in the United States; this is after experiencing the leveling effects of the "great compression" that swept through countries on both sides of the Atlantic. To be sure, top income increases have

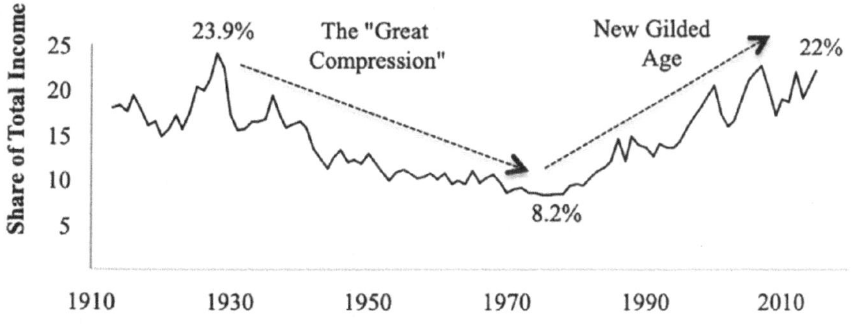

FIGURE 6.14 Top 1% share in the United States
Source: World Inequality Database (2019)

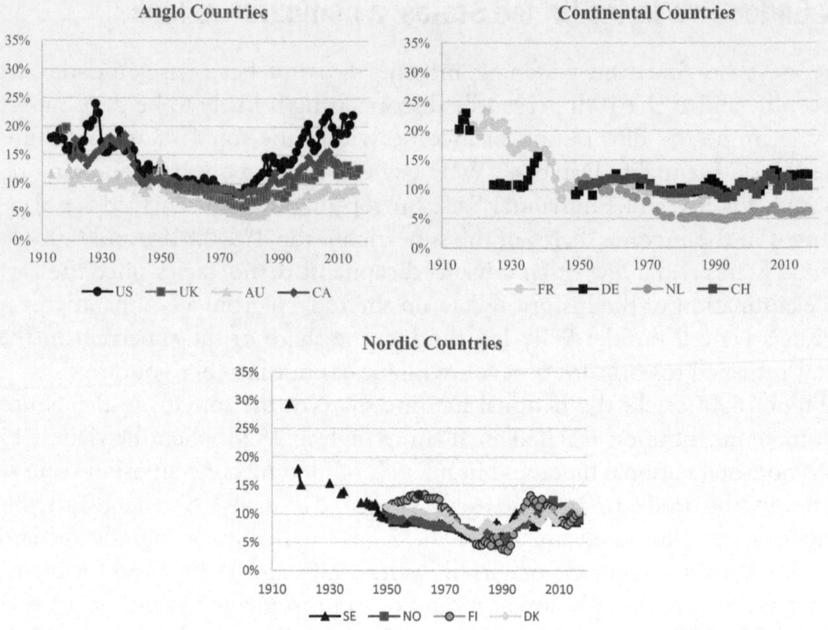

FIGURE 6.15 Top 1% share in other countries
Source: World Inequality Database (2019)

occurred in all the other countries, but none of them have increased by 2.5 times since the 1970s as it has in the United States. Key differences have emerged among the three groups of countries. The upward trend in the Anglo countries started in the late 1970s and early 1980s, earlier than in the countries in the other two clusters. Second, top income inequality has been comparatively stable in the continental countries since the mid-1990s. Between 1996 and 2017, the income share of the top 1% increased by 1 percentage point in France, the Netherlands, and Switzerland, and by 2 percentage points in Germany. Finally, top income inequality increased sharply in the Nordic countries in the 1990s and has trended downwards since the mid-2000s. For example, the 1% income share in Norway went from 5% in 1990 to 12% in 2000 to 9% in 2017; in Finland, it jumped from 4% to 13% in the 1990s and leveled off at around 9% in the 2010s.

What accounts for the New Gilded Age in the United States? Perhaps the best way to address this question is by first examining the factors that contributed to the "great compression." As it did for all other countries involved, World War II had an important leveling effect in the United States. Scheidel (2017: 6–7) summarizes why the two world wars had such an effect:

> The physical destruction wrought by industrial-scale warfare, confiscatory taxation, government intervention in the economy, inflation, disruption of global flows of goods and capital, and other factors all combined to wipe out elites' wealth and redistribute resources. They also served as uniquely powerful catalysts for equalizing policy change, providing powerful impetus to franchise extensions, unionization, and expansion of the welfare state.

The "conscription of income" during both world wars was justified on fairness grounds—the rich had to do their part if the burden of fighting fell on the shoulders of ordinary people (Scheve and Stasavage 2016). As Americans mobilized for war, the idea of equalizing sacrifices between the general public and the wealthy segment of the population gained political traction, leading to significant increases in top marginal income and inheritance taxes. For example, in the United States, the top marginal income tax rate (which is the tax rate applied on the last dollar earned) sharply increased from 7% in 1915 to 77% in 1918—the year after the country entered WWI—and from 81% in 1941 (the year it entered WWII) to 94% in 1944 (Tax Policy Center 2020). Estate taxes climbed from 70% in 1939 to 77% in 1941. Set at such high levels, these confiscatory taxes significantly limited the ability of high-income earners to achieve significant income gains. Moreover, these high taxation rates were not reversed soon after WWII ended, as it happened following WWI. The top marginal income tax maintained its WWII level until the early 1960s, and the high estate tax held steady until the early 1980s.

The Great Depression also generated a powerful leveling effect in the United States. The top income share dropped sharply from 23.9% in 1928 to 15% in 1931 where it stayed relatively unchanged until the outset of WWII. From a comparative perspective, the deconcentration effect of the economic crisis proved stronger in the United States than in other countries and even WWII. As Scheidel (2017: 148) observes, "the Great Depression played a greater role in equalizing income and wealth disparities relative to the wars themselves than among the other main belligerents." Still, we are left with the question of why the leveling effects of both the economic crisis and WWII extended well into the 1970s. There is nothing inevitable about the long-term leveling effects of an economic crisis. The Great Recession—which bears some important similarities with the Great Depression—caused the top income share to drop from 22.6% in 2007 to 17% in 2009 only to rebound to its pre-crisis level by 2012. The political economic literature offers insights on why the leveling effects of these earlier twentieth-century events stuck around for several decades.

Hacker and Pierson (2016) and Levy and Temin (2007) attribute the sustained leveling of income distribution to a meeting of minds among business, labor, and government regarding how the government and market should co-participate in fostering inclusive growth. For Levy and Temin, it was the "Treaty of Detroit" model—an institutional arrangement that combined labor-business compromises over industrial relations and norms of fair compensation—that facilitated income compression. For Hacker and Pierson, it was the embrace of a "mixed economy"—in which government and market played complementary roles in promoting broad public goals—that helped suppress income inequality. The postwar consensus that facilitated the coordination of actions between labor and business emerged against the backdrop of sustained productivity growth and the New Deal-era progressive regulatory framework which underpinned labor's bargaining power. The convergence of these factors, as Levy and Temin (2007: 4) note, enabled the "median compensation of full-time workers . . . and labor productivity . . . [to grow] at the same rate from 1950 to the late 1970s. Simultaneously, income equality increased as very high incomes . . . grew more slowly than labor productivity."

But why did business agree to the idea of a mixed economy? Hacker and Pierson identify a trilogy of reasons. Business reaped important advantages from the mixed economy—it promoted social peace, legitimized market capitalism, tamed business cycles, and leveled the competitive playing field by expanding unionization across industries. Further, because the idea of maximizing shareholder wealth was not yet an established principle of corporate governance, corporations enjoyed more leeway to work with labor to achieve common objectives. Finally, the combination of progressive policies and power of organized labor constrained the actions of corporate America. As Hacker and Pierson (2016: 146) remark, "Business leaders found themselves compelled to negotiate and seek acceptable solutions within a system where other voices would be heard." They also faced fairness norms that militated against high executive compensation, as Levy and Temin (2007) point out.

The "winner-take-all" economy

Economists and political scientists spotlight different, although not unrelated, factors to explain why top income concentration has reemerged since the 1980s. One fact is incontrovertible: the rising income share of the top 1% is the result of stronger growth in wage income relative to business or capital income (Kaplan and Rauh 2013; Keister 2014; Piketty and Saez 2006). According to a study by the Institute for Policy Studies, the CEO-to-worker compensation increased modestly from 20 in 1965 to 29.9 in 1978, but then skyrocketed to reach a high of 376.1 in 2000. CEO compensation relative to worker earnings dropped sharply during the Great Recession, from 345.3 in 2007 to 195.8 in 2009, only to rebound to 303.4 in 2014 (see Mishel and Davis 2015).

IN FOCUS BOX 6.2 CHARACTERISTICS OF THE "WINNER-TAKE-ALL" ECONOMY

The term "winner-take-all" economy is commonly used to describe the unique economic inequality trend in the United States since the early 1980s. Popularized by Hacker and Pierson (2011: 11–19), the winner-take-all economy depicts how the American market system has shifted from one in which the gains of economic growth were broadly distributed across income groups to one in which the rewards of growth are narrowly funneled to the top 10%, especially those in the highest 1%. Thus, a key feature of the winner-take-all economy is the "hyper-concentration" of income at the top. Another important characteristic is that the extraordinary income concentration is not episodic but rather secular—it is a long-term trend that transcends business and partisan cycles, gradually running-up income at the top of the income hierarchy. The other characteristic of the winner-take-all economy is that the lower- and middle-classes have reaped few rewards from it. "The economy has stopped working to provide security and prosperity" for them, as Hacker and Pierson (2011: 13) note.

Several reasons have been floated to explain why CEOs' compensations have increased significantly. Some accounts of why the winner-take-all economy has emerged focus on managers' increased ability to secure compensations that exceed their marginal economic product (Kaplan and Rauh 2013). According to the optimal contracting approach, the compensation packages of managers are designed to effectively incentivize managers to act in accord with owners' best interests—that is, maximize shareholder value. However, Bebchuk and Fried (2003) find suggestive evidence that managers can leverage their positional advantage to extract rents, resulting in compensations that exceed their marginal product.

Some have argued that the norms of fairness that were instrumental in guiding pay distribution between employees and managers have given way to practices leading to winner-take-all compensations (Hacker and Pierson 2016; Levy and Temin 2007). It is now common for CEOs' salaries to be tied to their companies' market capitalization. According to Gabaix and Landier (2008) and others, this is a key factor accounting for top income concentration in recent decades as the average size of S&P 500 companies has increased.

Another reason is that the drop in the top marginal income tax since the early 1980s has incentivized CEOs to secure larger incomes. As Piketty et al. (2011: 2) note, "When top marginal tax rates are very high, the net reward to a highly paid executive for bargaining for more compensation is modest. When top tax rates fell [after the 1970s], high earners started bargaining more aggressively to increase their compensation." Their data show that a strong negative relationship exists between change in top 1% income share and change in top marginal tax rate. The top income share increased the most in the United States and the United Kingdom from 1960–1964 to 2005–2009, the two countries that enacted the deepest cuts in top tax rates during this period.

Finally, managerial power has been enhanced as organized labor has become weaker. The business-labor relationship captured in the Treaty of Detroit had much to do with unions' sizable bargaining power, which was leveraged to ensure that corporate resources were more equitably distributed. In the face of diminished union power, management has had more leeway to reallocate resources in its direction.

Another category of explanations focuses on changes in the demand and supply of skilled labor. One strand of argument is related to skill-biased technological change (SBTC). Research on SBTC puts forth two arguments. One argument holds that the diffusion of information and communication technologies in various production activities has increased the demand for and wages of high-skilled labor. Further, the supply of skilled workers has fallen behind the demand for such workers, thus driving up their wage premium (Autor et al. 2008; Katz and Murphy 1992). The change in the nature of the "race between technological change and education," as Golding and Katz (2009: 4) note, has had a profound distributional effect. They summarize this point well: "Education ran faster during the first half of the century [thus ensuring broad-based prosperity] and technology sprinted ahead of limping education in the last 30 years [generating huge rewards for those possessing advanced skills]. The race produced economic expansion and also *determined which groups* received the fruits of growth" (italics added).

Another line of research related to SBTC spotlights the polarization effect of technological change on earnings distribution (Autor et al. 2006). According to the polarization claim, computing- and knowledge-intensive solutions complement high skill professions, substitute middle-skilled workers performing routine tasks, and has a minimal impact on low-skilled works involved in personal, manual services. As a result, the U.S. labor market is "polarizing into high-wage and low-wage jobs at the expense of middle-skill jobs," as Autor et al. (2006: 186) point out. The polarization of the employment structure contributes to greater inequality in the upper half of the earnings distribution, but moderates earnings inequality in the lower portion of the income distribution.

Some economists have also claimed that those in the upper echelon of the earnings distribution possess hard-to-find talents and expertise, explaining why their earnings are relatively higher (Kaplan and Rauh 2013; Gabaix and Landier 2008). According to the "superstar" argument, some reap huge rewards because they are able to leverage technologies and personal talents to perform on a broader scale than an average person can (Rosen 1981). As professional basketball superstars, LeBron James and Michael Jordan attracted tens of thousands of viewers each time they played because their audiences knew both players would deliver outstanding performances game after game. Hedge fund managers and CEOs of S&P 500 companies manage assets worth several billions and make high-stakes decisions that can spell disaster or bring windfall for their business and stakeholders alike. In short, according to the scarcity-of-talent argument, people like James and Jordan and corporate leaders are highly compensated because they bring unique competencies to their professional work that are not easily substitutable.

Although there is evidence to corroborate the SBTC and superstar arguments, it does not shed much light on why top income concentration is much greater in the United States than in other rich OECD countries. Why have the salaries of superstars, financiers, and corporate managers in Canada, France, Sweden, and other countries not run away from the rest of society as fast as they have in the United States?

IN FOCUS BOX 6.3 LABOR MARKET INSTITUTIONS AND TOP INCOME SHARE

Several pooled time series analyses have found evidence that labor market institutions help restrain the rise of top incomes. According to studies by Hope and Martelli (2019), Huber et al. (2017), Jaumotte and Buitron (2015), and Scheve and Stasavage (2009), strong and encompassing unions help counteract the technological and economic forces that are driving up top incomes in societies across affluent democracies. The first two studies also find evidence suggesting that wage coordination and centralized wage bargaining contain growing top income shares. In short, as Huber et al. (2017) note, "a strong labor movement can shave income off the very top of society."

The association between trade unions and top income share is not obvious; after all, corporate executive pay is not determined by collective bargaining agreements like the wages of workers further down the income distribution. Still, unions can contain the growth of top incomes through several mechanisms. First, by negotiating higher wages and better benefits for workers, unions in effect reduce the share of corporate resources that management and capital owners can redistribute in their favor. Second, the codetermination right, which entitles workers to be represented in corporate boards, gives workers a voice in executive compensation. Third, by publicizing fairness considerations, unions can exert pressure on CEOs to restrain executive pay growth when corporate performance is slower than expected or agree to union wage increases when corporate performance is better than expected.

A key takeaway of these studies is that the decline in the organizational power and political influence of blue-collar trade unions witnessed across rich OECD countries since the 1980s signifies the erosion of a crucial counterforce against growing top incomes. Importantly, the strength of organized labor represents one among several other factors that condition the impacts of ICT and financialization on top incomes. The cross-national research on this topic points to the importance of public policies, organized business, and electoral politics. The influence of these other factors can account for why there may or may not be an acceleration of top income concentration following deunionization or why there is growing top income even though unionization has been relatively stable.

Public policies

To address this question, political scientists are much more likely than economists to emphasize the role of public policies and politics. Much is known about how public policies such as taxation and social welfare can redistribute income, a topic we will address in the next chapter. Here, we are interested in identifying those public policies that have played a central role in shaping the distribution of gains in market income.

Many have singled out financial deregulation as a key culprit for rising inequality (Bonica et al., 2013; Philippon and Reshef 2012). Since the early 1980s, a number of legislative reforms have unwound key New Deal-era regulations. These regulations were intended to promote investor confidence by restricting risk-taking behavior and to "align private ambitions more closely with broad economic goals such as financial stability," as Hacker and Pierson (2011: 68) note. The Glass-Steagall Act of 1933 that separated commercial and investment banking was gradually relaxed through a succession of legislative changes starting in the late 1980s until it was eventually repealed by the Gramm-Leach-Bliley Act of 1999. Both the 1980 Depository Institutions Deregulation and Monetary Control Act and the 1982 Garn-St. Germain Depository Institutions Act eliminated caps on interest rates, allowed for adjustable rate mortgages, and permitted cross-state acquisitions of banks. The 1994 Riegle-Neal Interstate Banking and Branching Efficiency Act eliminated New Deal-era restrictions on interstate banking and branching. Further, the Commodity Futures Modernization Act of 2000 deregulated the over-the-counter derivatives markets such as the market for credit default swaps.

These financial reforms, coupled with the invention of new financial instruments such as mortgage-backed securities and collateralized debt obligations, have contributed to the rapid growth of financial capitalism in the United States since the early 1980s. The fact that there are more individuals in the top 1% who have made their fortunes in finance in recent decades is not a coincidence. The policy reforms that reworked the rules guiding America's post-1970s financial system made it possible for people who work in finance to reap exorbitant rewards.

By way of tax reforms and policy drift, the American taxation code has conferred sizable tax benefits to affluent taxpayers. A series of legislative measures since the late 1970s has significantly reduced the progressivity of the tax code. As a result, the average tax rate for someone in the top 0.01% dropped from around 70% in the late 1970s to about 40% by the mid-1980s. The average tax rate for someone representing the top 1% dropped to 35% in the mid-1980s after hovering around 46% in the 1970s. What is more, the tax code has enabled private equity and hedge fund managers to treat a portion of their earnings as capital gains and dividends which carry a much lower tax liability. As Hacker and Pierson (2010: 185) remark, "although this loophole is widely viewed as indefensible," lawmakers have been slow to close it in the face of political resistance.

The corporate scandals in the early 2000s involving Enron, Tyco, and Worldcom brought into sharp relief the inadequacy of the existing corporate governance regulations in ensuring that the conduct of corporate managers is aligned with the interests of shareholders. In particular, these scandals illustrated how rules governing executive compensation could incentivize corporate executives to resort to fraudulent practices. The Sarbanes-Oxley Act of 2002 instituted important measures to enhance independent monitoring and transparency of corporate finances. However, the new law failed to enhance shareholders' ability to rein in managers' pay prerogatives. The 2010 Dodd-Frank financial regulation law also did little to regulate executive compensation even though there was ample evidence that linked increases in the earnings of executives to the sorts of excessive risk-taking activities that resulted in the financial meltdown in 2007–2009.

Electoral politics

There is an important piece of the puzzle we have not yet addressed. Why did public officials behave the way they did? Scholars have sought out answers by either looking into electoral politics or the politics of policymaking. Whereas electoral politics draws attention to the relevance of partisanship and voter preferences, the latter emphasizes the role of business power in the policymaking arena.

Bartels (2008) argues that income inequality in the United States has been shaped by partisan politics. The real incomes of low- and middle-class families have increased faster under Democratic than under Republican presidents, a pattern Bartels attributes to the distinct policy priorities of both parties. Democrats have consistently fought to increase the minimum wage and preserve the progressivity of income taxes.

However, the partisan cycles in inequality found in Bartels's study do not overlap with the historical trend of the top 1% income share. In fact, there is no evidence that its recent evolution has been shaped by the party controlling the presidency. Both parties appear to have aided and abetted the run-up of top incomes with the policies they have promoted. It was during the Clinton presidency that major financial deregulation laws were enacted. Further, opportunities to rein in rising top incomes through corporate governance and executive pay legislative reforms were allowed to pass by during the Obama presidency.

That both parties are linked to policy measures that have facilitated runaway top income inequality may be due to voter preferences. Because voter agitation toward economic inequality has been muted if not sporadic, the issue of inequality has escaped politicization for the most part, taking pressure off Democrats to take a tougher stance on top income inequality. As Bonica et al. (2013: 108) observe, "efforts to reduce inequality are not especially popular . . . there has been no groundswell of political support for sharp reforms of the financial sector." Rather than expressing blanket resentment toward the superrich, voter anger has tended to be triggered by news of an accounting scandal like the one involving Enron, or news of a government bailout of banks as the Troubled Asset Relief Program was designed to do, or news of predatory pricing such as the price hike of the popular pharmaceutical drug, the EpiPen—a device that injects epinephrine. "Political animus toward the 1 percent," as Bonica et al. (2013: 108) remark, "is largely directed at those perceived to have caused direct harm to the general public."

The absence of public pressure on lawmakers to reverse top income concentration may also be influenced by what has been happening to the relative income position of American voters. McCarty et al. (2016) have argued that the influx of immigrants in the United States, many of whom are poor, has had the effect of driving down the national average income relative to the income of the median American voter. As they put it, "the relative income of the median income *voter* in the United States did not deteriorate over a long period of rising inequality" (italics original, McCarty et al. 2016: 123–124). Arguably, the lack of a groundswell of public support to combat inequality may be related to the fact that many American voters do not feel as though rising inequality has undermined their material well-being.

Electoral politics accounts offer insights on why there has been little political push back against rising top income. What remains underexplored is why the actions of public officials, through legislation and inaction, end up working to the advantage of top income earners. We can gain analytical leverage on this question by considering the instrumental power of business.

Business power

Culpepper and Reinke (2014) draw a distinction between two forms of instrumental capabilities exercised by business. Strategic instrumental power arises when businesses and their associations deliberately deploy their organizational and financial resources to secure desired policy outcomes. Automatic instrumental power comes about when public officials internalize business logic in their decision-making process. This form of business power stems from three sources: public officials operating according to pro-business conceptual or ideological frameworks, the practice of public-private revolving door, and cultural capture which is cultivated through the interactions that public officials have with private sector actors.

Hacker and Pierson's (2010) "politics as organized combat" argument spotlights how the strategic use of campaign contributions and targeted lobbying has enabled business groups to succeed in securing favorable policy outcomes. Although the number of small donors has been on the rise since the early 1980s, the top 0.01% of the voting age population has contributed upwards of 40% of total political giving (Bonica et al., 2013: 111). Business political contributions have flowed to Democrats and Republicans alike however for different strategic reasons. As Hacker and Pierson (2010: 177–178) explain, contributions to the GOP are viewed by corporate elites as an investment in fostering "a cadre of elected officials committed to advancing a deregulatory and tax-cutting agenda." On the other hand, corporate money going to Democrats has been "a form of insurance . . . to minimize any prospect of distasteful legislation."

Corporate lobbying has also shaped policymaking outcomes in profound ways. As the organizational capacity of unions—a key champion of lower- and middle-class interests—atrophied starting in the 1970s, those of business groups took flight. The number of firms with registered lobbyists in Washington reached 2,445 in 1982, nearly 13 times the number of corporate lobbyists in 1971 (Hacker and Pierson 2010). Today's leading corporate interest groups such as the National Association of Manufacturers and the Chamber of Commerce came about as a result of significant organizational capacity building in the 1970s and early 1980s. Armed with mightier organizational resources than middle- and lower-class interest groups, business organizations have been able to promote and defend their interests by shaping the terms of discourse on crucial pieces of legislation, influencing the procedural votes of lawmakers, discouraging legislative updating of policies deemed harmful to business interests, and orchestrating information campaigns to influence public attitudes on policy developments.

The strategic deployment of lobbying and political giving has helped business win the support of key Democrats and moved the party to the right on economic issues.

For example, Senator Joe Liberman, a leading Democrat, led the Senate in blocking a proposal requesting that companies expense stock options given to executives, a measure that would have introduced greater transparency in how corporate leaders are compensated. It is only in the wake of the accounting scandals of the early 2000s that Senate Democrats' oppositional stance was reversed. President Obama's effort in 2010 to close the "carried-interest" loophole faced resistance from Chuck Schumer and Max Baucus, high-ranking Senate Democrats who received large campaign contributions from the financial sector. In response to the "shifting balance of organized power" in favor of business interest, Hacker and Pierson (2010: 173) remark that the Democratic Party has often adopted industry-friendly positions on issues such as corporate governance, taxation, global trade, and finance. In sum, the rightward shift of the center of political gravity in American politics can be traced to the political ascent of organized business interests, according to proponents of the "politics as organized combat" argument.

Another interpretation of why American politics has accommodated rising top income inequality focuses on the views and beliefs that guide public officials. Cultural capture is often invoked to explain why regulatory practices appear to promote business interests at the expense of the public interest. At the heart of cultural capture is a mechanism in which regulators internalize conceptual frameworks, worldviews, or beliefs shared by the very industries they are mandated to regulate. In his study on the behavior of financial sector regulators, Kwak (2014) notes that regulatory officials can become receptive to the views of industry leaders because endorsing them confers "perceived status benefits." Further, these are views communicated by individuals whom regulators identify to be in their in-group and thus should be trusted. Of note, enforcement of financial regulations often requires regulators to be embedded in the financial institutions they are overseeing, a practice sure to foster stronger group identification than in other industries where there is greater separation between regulators and regulatees.

The key policy implication of the cultural capture argument is that regulators are unlikely to call attention to runaway inequality since the high returns that financial executives are able to generate can be interpreted as a sign of effective regulatory performance. Another reason regulators stir away from the issue of compensation is that today's regulators may become tomorrow's managers in leading financial firms. The prospect of joining the private sector in the near future can create a powerful disincentive to "rock the boat"—that is, spotlight the problems that are not in the public's interest. As Bonica et al. (2013: 117) remark, "the revolving door, even with the best of intentions, clouds [regulators'] decision making."

Conclusion

Income inequality has risen across rich OECD countries. A closer look at this common trend, however, reveals that inequality has been increasing faster in some countries than in others and that there remains a significant gap between the least and most inegalitarian countries. Structural-economic factors such as technological change, financialization, the rise of the knowledge economy, and economic globalization have been singled out in the literature as key culprits of the rise in inequality in advanced political economies. The main drawback with this line of argument is that it does not provide much analytical leverage on the question of why there are notable differences in the inequality trajectories of affluent democracies even though they have all been exposed to the same structural-economic factors.

To address this question, CPE scholars have focused on the role of labor market institutions. This strand of research suggests that strong and encompassing unions coupled with coordinated collective bargaining and codetermination rights have helped mitigate the inequality inducing effects of the structural-economic transformations that have occurred since the 1970s. Moreover, researchers have explored how political factors influence a country's income distribution. In this chapter, we explored how electoral politics, public policy, and interest group politics in the United States have contributed to the rise of top incomes.

Key terms

Conscription of income

Descriptive representation

Gini coefficient

Great compression

Income

Okun's trade-off

Skill-biased technological change

Substantive representation

Winner-take-all economy

Discussion questions

- Why should we be concerned about rising income inequality?
- Compare and contrast the Anglo, continental, and Nordic countries with respect to wage and top-income distribution since the early 1980s.
- What factors can account for the differences in the inequality trajectories of advanced political economies?
- Discuss the various sources of the New Gilded Age in the United States. Which one do you find most insightful?

Further reading

Bartels, Larry. 2018. *Unequal Democracy: The Political Economy of the New Gilded Age*. 2nd edition. Princeton, NJ: Princeton University Press.

Explores the political causes and effects of rising inequality in the United States.

Culpepper, Pepper. 2011. *Quiet Politics and Business Power*. New York: Cambridge University Press.

Details how organized business in Japan and Europe have quietly shaped corporate governance regulations.

Hoffman, Florian, David S. Lee, and Thomas Lemieux. 2020. "Growing Income Inequality in the United States and Other Advanced Economies." *Journal of Economic Perspectives* 34(4): 52–78.

Provides an assessment of how the rise in inequality is linked to changes in labor versus non-labor market income.

McCarty, Nolan, Keith T. Poole, and Howard Rosenthal. 2016. *Polarized America: The Dance of Ideology and Unequal Riches*. 2nd edition. Cambridge, MA: The MIT Press.

Investigates the connections among economic inequality, polarization, immigration, and public policy.

CHAPTER

7 Redistribution

The previous chapter focused on market income inequality and its determinants. This chapter will focus on the reduction of inequality attributed to the redistributive effects of the tax-transfer systems in OECD countries. The concept of redistribution boils down to the following: the reduction of market income inequality by way of government income transfers that benefit low-income households and by way of progressive taxation. As a result of redistribution, disposable income inequality is lower than market income inequality.

We begin the chapter by going over some basic issues about how to measure redistribution. Next, we will discuss trends in redistribution from both cross-national and cross-temporal perspectives. The chapter then introduces readers to the Meltzer-Richard-Romer (MRR) model, a work-horse model of redistribution, and evaluates it against recent data. The fourth section will elaborate on different types of welfare state regimes, compare and contrast their redistributive effects, and briefly discuss trends in redistribution in recent decades against the backdrop of welfare state retrenchment. The last two sections will survey determinants of redistribution. While the penultimate section focuses on determinants of individual preferences for redistribution, the last section addresses macro-level factors that shape redistributive spending.

Measuring redistribution

In this chapter, redistribution is measured as the difference between the gini coefficient of market income (referred to as pre-fisc gini in table 7.1) and gini coefficient of disposable income (referred to as post-fisc gini in table 7.1).

There are two ways of measuring that difference. One way is by simply calculating the absolute difference: [pre-fisc gini − post-fisc gini]. The other is by calculating the proportional reduction in inequality: [((pre-fisc gini − post-fisc gini)/pre-fisc gini) × 100]. The percentage reduction method is commonly used in the literature for it provides a more accurate measure of redistributive efforts (Huber et al. 2014; Iversen and Soskice 2009). However, Kenworthy and Pontusson (2005: 450) have questioned

DOI: 10.4324/9780429199462-7

the merits of using this method to calculate redistribution and change in inequality, arguing that "absolute measures of change [in inequality] are easier to interpret than relative measures and also more substantively sensible."

IN FOCUS BOX 7.1 MINDING THE INITIAL LEVEL OF INEQUALITY

Consider the following example. Let's say that the gini coefficient of market income increased from .273 to .349 in country A and from .369 to .445 in country B between two points in time. In absolute terms, market inequality increased by .076 in both countries. However, when this change is expressed in percentage terms, notice that inequality in country A (the more egalitarian country out of two countries) increased by 27.8% while inequality in country B increased by 20.6%. We end up with a similar result when calculating redistribution. Let's say the pre-fisc gini and post-fisc gini are .273 and .212, respectively, in country A. In country B, pre-fisc gini and post-fisc gini are .335 and .274, respectively. In absolute terms, redistribution amounts to .061 in both countries. Expressed in percentage terms, country A's redistribution equaled 22.3% while country B's amounted to 18.2%. As both examples illustrate, the difference between countries A and B relates to "initial levels rather than the extent of change" (Kenworthy and Pontusson 2005: 450). To sum up, when the percentage change method is used, we need to be mindful of the initial level of inequality when assessing the extent of redistribution.

Unlike the previous chapter which focused on earnings from labor, in this chapter we consider all sources of income including income from social benefits such as unemployment insurance, disabilities payment, and pension. Such social transfers play an important role, as we will see, in reducing inequality. There are two components of the welfare state regime that are not considered even though they help reduce inequality. Public services such as health care, childcare, elderly care, and education are omitted because they do not directly change the distribution of income via cash payment or tax. However, as Kenworthy and Pontusson (2005: 455) note, "to the extent they are provided at low or no cost and are universally available, services are equivalent to a flat-rate benefit given to each household, which reduces the degree of consumption inequality." Thus, one should bear in mind that the data on redistribution that we will be using in this chapter underreport the extent of redistribution, particularly in countries whose welfare states provide extensive public services like those in the Nordic countries.

Another key concept relates to the measurement of income distribution. Among the many debates that have shaped comparative political economy, one is especially pertinent for us in this chapter: Does market inequality influence redistribution? Some scholars have opted to use income deciles to measure market inequality. For example, Iversen and Soskice (2009) use the 50–10 and 90–50 wage ratios to explore the association between market inequality and redistribution, while Moene and Wallerstein (2008b) use the 90–10 wage ratio. Alternatively, to analyze the same association, Alesina and Glaser (2004), Bradley et al. (2003), Huber et al. (2014), Kenworthy and Pontusson (2005), and Pontusson (2005) employ the gini coefficient.

As it turns out, how income distribution is measured will affect the association between inequality and redistribution.

In this chapter, the main unit of analysis will be working-age households rather than working-age individuals. This difference is not trivial—the extent of inequality will be greater using the former unit even if both units are measured using the gini coefficient. This is the case because the working-age household measure captures different employment statuses (unemployed, part-time, full-time, self-employment) and sources of earnings (labor and non-labor such as property and investments).

Inequality and redistribution from cross-national and cross-temporal perspectives

Table 7.1 provides cross-national data on inequality and redistribution for four time periods. The data on pre- and post-fisc inequality come from the Luxembourg Income Study (LIS) database and are compiled in the Comparative Political Data Set 1960–2016 (Update 2018) organized by Armingeon et al. (2018). LIS income data

TABLE 7.1 Inequality and redistribution among working age households

	1980s			**1990s**			**2000s**			**2010s**		
	Pre-fisc Gini	Post-fisc Gini	Redistribution	Pre-fisc Gini	Post-fisc Gini	Redistribution	Pre-fisc Gini	Post-fisc Gini	Redistribution	Pre-fisc Gini	Post-fisc Gini	Redistribution
Nordic												
Denmark	31.3	21.7	30.7	34.5	20.2	41.4	34.3	20.7	39.7	36.4	22.9	37.1
Finland	31.0	18.9	39.0	36.3	19.7	45.7	38.1	24.1	36.7	38.1	24.7	35.2
Norway	27.3	21.1	22.7	31.1	21.5	30.9	35.2	23.3	33.8	35.8	23.1	35.5
Sweden	31.1	18.9	39.2	37.9	21.0	44.6	37.1	22.8	38.5	37.0	26.8	27.6
Mean	*30.2*	*20.2*	*32.9*	*35.0*	*20.6*	*40.7*	*36.2*	*22.7*	*37.2*	*36.8*	*24.4*	*33.9*
Continental												
France	42.4	29.9	29.5	41.7	28.2	32.4	40.5	27.1	33.1	42.6	28.7	32.6
Germany	33.5	23.8	29.0	36.2	24.7	31.8	39.5	26.5	32.9	40.5	27.9	31.1
Netherlands	41.7	24.1	42.2	36.1	23.8	34.1	37.1	25.9	30.2	36.6	24.9	32.0
Switzerland	33.0	29.6	10.3	32.3	28.0	13.3	32.1	26.7	16.7	33.8	27.9	17.5
Mean	*37.7*	*26.9*	*27.8*	*36.6*	*26.2*	*27.9*	*37.3*	*26.6*	*28.2*	*38.4*	*27.4*	*28.3*
Anglo												
Australia	37.0	27.5	25.7	40.7	28.7	29.5	41.6	29.9	28.1	41.2	30.4	26.2
Canada	34.2	26.7	21.9	38.6	28.0	27.5	40.7	30.5	25.1	41.2	31.0	24.8
United Kingdom	36.9	26.4	28.5	45.0	32.6	27.6	44.6	32.9	26.2	46.2	33.0	28.6
United States	39.3	30.8	21.6	42.8	34.0	20.6	43.2	34.6	19.9	45.8	36.1	21.2
Mean	*36.9*	*27.9*	*24.4*	*41.8*	*30.8*	*26.3*	*42.5*	*32.0*	*24.8*	*43.6*	*32.6*	*25.2*

Notes: Averages calculated by the author. The country averages for 2010s cover the years up to 2015. OECD data were used to calculate the pre- and post-fisc gini coefficients for Sweden from 2010 to 2016.

Sources: Armingeon et al. (2018) and OECD, IDD (2019b).

are available for different years rather than annually and are equivalized using the square root of the number of persons in the household to take account of the variance in household size. The data are based on incomes of households with members aged 18 to 65.

Focusing first on pre-fisc (pretax-pretransfer) inequality levels across time using the group mean as a reference point, the Nordic country cluster maintained the lowest levels from the 1980s to the 2010s. However, the gap between the Nordic and continental countries decreased during this time. The convergence was due to the fact that the Nordic cluster witnessed a 21.8% increase in pre-fisc inequality between the 1980s and 2010s, while the pre-fisc inequality average for the continental group barely increased. The Anglo group's reputation for having higher inequality levels was not borne out in the 1980s but became noticeable starting in the 1990s.

Turning to post-fisc (posttax-posttransfer) inequality levels, again using the group mean, we see that the Nordic cluster consistently maintained the lowest levels, the Anglo group had the highest levels, and the continental group was in the middle. In terms of change, the Nordic cluster faced the highest increase (20.8%), followed by the Anglo cluster (16.8%), while the continental group's level barely increased (1.6%). Because of these divergent trends, the differences in post-fisc inequality between the Nordic and continental groups decreased from the 1990s to the 2010s. If the Nordic group saw the highest increases in pre-fisc inequality, then why did it not lose significant ground relative to the continental group and especially to the Anglo countries in terms of level of post-fisc inequality? It is because of the magnitude of redistribution in the Nordic countries.

The Nordic group offset rising inequality in market income by adjusting the extent of redistribution. Redistribution increased sharply between the 1980s and 1990s (23.7%) at the same time pre-fisc inequality also rose significantly (15.9%), but then dropped between the 2000s and 2010s as the rate of increase in pre-fisc inequality slowed. As for the continental cluster, redistribution and pre-fisc inequality were relatively stable between the 1980s and 2010s. In the Anglo group, although redistribution and pre-inequality generally moved in the same direction, redistributive efforts were not as robust as in the Nordic group.

Among the Nordic countries, Norway's level of pre-fisc inequality increased the most from the 1980s to the 2010s. However, despite increasing by 31.1% during this period, the country's average inequality levels during these decades remained below the group average. Sweden experienced the largest increase in post-fisc inequality, increasing by 41.8%. The highest levels of inequality reduction were witnessed in the 1990s, a decade in which pre-fisc inequality increased sharply in many Nordic countries. Norway's level of redistribution appears to be the most responsive to changes in pre-fisc inequality levels since the 1980s. Sweden scaled back its redistribution efforts starting in the 2000s; this can explain why the country's post-fisc inequality increased by 18% between the 2000s and 2010s.

Within the continental group, France had the distinction of having the highest levels of pre-fisc inequality while Switzerland stood out for having the lowest levels from the 1980s to the 2010s. Germany's and the Netherlands' pre-fisc inequality levels moved in opposite directions during these decades. Whereas Germany's steadily climbed (amounting to an overall increase of 21%), the

Netherlands' dropped (an overall decline of 12.2%). With regard to post-fisc inequality levels, Switzerland and France saw gradual decreases from the 1980s to 2000s, Germany experienced a steady increase, and the Netherlands recorded relatively stable levels.

Levels of redistribution have converged over time in continental countries. In the 1980s, the extent of redistribution in the Netherlands was comparable to the Nordic average in the 1990s while Switzerland's redistribution efforts was the lowest and remained so up to the 2010s. The level of redistribution in the Netherlands dropped sharply between the 1980s and 1990s, a period in which the Dutch economy experienced a drop in pre-fisc inequality. Switzerland's redistribution level gradually increased, but it did not appear to coincide with rising levels of pre-fisc inequality. On the other hand, France's redistributive efforts gradually increased amid persistently high pre-fisc inequality, bringing the country's post-fisc gini levels closer to the continental average in the 1990s and 2000s.

Although the Anglo country averages for pre- and post-fisc inequality were similar to those of continental countries in the 1980s, inequality levels thereafter trended up for Anglo countries. By the 2010s, the United Kingdom and the United States had the highest levels of inequality. Between the 1980s and 2010s, the United States consistently had the highest levels of post-fisc inequality levels, but its pre-fisc inequality levels were surpassed by the United Kingdom and were not significantly higher than those in the Nordic and continental countries. Redistribution levels in the Anglo countries were lower than in the other two country clusters with the exception of Switzerland. During this time period, the degree of inequality reduction in Australia and the United Kingdom was similar to the continental country average.

While table 7.1 suggests that there is a relationship between inequality and redistribution, we need a theoretical model to explain why changes in inequality seem to be associated with changes in redistribution.

A basic model of redistribution

The idea that rising income inequality results in higher levels of redistribution in democracies was first elaborated by Meltzer and Richard (1981) and Romer (1975). Referred here as the MRR model, it offers a simplified view of how democratic politics can compensate against worsening income distribution. First, the MRR model assumes that government redistribution is financed by a proportional tax—so that the tax liability of individuals increases as their market income rises—and is dispensed equally to all members of society in the form of a flat-rate (lump-sum) benefit. The implication of this assumption is that those who earn more than the mean income face a net cost of taxation—that is, what they contribute in taxes exceeds what they receive in benefits. On the other hand, those who earn less than the mean income face a net benefit of taxation—that is, the value of redistributive benefits exceeds the cost of taxation—as long as taxes are not so high that they discourage people from working. This is referred to as the disincentive effect of redistributive taxation.

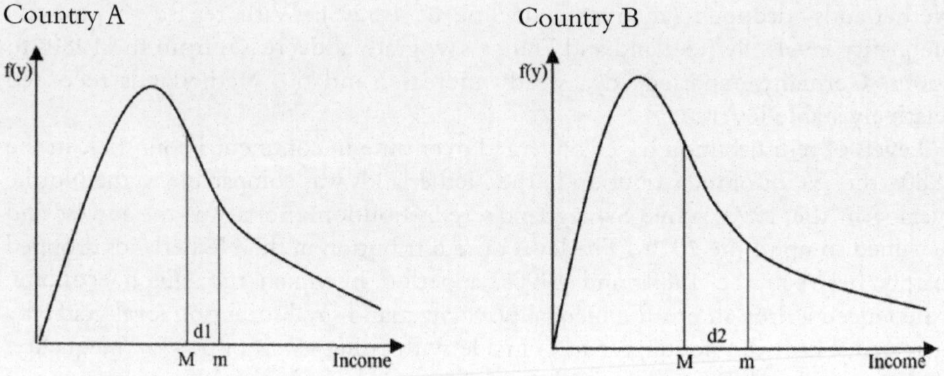

FIGURE 7.1 Right-skewed income distribution

Source: Beramendi, Pablo, and Christopher J. Anderson. 2008. eds, Democracy, Inequality, and Representation: A Comparative Perspective (pg. 316). © Russell Sage Foundation, 112 East 64th Street, New York, NY 10065. Reprinted with Permission.

Another key assumption is that the distribution of income before taxes and social transfers is skewed to the right, as illustrated in figure 7.1. The incomes of citizens are arrayed from zero (at the origin) to the highest incomes along the horizontal axis, while the vertical axis captures the frequency of recipients with such incomes. To say that income distribution is right-skewed simply means that there is a large proportion of the population with low incomes and an increasingly smaller proportion of the population at higher income levels—representing the long tail. Because incomes are distributed this way, the mean income (m) is larger than the median income (M), which is the case in countries A and B.

However, note that the gap between the mean and median in country A is less than in country B (d2>d1) even though we are assuming here that the mean income is the same in both countries. What differs is the distance of the median incomes: in country A, the median income is closer to the mean than in country B because its income is less unequally distributed. Graphically, the shorter, fatter tail of the income distribution in country A illustrates this. According to the logic of the MRR model, as the distance between the median and mean incomes increases, the median income earner is expected to support more redistribution up to the point where the taxation liability that is incurred by society in order to finance social benefits begins to undermine economic prosperity. In short, we would expect to find greater redistribution in country B than in country A.

Finally, the MRR model assumes that democratic politics operates as depicted by the Downsian median voter theory. Redistributive policies are determined by an electoral process in which voters possess two qualities: first, they are assumed to have well-formed preferences over redistribution that are defined by their income relative to the average income; and, second, voters are assumed to be able to discern the efficiency costs of taxation. By invoking the median voter in majoritarian politics, the MRR model does not just elaborate the behavioral foundation of how individuals form their redistributive preferences, it also provides a macro-level explanation of the extent of redistribution. As Dimick et al. (2018: 3–4) observe, the MRR model is able to predict redistributive outcomes by way of "aggregat[ing] individual preferences through a highly simplified model of democratic decision making: The median voter (not necessarily the voter with median income) is the decisive voter, and therefore, the person whose preferences have the most important implications for policy." To the extent that political parties are office seekers in a Downsian two-party contest, it is the preference of the median voter, not partisanship, which ultimately determines taxation and redistribution. The MRR model predicts that the median voter will want more redistribution the more skewed the income distribution and the lower the disincentive effect of taxation.

Voter turnout plays an important role in determining the income profile of the median voter in an election. In a low voter turnout situation, the income of the median voter will be closer to the mean income because a large proportion of the non-voters are poor, leaving the electorate more affluent than the voting-eligible population. By the logic of the MRR model, electoral politics in a low-turnout setting is expected to lead to some scaling back of redistribution. In contrast, when turnout is high because of the participation of low-income citizens, the median voter's income will be further below the mean income, which the MRR model predicts should result in greater redistribution.

IN FOCUS BOX 7.2 EVALUATING THE MRR MODEL

How does the MRR model stand up to empirical evidence? Figure 7.2 plots average redistribution against average earnings inequality between the early 1980s and mid-2010s. It shows that countries with lower earnings inequality such as Denmark, Finland, and Sweden redistribute more than countries with more unequal distributions of earnings like Canada and the United States. Contrary to what the MRR model posits, figure 7.2 suggests that a negative association exists between income inequality and redistribution, a phenomenon that Iversen and Soskice (2009) refer to as the "Robin Hood paradox."

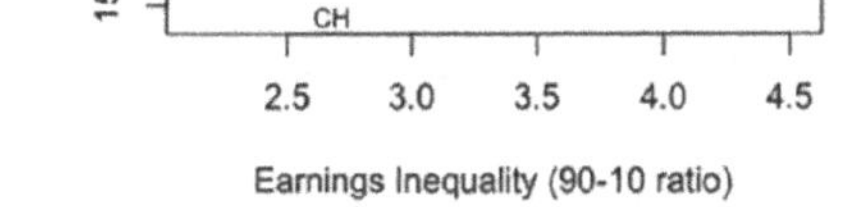

FIGURE 7.2 Average redistribution and earnings inequality, 1980s to 2010s

Note: r = –0.59, sig @ 0.05

Sources: Table 7.1 and table 6.1.

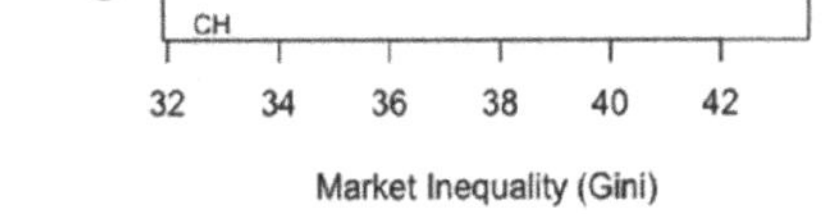

FIGURE 7.3 Average redistribution and market inequality, 1980s to 2010s

Note: r = 0.22

Source: Table 7.1.

The redistribution paradox that Iversen and Soskice observe, however, is sensitive to how redistribution and market inequality are measured. Their analysis examined the association between 90–50 earnings ratio for full-time workers (a proxy for market inequality) and redistribution measured as the proportional reduction in inequality from 1970 to 1995. When the 90–10 ratio is used against redistribution, as figure 7.2 does, we end up with the same result as Iversen and Soskice. However, in seeking "to recast the empirical basis of this debate" regarding the redistribution paradox, Kenworthy and Pontusson (2005) propose measuring inequality on a household basis using the gini coefficient of market income in order "to capture the distributive effects of employment (or nonemployment)." Further, they use the absolute approach to measure redistribution—pre-fisc inequality minus post-fisc inequality.

Following the advice of Kenworthy and Pontusson (2005), figure 7.3 plots average redistribution using the average absolute redistribution against average gini coefficient of household market income. Note that the relationship is now positive albeit weak, which is a result that Kenworthy and Pontusson also found in their study of OECD countries between 1979 and 2000. If we focus on the position of Germany, Norway, and the United Kingdom relative to the best-fit line, we see that redistribution increases as market inequality rises. We need to apply caution here as the scatterplot shows that many countries are too dispersed around the best-fit line to confirm the underlying logic of the MRR model.

Figures 7.4 and 7.5 look at the association between changes in inequality and redistribution. Figure 7.4 plots percentage change in redistribution against percentage change in market inequality between the 1980s and 2010s. The positive association is quite weak; Norway and Switzerland are well out of range of the best-fit line. Many countries appear to defy the logic of the MRR model, most especially Switzerland and Sweden. However, the positions of Denmark, France, the Netherlands, and Norway appear to be consistent with the predictions of the MRR model.

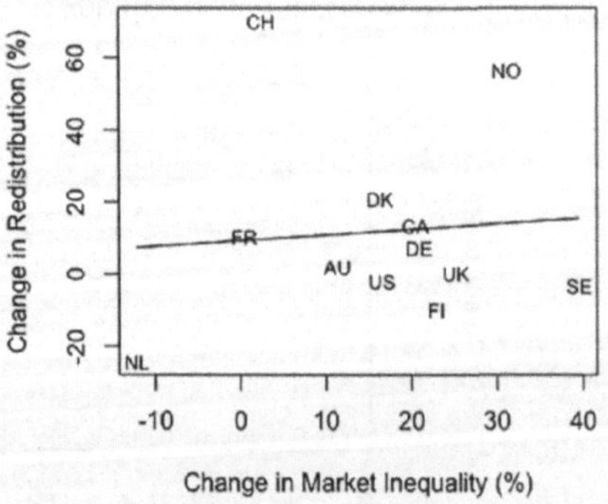

FIGURE 7.4 Percentage changes in market inequality and redistribution, 1980s–2010s

Note: r = .08

Source: Table 7.1.

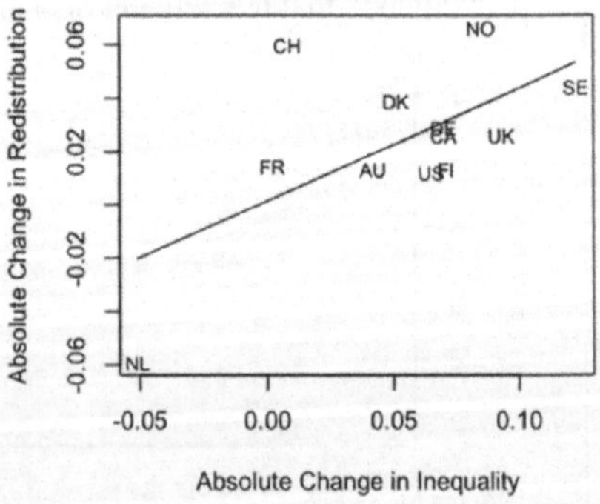

FIGURE 7.5 Absolute changes in market inequality and redistribution, 1980s–2010s

Note: r = .62, sig @ 0.05

Source: Table 7.1.

Figure 7.5 plots absolute change in redistribution against absolute change in inequality between the 1980s and 2010s. The relationship is stronger, with many countries clustered closer to the best-fit line. Kenworthy and Pontusson (2005: 458) also found a similar pattern between the late 1970s and 2000. As they point out, "redistribution tended to increase in response to the rise in household market inequality. And it did so in proportion to the degree of increase in inequality, producing a strong positive association between changes in market inequality and changes in redistribution" (Kenworthy and Pontusson 2005: 461). What they observed up to 2000 appears to have held well into the 2010s.

To sum up, there is some evidence in support of the MRR model. However, the evidence we have gleaned in the preceding In Focus Box raises an important question: What accounts for the cross-national and cross-temporal differences in the co-movement of inequality and redistribution? Part of the answer is that the welfare state, voter turnout, partisanship, social identity, cultural norms, and policy constraints shape the link between distribution and redistribution. Another factor is that people's exposure to economic risk may have a greater impact on popular support for redistribution than relative income. We address these points in the next sections.

Welfare states

Most contemporary works in the subfield of comparative political economy of the welfare state have been influenced in some form or another by Esping-Andersen's (1990) pioneering work which details three types of welfare states. Social democratic, Christian democratic, and liberal welfare states—which correspond in general with the Nordic, continental, and Anglo country clusters, respectively—are distinguished by their levels of de-commodification and stratification. De-commodification refers to the ability of individuals or households to "uphold a socially acceptable standard of living independently of market participation" (Esping-Andersen 1990: 37). Social welfare is also "an active force in the ordering of social relations" insofar as it can promote equality of status via inclusive, solidaristic programs or foster dualism via programs that stigmatize or differentially treat claimants (ibid: 23). We can also add another element of contrast—the three welfare state types achieve different degrees of inequality reduction.

Comparing welfare states

The extent to which welfare states achieve de-commodification, stratification, and redistribution hinges, to a large extent, on the rules of eligibility and scope and generosity of social programs. Three different eligibility rules are used to determine who has access to social benefits: means-testing, social insurance, and universal entitlement. In means-testing arrangements, which are widely used in liberal welfare states, entitlement to social benefits (primarily social assistance that target low-income households and individuals) is based on demonstrated need. Because the benefits delivered through means-tested programs provide a minimal safety net of last resort and their recipients face social stigma, this type of arrangement is designed to discourage reliance on public social benefits and render participation in the labor market the primary source of well-being for individuals and households. By design, social assistance benefits replace a relatively small percent of market income and are provided for a short duration. Therefore, means-testing leads to lower redistribution and welfare generosity, features commonly found in liberal welfare states.

In social insurance arrangements, the right to social benefits is based on prior contribution. For example, to receive public pension and unemployment benefits, people must contribute to both programs usually by way of paying a payroll or social security tax and the size of the benefits that people are entitled to is often determined by how much they have contributed. Christian democratic welfare states, which are based on the social insurance model, by design will differentially treat individuals based on their employment profiles, offering generous social insurance benefits to long-term workers, but requiring those with shorter and scattered work stints to fall back on means-tested social assistance. This type of welfare state seeks to ensure income stabilization for full-time workers facing labor market risks, not universal sharing of risks. Thus, dualism and high levels of benefit generosity can coexist in such welfare states.

The third type of eligibility rule is referred to as universal entitlement. This eligibility rule is based on the principle of social citizenship, which calls for the promotion of social equality and solidarity via universal risk-pooling. Universal entitlements such as basic retirement pension, education, child allowances, and income support for parental leave are available to all citizens or residents irrespective of past contribution or income. Because of their universalistic and social citizenship features, social democratic welfare states can achieve relatively high levels of de-commodification and redistribution thanks to the universal access to social benefits, the flat-rate nature of such benefits, and higher levels of public social spending.

Welfare states can also be differentiated based on their use of cash benefits and public services in their efforts to provide for the well-being of people. OECD data on social expenditures are broken down into several categories: old age, survivors, incapacity related, health, family, active labor market programs, unemployment, housing, and other social policy areas. For each of these categories, with the exception of health, the OECD calculates benefits in the form of cash transfer and of service. As Huber and Stephens (2001: 42) note, many social services such as childcare, elderly care, and home-help services for the disabled are based on the principle of citizenship rights while cash transfer benefits are contingent on prior employment and income. Moreover, the government or private sector (through government-mandates) can provide social services.

Private provision of social benefits, which the OECD refers to as private social expenditures, makes eligibility to such benefits conditional upon employment. The OECD defines private social expenditure as "social benefits delivered through the private sector [, which] can be mandatory (stipulated by law) or voluntary." We are especially interested in mandatory private expenditures (as a percentage of GDP) since it constitutes the largest portion of total private spending. The three most common private mandatory programs are compulsory private health insurance, compulsory pension contribution, and sickness payment by employers. The amount of private social benefits a person can receive is closely associated with the type of occupation held by an individual. Individuals in high-paying occupations tend to receive more generous benefits than individuals in low-paying occupations. Unless the government steps in to supplement private insurance schemes, a two-tier system can emerge whereby some are well protected while many others are not.

Comparative data on social welfare

Table 7.2 provides data on different features of modern welfare states. Many of the attributes we have elaborated regarding social democratic, Christian democratic, and liberal welfares are corroborated by the data. Public social spending as a percentage of GDP is highest in the Nordic countries and lowest in Anglo countries. Social spending has increased overall in the continental and Anglo countries, but decreased in Nordic countries between the early 1990s and late 2000s. As a result, the difference in social spending between the Nordic and continental countries has narrowed but the gap between the two country groups and the Anglo countries remains conspicuous. With the exception of Denmark and France, high spending countries have seen a drop in social spending levels, while the opposite has occurred in low spending countries.

Welfare generosity, which gives us an idea about the extent of de-commodification, has been higher in the Nordic countries than in the continental and Anglo countries. On average, the level of benefit generosity dropped in the Nordic countries but remained stable among the continental and Anglo countries, leading the Nordic and continental groups to have similar generosity levels by the late 2000s. Norway and Sweden had generosity levels above 40 in the early 1990s; only Norway was at that level by the late 2000s. Of note, social spending and benefit generosity did not move in the same direction in half of the countries in the sample. In the Netherlands and Norway, benefit generosity increased while spending levels dropped. In Australia, Denmark, France, and Germany, social spending increased while benefit generosity decreased.

Modern welfare states provide social benefits through a combination of cash transfers and public services. Cash transfers refer to a payment an individual receives from the government as a result of being enrolled in a public pension, unemployment insurance, sickness and disabilities insurance, or other income supporting program. Table 7.2 shows that cash benefits as a percentage of GDP were slightly higher in Nordic countries than in continental countries in the early 1990s but were virtually identical in the mid-2010s due to cash benefit cutbacks in Norway and Sweden. The sharpest drops in cash benefits occurred in the Netherlands and Sweden, while the largest increases took place in Denmark, France, and Switzerland.

Between the early 1990s and mid-2010s, the size of the public service sector was consistently larger in the Nordic countries, although public services in France, Germany, and the United Kingdom reached Nordic country levels by the mid-2010s. Expenditures on public services in the Anglo countries surpassed those of continental countries in the mid-2010s, which was due to higher public health-related expenses. With respect to public services net of health spending, we see that the Nordic countries continued to outspend the continental and Anglo countries.

TABLE 7.2 Dimensions of the welfare state

	Public Social Spending[1]		**Welfare Generosity[2]**		**Cash Benefits[3]**		**Public Services[4]**		**Replacement Rate[5]**		**Private Social Spending[6]**		
	Early 1990s	Late 2000s	Early 1990s	Late 2000s	Early 1990s	Mid-2010s	Early 1990s	Mid-2010s	Early 1990s	Late 2000s	Mid-2010s (A)	(B)	(C)
Nordic	*27.8*	*25.9*	*39.9*	*36.6*	*14.6*	*13.8*	*9.8*	*12.6 (6.3)*	*76.5*	*68.0*	*3.0*	*1.4*	
Denmark	26.8	27.8	36.7	33.5	11.5	13.7	10.0	13.3 (6.6)	90.0	73.0	4.4	2.6	—
Finland	28.8	26.5	35.6	33.7	17.2	18.0	9.4	11.4 (5.7)	63.8	56.8	1.5	—	—
Norway	23.3	21.2	41.8	43.0	13.4	12.5	8.3	11.7 (5.3)	62.0	64.6	2.5	1.3	—
Sweden	32.3	28.2	45.7	36.2	16.1	11.2	11.4	13.9 (7.6)	90.0	77.5	3.6	0.4	—
Continental	*22.5*	*24.2*	*36.7*	*36.3*	*13.5*	*13.7*	*6.9*	*8.1 (2.5)*	*59.0*	*63.8*	*8.0*	*2.1*	*3.7*
France	25.8	30.5	38.9	38.0	15.6	19.3	8.5	11.6 (*2.8*)	60.0	63.7	3.5	0.2	0.0
Germany	23.8	26.0	36.3	32.2	13.6	13.5	7.8	10.7 (*2.6*)	40.0	40.1	3.5	1.4	0.8
Netherlands	25.7	21.7	36.3	38.1	16.3	11.4	6.5	5.5 (*2.8*)	70.0	71.6	13.4	0.7	5.7
Switzerland	14.7	18.7	35.1	36.9	8.3	10.6	4.6	4.7 (1.7)	65.8	80.0	11.5	6.0	4.5
Anglo	*16.8*	*18.7*	*24.1*	*24.1*	*9.0*	*9.4*	*6.6*	*9.6 (2.1)*	*36.2*	*30.2*	*7.3*	*1.9*	
Australia	14.3	17.3	22.2	20.8	7.8	9.0	6.0	9.3 (*2.9*)	31.3	24.2	5.8	4.7	—
Canada	19.9	18.0	26.6	25.8	11.0	9.3	7.7	8.1 (*0.8*)	57.7	46.0	4.7	—	—
United Kingdom	18.5	22.2	26.4	28.1	9.2	10.3	6.6	11.1 (*3.4*)	27.9	20.5	6.2	0.9	0.0
United States	14.3	17.4	21.1	21.5	7.9	9.0	5.9	9.7 (*1.3*)	27.8	30.2	12.5	0.2	5.6

Definitions and sources:

[1] Total public social expenditure as a percentage of GDP. *Source*: Brady et al. (2020).

[2] Overall social benefit generosity, calculated by summing the indices of unemployment benefit generosity, sickness benefit generosity, and pension benefit generosity. *Source*: Scruggs et al. (2017).

[3] Cash benefits, as a percentage of GDP, represent public pensions and income support to the working age population. *Source*: OECD, SOCX (2019).

[4] Public services, as a percentage of GDP, represent public provision of health care, elderly care, childcare, job training, family support, and other services. Numbers between parentheses represent public service without public expenses on health care. *Source*: OECD, SOCX (2019).

[5] Gross replacement rate of unemployment insurance for the first year of unemployment, calculated by taking the average annual insurance benefit received by individuals from different family types who earn two-thirds of the average annual earnings of a production worker. *Source*: Brady et al. (2020).

[6] Private social spending as a percentage of GDP. (A) combines gross mandatory private and gross voluntary private expenditures. (B) private spending on cash benefits. (C) private spending on health. *Source*: OECD, SOCX (2019).

An important question to ask is, how much of an individual's labor market income is replaced by cash benefits? Table 7.2 provides data on the replacement rate of unemployment. The measure used looks at the replacement rate for low-income workers (those who earn two-thirds of the average annual earnings of a production worker) rather than for an average worker. As Huber and Stephens (2001: 92) note, given social democratic welfare states' emphasis on universalism and egalitarianism, "those with minimum qualifying conditions [such as people with intermittent work record] were much better" under this type of welfare state. Indeed, the Nordic averages in the early 1990s and late 2000s were higher than those of the continental group, and twice as high as those of the Anglo group. There was some convergence in the replacement rates by the late 2000s between the Nordic and continental countries because all continental countries increased their rates while high-rate countries like Denmark and Sweden significantly lowered theirs. Interestingly, there is a fair amount of variance within each group. Among the Anglo countries, Canada stands out for having a rate that is much higher than the group average. Among the continental countries, Germany stands out for its relatively low average rate. Among the Nordic countries, Finland and Norway stand well below Denmark and Sweden.

Table 7.2 also provides comparative data on private social spending. On average, the continental and Anglo countries rely more on private social spending than the Nordic countries. The two lowest private social spenders were Finland and Norway while the two highest were the Netherlands and the United States. Most countries used mandatory private cash transfers however for different ends. In Germany, the Netherlands, Norway, Sweden, and the United States, the bulk of private cash transfers were associated with incapacity-related programs. In Australia, Great Britain, and Switzerland, almost all private cash transfers took the form of pension contributions. In Denmark, private cash transfers were tied to survivors' payments. Fewer than half of the countries recorded mandatory private sector service-related expenditures in the mid-2010s. In Germany, the Netherlands, Switzerland, and the United States, about all of these expenses were related to health care.

The redistributive effects of the tax-transfer system

There are notable cross-national differences in the degree to which the tax-transfer systems of OECD countries reduce market income inequality. Table 7.3 breaks down redistribution into two components: percentage change in gini coefficient caused by taxes and percentage change in gini coefficient caused by transfers.

Taxes have different effects across OECD countries. In Denmark, Finland, the Netherlands, Sweden, and Switzerland, taxes actually increase inequality. For example, Sweden's pre-fisc gini in 2005 was 37.1 while its post-tax, pre-transfer gini was 38.8, amounting to a 4.6% increase in inequality. Similarly, Switzerland's pre-fisc gini in 2007 stood at 32.7 while its post-tax, pre-transfer gini reached 34.3, representing a 4.9% increase in inequality. On the other hand, taxes helped reduce inequality in all Anglo countries, Norway, Germany, and France. In the United States, where taxes were on average highly redistributive in the 2000s, the pre-fisc gini in 2004 was 43.7 while the pre-transfer, post-tax gini was 39.6, amounting to a 9.4% reduction in inequality.

The fact that taxes worsen inequality in many European countries and ameliorate inequality in the Anglo countries might be a surprise to many. A commonplace view holds that many European countries fund their expensive welfare states by taxing the rich while Anglo countries do minimal redistribution presumably because they opt not to tax the rich. In fact, it is exactly the opposite: high-redistribution countries rely more on regressive taxes while low-redistribution countries rely more on progressive taxes. Figure 7.6 plots household tax progressivity against redistribution in the 2000s. Lower values along the horizontal axis represent less progressive (more regressive) household taxes, meaning a larger portion of taxes falls on lower income groups; higher values signify that affluent income groups pay a larger proportion of overall taxes.

If we put aside Switzerland, what emerges is a strong, negative relationship between tax progressivity and redistribution. In the region representing high

TABLE 7.3 Average redistribution effects of taxes and transfers, 2000s

	Taxes	Transfers
Nordic	*-2.5*	*38.6*
Denmark	-3.8	41.8
Finland	-0.3	36.9
Norway	0.7	33.2
Sweden	-6.5	42.3
Continental	*0.5*	*28.3*
France	3.8	30.5
Germany	7.3	27.8
Netherlands	-4.1	34.0
Switzerland	-5.0	20.7
Anglo	*5.3*	*20.6*
Australia	4.8	24.6
Canada	5.3	20.8
United Kingdom	1.8	25.1
United States	9.2	11.7

Note: calculated by the author.

Source: Armingeon et al. (2018).

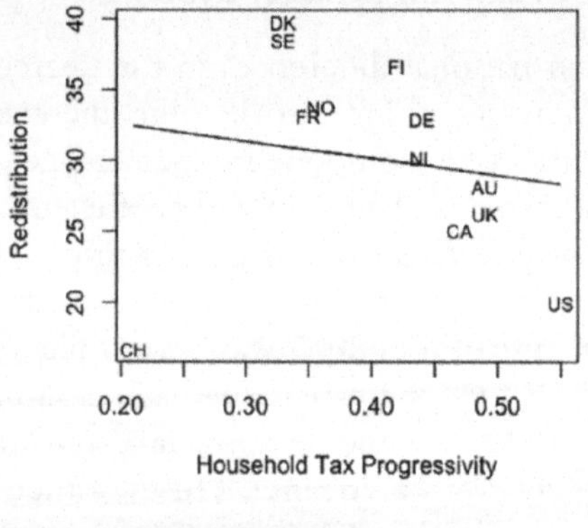

FIGURE 7.6 Tax progressivity and redistribution, 2000s
Notes: r = –0.16; (r = –0.90, sig @ 0.00 without Switzerland)
Sources: Table 7.1; and Beramendi and Rehm (2015).

redistribution/low progressive taxes, we find the Nordic countries and France; in the region with low redistribution/high progressive taxes, we find the Anglo countries. The key takeaway, as Martin and Hertel-Fernandez (2014) note, is that the Nordic countries fund their egalitarian policies not "through soak-the-rich, steeply progressive taxes" but rather via "broad-based taxes that ask all workers to contribute to a generous welfare state." Beramendi and Rehm (2016) remark that this combination of redistributive spending and regressive taxes helps engender broad public support for redistribution in those countries because it mitigates cross-class conflicts over who pays and who benefits.

As table 7.3 shows, the bulk of redistribution is done through transfers. The pattern that emerges is familiar. The Nordic welfare states on average redistribute

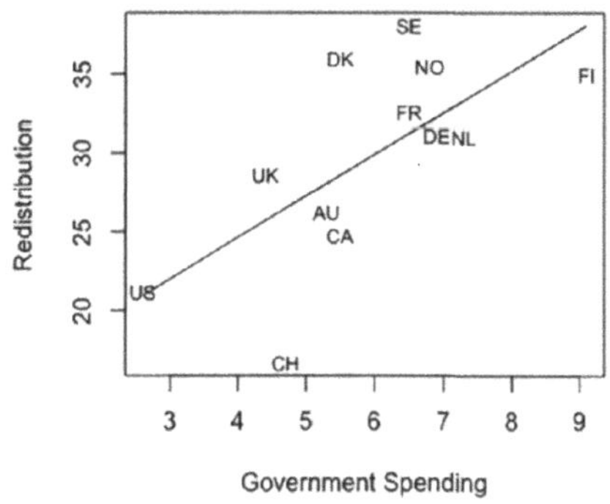

FIGURE 7.7 Average government spending and redistribution, late 1990s to late 2000s
Note: r = 0.67, sig @ 0.01

Sources: Table 7.1 and OECD SOCX (2019a).

more than the Anglo and continental countries. As Pontusson (2005: 156) observes using earlier data, government spending on cash transfers "provides a very good predictor of redistribution." Figure 7.7 plots average government spending on transfers net of old age pension as a percentage of GDP against redistribution from the late 1990s to late 2000s. Higher government spending is associated with higher levels of redistribution as seen in the Nordic countries; lower spending is related to lower redistribution levels as depicted in the Anglo countries.

Redistribution in times of welfare state restructuring

Until the 1970s, governments in affluent OECD countries faced an expansionist fiscal regime. The development of welfare states in the postwar period took place against the backdrop of steady economic growth and increasing tax revenue. Both made the expansion of social welfare fiscally sustainable. The politics of welfare state expansion has been likened to a "process of political credit claiming." In the postwar period, politicians reaped electoral gains for backing social programs that delivered material benefits to various clientele groups—such as recipients of pension, unemployment insurance, disabilities, health, and social assistance (Pierson 1996: 144). Not only did these clientele groups reward politicians, societies came to view the welfare state as a key pillar of modern democratic capitalism, guaranteeing citizenship rights and engendering social stability (Pierson 2001a).

Since the 1970s, policymakers have faced various "problem pressures" that have forced them to undertake social welfare reforms (Huber and Stephens 2015). First, the combination of slower economic growth, weak wage growth among lower and middle classes, and high tax rates has made it difficult for governments to find additional tax revenues to fund rising public expenses fueled in part by past commitments. Second, societies in affluent countries face new social risks stemming from an ageing population, increased incidence of single-parent families, lower fertility rates, higher female labor market participation, and larger immigrant populations. Finally, societies have had to cope with the unsettling effects of transitioning to globalized, service-oriented economies—specifically, deindustrialization, increase in non-standard employment, the substitution effect of technological innovation on occupations, the job dislocation effect of import competition, and offshoring of jobs.

Responding to these economic and demographic challenges has been politically difficult, a process Pierson (1996: 145) calls "an exercise in blame avoidance." While welfare state adjustment disproportionately inflicts costs on specific groups in the electorate such as pensioners and public service employees, its benefits are diffused and typically not felt immediately. As a result, politicians who undertake welfare state reforms risk facing a political backlash from mobilized welfare state clientele groups and can become the target of electoral retribution.

Pierson (2001b) identifies three dimensions of welfare state restructuring: cost containment, re-commodification, and recalibration. Whereas cost containment focuses on controlling social spending levels, re-commodification involves augmenting people's reliance on the labor market for their well-being and taking on greater responsibility for insuring themselves against various risk contingencies. Recalibration focuses on adapting welfare states to better meet contemporary social needs and demands, many of which stem from transitioning to a service economy and demographic changes.

One of the effects of welfare state restructuring is that it impacts total social spending levels. Cost containment and re-commodification decelerate social spending. To the extent that updating of social welfare (a form of recalibration) can involve the creation or expansion of social programs such as childcare and elderly care, social spending levels may stay the same or increase. Table 7.4 provides data on average annual growth of total public social spending per capita for four time periods. The average annual growth rates dropped in each group between the

TABLE 7.4 Average annual growth of total social spending per capita

	1980–1990	1990–2000	2000–2010	2010–2015
Nordic	*4.1*	*1.8*	*2.2*	*1.7*
Denmark	2.9	3.2	2.3	0.9
Finland	5.6	0.4	3.3	1.7
Norway	4.9	2.1	1.7	2.9
Sweden	2.9	1.3	1.4	1.3
Continental	*2.8*	*1.9*	*1.4*	*0.9*
France	6.2	2.9	1.8	1.1
Germany	1.9	2.9	1.3	0.5
Netherlands	2.0	0.1	0.5	0.4
Switzerland	1.1	2.1	1.9	1.7
Anglo	*3.3*	*2.7*	*2.7*	*1.6*
Australia	4.0	5.7	0.7	3.5
Canada	4.1	0.9	2.0	1.2
United Kingdom	2.4	2.6	4.2	0.6
United States	2.5	2.6	3.9	0.9

Note: Per capita figures are at constant prices (2010) and constant PPPs (2010), in US dollars. Averages calculated by the author.

Source: OECD SOCX (2019).

1980s and 1990s, a period coinciding with the beginning of welfare state retrenchment in many countries. Unlike the Nordic and Anglo groups, the continental group saw consecutive declines in average annual growth over the four time periods. Within the Nordic group, Finland and Norway saw the biggest changes in average growth rates across the four time periods. Within the continental group, there has been more stability in spending growth rates over time, with the exception of France between the 1980s and 1990s. There has been more variance in growth rates among the Anglo countries over time, with Australia and Canada experiencing sharp drops. Moreover, contrary to what many believe, spending growth rates actually increased consecutively from the 1980s to 2000s in the United Kingdom and the United States.

This last point is consistent with a broader pattern we see among OECD countries, namely earlier spending levels seem to have an effect on subsequent spending growth. Figure 7.8 plots social spending as a percentage of GDP in 1980 against average growth of social spending per head between 1980 and 2015. In general, high-spending countries in 1980 such as Denmark, Germany, the Netherlands, and Sweden experienced lower subsequent spending growth than lower-spending countries such as Australia, Finland, Norway, United Kingdom, and the United States. In effect, smaller welfare states in the early 1980s grew faster in subsequent decades while larger welfare states grew slower.

How has the restructuring of welfare states since the 1980s impacted redistribution in OECD countries? The short answer is that the social policy reforms instituted since the 1980s have affected welfare states differently. Figure 7.9 shows that redistribution in Finland, the Netherlands, Sweden, the United Kingdom, and the United States in the 2000s was lower relative to their levels in the 1980s. In the Netherlands' case, the change was significant, dropping from 42.2% in the 1980s to 30.2% in the 2000s. On the other hand, redistribution increased in the remaining seven countries, climbing significantly in Switzerland (from 10.3% to 16.7%) and in Denmark (from 30.7% to 39.7%).

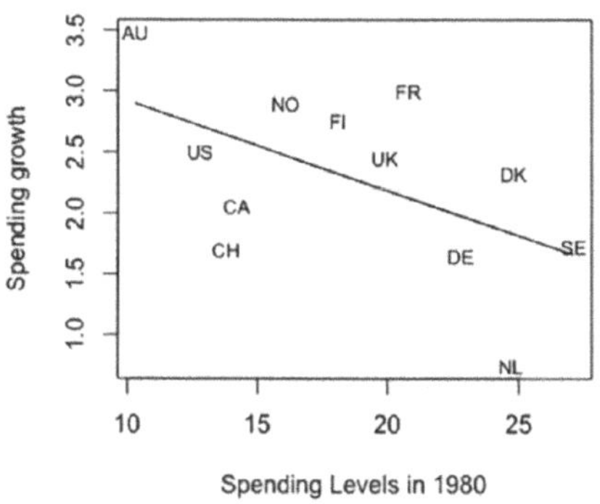

FIGURE 7.8 Spending level in 1980 and spending growth per person, 1980–2015

Note: r = −0.537, sig @ 0.05

Sources: Table 7.4; and OECD SOCX (2019a).

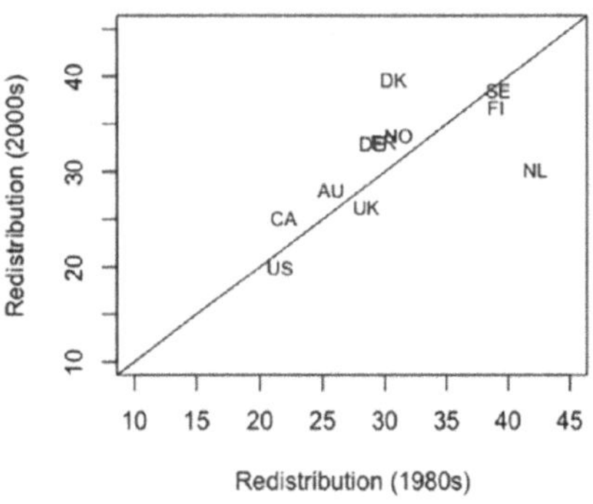

FIGURE 7.9 Redistribution in the 1980s versus in the 2000s

Source: Table 7.1.

Determinants of preferences for redistribution

In the previous section, we explored how the cross-national differences in the level and scope of redistribution is shaped by welfare state regimes. Thus, the focus up to now has been at the aggregate level—looking at the connection between policies and outcomes. In this section, we focus on the microfoundations of redistribution—the formation of individual preferences for redistribution.

Most comparative micro-level studies use survey data from the International Social Survey Programme (ISSP) to evaluate their conjectures about the determinants of redistributive preferences. Some scholars have used data generated from the following question which appears in the ISSP-Social Inequality surveys conducted in 1987, 1992, 1999, and 2009: "It is the responsibility of the government to reduce the differences in income between people with high incomes and those with low incomes." Respondents are asked to choose from one of the following five possible answers: "strongly agree, agree, neither agree nor disagree, disagree, strongly disagree." The other relevant question, which appears in the ISSP-Role of Government module surveys in 1985, 1990, 1996, 2006, and 2016 is: "On the whole, do you think it should or should not be the government's responsibility to reduce income differences between the rich and the poor?" Here, the question contains four possible answers: "definitely should be, probably should be, probably should not be, definitely should not be." ISSP also enables researchers to track individual preferences for specific social programs such as unemployment benefits or public pension.

Table 7.5 provides data on the proportion of people who support redistribution. The data were collected from the ISSP-Role of Government module surveys. Some of the countries we have looked at in previous sections like Denmark, Finland, and the Netherlands are not included for lack of data. Moreover, some yearly data are missing for Canada, France, Sweden, and Switzerland. In general, Europeans are more supportive of redistribution than non-Europeans. The average level of support in the United States is quite low (47.8%) compared to France (77.1%) and Norway (74.4%). Of note, the group-level differences we have detected in previous sections of this chapter do not appear to exist when we look at micro-level data. For example, the share of the population who support redistribution is similar between Sweden and Switzerland and between Great Britain and Norway.

Is the positive association between inequality and redistribution observed at the aggregate level also seen at the micro-level? Recall that the data we examined in previous sections suggested higher levels of (and increases in) market inequality tend

TABLE 7.5 Percentage of people who support redistribution

Year	Australia	Canada	France	Germany	Norway	Sweden	Switzerland	United Kingdom	United States
1985	53.8	—	—	67.4	—	—	—	74.6	38.5
1990	51.2	—	—	69.1	71.7	—	—	73.8	44.5
1996	51.7	50.5	74.2	69.4	73.3	70.6	60.4	67.7	48.0
2006	60.6	67.8	77.7	72.1	74.2	67.7	69.3	69.4	52.2
2016	60.0	—	79.5	80.9	78.2	66.7	69.3	79.5	56.0
Mean	*55.5*	*59.2*	*77.1*	*71.8*	*74.4*	*68.3*	*66.3*	*73.0*	*47.8*

Source: ISSP-Role of Government module surveys, multiple years.

to be correlated with higher levels of (and increases in) redistribution. Neither figure 7.10 nor 7.11 offer evidence that such an association exists at the micro-level. In fact, figure 7.10 points to a negative relationship between redistribution preferences and market inequality: support for redistribution drops as inequality rises.

Further, change in inequality does not appear to be related to change in redistribution preferences, as illustrated in figure 7.11. Although the increase in inequality in Canada and Switzerland was similar, the increase in support for redistribution in Canada was twice as large as in Switzerland. Norway and Sweden experienced similar market inequality changes, yet redistribution preferences in Sweden dropped. Income inequality increased by almost the same amount in Great Britain and the United States and reached comparable levels by the mid-2010s, but there was nearly a 39-point difference between the two countries in terms of public support for redistribution.

Do these results mean that the distribution of income does not influence a person's redistribution preference? The studies we will review next suggest that relative income does matter but its effects on preference for redistribution is mediated by various factors. This explains why there is much cross-national and cross-temporal diversity among OECD countries with regard to the degree to which income is related to redistributive attitudes. Several scholars have posited that individual preferences for redistribution are shaped by one's exposure to labor market risks. Accordingly, social welfare is not simply viewed in terms of performing an inequality reduction function but also an insurance function. Another strand of scholarship examines the role of identity and group homogeneity in shaping preferences for redistribution. Specifically, people's support of redistribution to the poor is influenced by their sense of social affinity, whether they have a common religious, racial, or ethnic identity with them. Thus, redistribution preferences are reflective of income interacting with other individual- and contextual-level determinants. What follows is a discussion of a selected body of literature related to both strands of thinking about the formation of redistributive preferences.

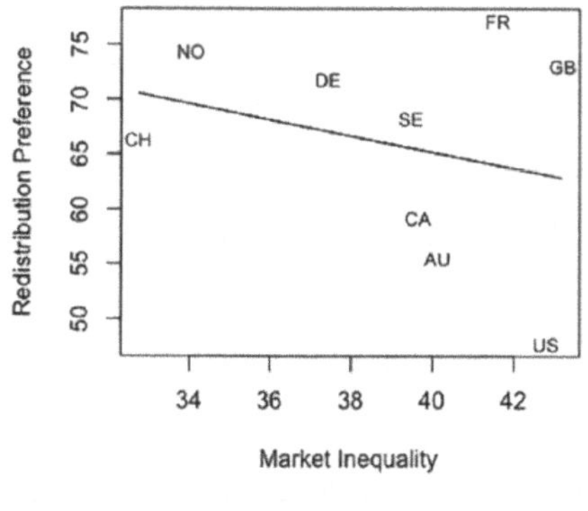

FIGURE 7.10 Average market inequality and redistribution preferences, between 1980s and 2010s

Note: r = −0.274

Sources: Tables 7.1 and 7.6.

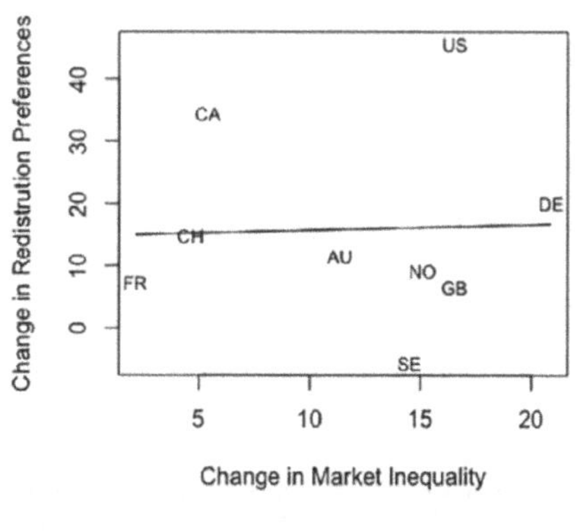

FIGURE 7.11 Changes in redistribution preferences and market inequality

Note: r = 0.037

Sources: Tables 7.1 and 7.6.

Insurance models

Based on the logic of the MRR model, which we elaborated at the beginning of the chapter, lower-income individuals are expected to support redistribution while higher-income individuals are not. However, what if social welfare had a dual function: to reduce the income gap between the rich and poor and to redistribute the risk of income loss? Baldwin (1990: 1) was among the first to elaborate the insurance view of social spending: "The modern welfare state decisively advanced society's ability to treat each of its members equally . . . less by redistributing wealth than by reapportioning the costs of risk and mischance." According to the insurance approach to social welfare, individuals focus on the future utility of social protection, not on the current utility as the MRR model assumes. The willingness to pay for social protection today is based on the probability that one will need it to hedge against future risks. Thus, the material self-interest of individuals has an intertemporal element when redistribution is viewed as a mechanism to mitigate risk.

Moene and Wallerstein (2008a, 2008b) develop a model that combines redistributive and insurance motives to predict the relationship between income inequality and public support for welfare expenditures. They distinguish between two types of welfare programs: programs that insure people against income loss due to layoffs, accidents, or illness and programs that benefit the public at large, whether employed or not, such as health care, pension, family benefits, and means-tested social assistance. Moene and Wallerstein find that higher market inequality (whereby the income gap between the median and average income widens) is associated with lower support for programs that insure people against income loss, while inequality has little or no association with support for programs that benefit the public at large. A key assumption underpinning their model is that demand for insurance rises as income increases. This explains why rising inequality decreases support for insurance programs—the willingness of the median income earner to purchase insurance (via taxes) declines as their income falls further below the mean income. Using the same logic, their model predicts and their empirical evidence confirm that demand for redistributive insurance is greater in more egalitarian societies.

Iversen and Soskice (2001) probe how the variance in the redistribution preferences among workers is linked to differences in the composition of skills among them. They argue that workers who have invested in less portable skills, such as those specific to industries or firms, are more exposed to labor market risks. Therefore, they will be more supportive of social protection than workers who possess general skills which are more marketable across occupations (see also Cusack et al. 2006). The idea is that those who have invested in specific skills face a higher cost of layoff because the market value of their skills is tied to the industry or firm in which they were previously employed. They might face longer unemployment spells as they search for jobs that fit their specific skills. Iversen and Soskice discover strong suggestive evidence that workers who possess higher levels of skill specification support greater social protection.

Furthermore, drawing on the logic of MRR, Iversen and Soskice posit that income is inversely related to demand for redistribution, as illustrated in figure 7.12. The vertical axis represents preference for redistributive spending, while the horizontal axis marks the income of the median voter (M) and the mean income (m). The figure also plots the relationship between redistribution preference and income

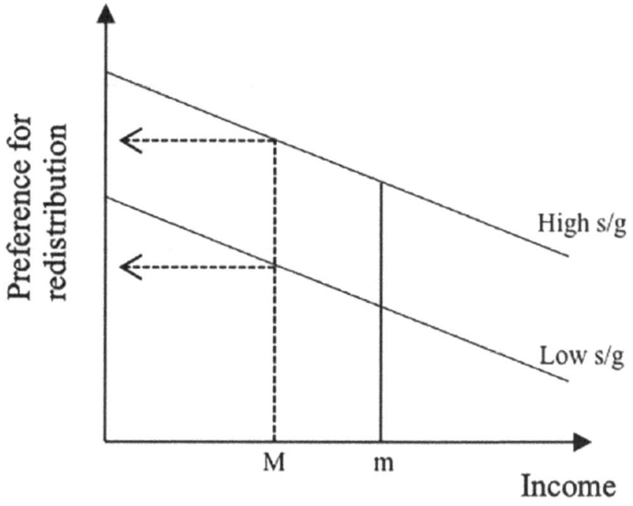

FIGURE 7.12 Iversen and Soskice's asset model
Source: Iversen, Torben, and David Soskice. 2001. "An Asset Theory of Social Policy Preferences." American Political Science Review 95(4): 878. Reproduced with permission.

for a low and a high ratio of specific to general skills (s/g). Note that for either low s/g or high s/g, income and support for redistribution are negatively related. However, among high-income workers, the degree of support for redistribution varies depending on whether they possess specific skills. Moreover, the median worker is expected to be more supportive of redistribution in a high s/g setting.

Rehm's (2011) study aims to identify the key factors shaping individual preferences for unemployment benefits. Rehm finds evidence suggesting that support for more unemployment benefits decreases with income but increases with the risk of unemployment. In this study, the unemployment rate at the occupational level—for example, among professionals, service workers, plant workers—serves as an estimator of an individual's unemployment risk. According to Rehm, because an individual's exposure to the risk of unemployment declines as income rises, higher-income individuals are net losers of unemployment insurance programs.

Based on his statistical results, Rehm estimates that moving from low to high income decreases the probability of preferring more or much more public spending on unemployment benefits from 0.47 to 0.25. Further, moving from low to high unemployment risk is predicted to increase the probability of support from 0.32 to 0.50. Rehm probes how individual support for unemployment benefit translates into actual policy outcomes. He argues that if a majority of individuals is more or less at risk of becoming unemployed, which implies that poor, middle-class, and perhaps certain well-off citizens can anticipate benefiting from unemployment benefits, their combined electoral influence pressures governments to increase unemployment benefits. Rehm finds that countries with more (less) equally distributed unemployment risks have higher (lower) unemployment replacement rates.

The studies we have reviewed so far contend that individuals support social protection to hedge against the probability of unemployment or low marketability of specific skills. Rueda and Thewissen (2018) argue that demand for redistribution can also be shaped by the degree to which one's job is susceptible to the risk of automation. Occupations that are more routine task intensive such as office and customer services clerks and various occupational trades (metal, machinery, printing, and precision) workers are more vulnerable to being automated. Technological innovations have made it possible for these occupations, which are largely devoid of "complex and abstract task structures," to "be partitioned into step-by-step rules" and substituted by computers or robots (ibid: 140).

They find that individuals who work in routine occupations are more inclined to support redistribution. Moreover, the occupational risk of automation has a stronger positive effect on support for redistribution than the effect associated with skill specific risk. Although their data suggest that higher wages and skills are found in occupations with low routine task intensity, they warn that such a relationship is rather weak. Included among the less routine occupations are higher-paying, higher-skilled professions like general managers, health practitioners, and engineers but also lower-paying, lower-skilled professions such as drivers and personal and protective services workers.

Social affinity models

Another strand of research on social welfare holds that people's level of support for redistribution is influenced by the identity of the beneficiaries of redistribution. This literature documents that people are likely to feel generous or altruistic toward others if they share a common identity with them or if there is no social "distance" between them "along some salient dimension," as Alesina and Glaser (2004: 134) point out. In focusing on racial and ethnic differences, they note that "when there are significant numbers of minorities among the poor, then the majority population can be roused against transferring money to people who are different from themselves" (ibid). The majority's reluctance to support redistribution is not due strictly to their material self-interest but rather by the fact that the poor and members of the majority are divided along racial or ethnic lines. In fact, many scholars who have developed social affinity models argue that individuals are willing at times to be altruistic toward the less fortunate with whom they share common experiences or common identities, what some refer to as parochial altruism (Lupu and Pontusson 2011; Rueda 2018).

Drawing on the concept of social affinity, Lupu and Pontusson (2011) argue that support for redistribution among middle-income voters rises when the income distance between the middle and poor become compressed and the income distance between the middle and the rich becomes more dispersed. The proximity of income between the poor and middle-income voters—a more compressed 50–10 earnings ratio—is what rouses feelings of social affinity among middle-income individuals with the poor and prompts them to support redistribution. This income-based social affinity and middle-income support for redistribution dissipate, however, when the 50–10 ratio increases and income differences in the upper half of the income distribution get smaller. In short, their study sheds light on the question of why support for redistribution among middle-income voters varies cross-nationally and cross-temporally. Their micro-level model also provides insight on why redistributive spending is higher in some OECD countries than others and varies within countries across time. Their evidence suggests that "governments . . . tend to pursue more redistributive policies when the structure of inequality favors a coalition between middle-income voters and the poor" (ibid: 332).

Using individual-level data from the European Social Survey from 2002 to 2012, Rueda (2018) investigates how the level of population homogeneity influences the redistribution preferences of the poor and the rich. One school of thought is that the poor and the rich reap "moral" benefits by supporting redistribution when group homogeneity is high. Such parochial altruism—willingness to care for the well-being of in-group members—results in higher support for redistribution among the poor and rich alike. Another line of argument holds that the poor withdraw their support for more redistribution when group heterogeneity is high, essentially forfeiting the additional benefits they would have obtained from greater redistribution.

Rueda offers an alternative argument. Ethnocultural considerations have a greater effect on the redistributive preferences of the rich than on those of the poor. The support for redistribution among the rich increases (decreases) when societies are more (less) homogeneous. In contrast, the poor's level of redistribution support barely changes as societies become less or more heterogenous. The fact that the redistributive attitudes of the poor remain stable in the face of different levels of group homogeneity, as Rueda (2018: 236) notes, suggests that "poor altruism is trumped by material incentives." For affluent voters, however, support for redistribution is conditioned by the level of group homogeneity.

In addition to income, risk, and group homogeneity, factors such as homeownership and religiosity have been shown to influence attitudes on redistribution. Ansell (2014) argues that homeownership equips individuals with self-supplied means to hedge against various life risks. Because rising home prices add to individuals' stock of wealth and enable them to obtain larger home equity loans, homeownership can lessen individuals' reliance on public forms of insurance. As a result, homeowners are likely to be less supportive of public social protection during housing booms, an argument Ansell corroborates using survey data from the United States, the United Kingdom, and ISSP.

Scheve and Stasavage (2006) contend that religious individuals are able to fall back on their faith and communal material assistance to support themselves against adverse circumstances. Given the private buffer effect of religious participation, the authors show that religious people, in contrast to secular individuals, are less likely to support public provision of social insurance. Rehm (2011) and Rueda (2018) also find evidence of religiosity's dampening effect on redistribution preferences.

It is commonplace for statistical analyses on redistribution to control for age, gender, and education for they have been found to shape redistribution preferences. Income and job security are likely to weigh more heavily on the minds of older individuals than younger individuals partly because they are closer to retirement and they face more obstacles in seeking reemployment. Women have greater propensity to favor redistribution because they are more likely to be out of the labor market for a longer time than men given their role as primary caregivers in a family. Individuals with higher levels of education are less likely to support redistribution primarily because they can leverage their talents and skills to secure better paying and longer-term employment that come with greater job security.

In addition to these demographic factors, several economic factors influence individual support for redistribution. The unemployed, who are currently drawing on public transfers, are more supportive of redistribution. In contrast, the self-employed, who rely on hired hands and flexible labor markets, are more likely to oppose redistribution. Finally, union workers express greater support for redistribution since it provides a layer of protection against the kinds of labor market risks they are exposed to and reinforces unionism's egalitarian values.

Macro-level determinants of redistribution

A key takeaway of the recent literature exploring the microfoundations of redistribution is that preferences for redistribution are not mere reflections of individuals' desires to maximize current income. Individual preferences can reflect insurance motives, in which case material self-interest is defined intertemporally, or can reflect other-regarding motives such as parochial altruism. Still, this literature has been faulted, in the words of Pontusson and Weisstanner (2018: 33–34) "for losing sight of redistribution as a macro-level outcome." Their criticism is two-fold. First, they note that until recently much of the literature on redistribution preferences did not investigate systematically how individual preferences affect political behavior, are aggregated nationally, and brought to bear on policy outcomes (notable exceptions are Ansell 2014; Lupu and Pontusson 2011; Rehm 2011). Second, they are skeptical of the notion that redistribution outcomes can be traced back directly to voter preferences. Next, we explore selected works that connect micro- and macro-level analysis of redistribution.

Political-institutional factors

There are several political-institutional factors that influence redistribution—partisanship, voter turnout, proportionality, and vocational training systems. We will elaborate the first two factors in detail and conclude with briefer treatments of the last two. The literature on redistribution asserts that Left and Christian democratic governments distinctly shape redistribution. Specifically, Bradley et al. (2003) and Huber and Stephens (2014) observe that while welfare state expansion in the postwar period has occurred during both incumbencies, social democratic parties have been more committed to inequality reduction than Christian democratic parties, who instead prioritize income stabilization. As a result, longer periods of left-wing governments have been linked to welfare states whose tax-transfer structures lead to more redistribution than in countries with longer Christian democratic incumbencies.

Figure 7.13 looks at the association between average redistribution and frequency of Left governments between 1980 and 2010. Redistribution levels are higher in countries that have had longer periods of Left governments. Although simple correlations and pooled data analyses (Bradley et al. 2003; Cusack et al. 2006; Huber and Stephens 2014) suggest partisanship is a determinant of the cross-national differences in the level of redistribution, it does not offer much analytical leverage in terms of explaining change in redistribution. Kenworthy and Pontusson (2005: 455) note that the increase in redistribution seen in several rich OECD countries between the 1980s and 1990s coincides with a general decline in Left incumbency during that time. Moreover, some of the countries that saw large increases in redistribution during this time period, such as Australia and Germany, "are not distinguished by a history of Left-party dominance or . . . by significant political advances by Left parties" (ibid).

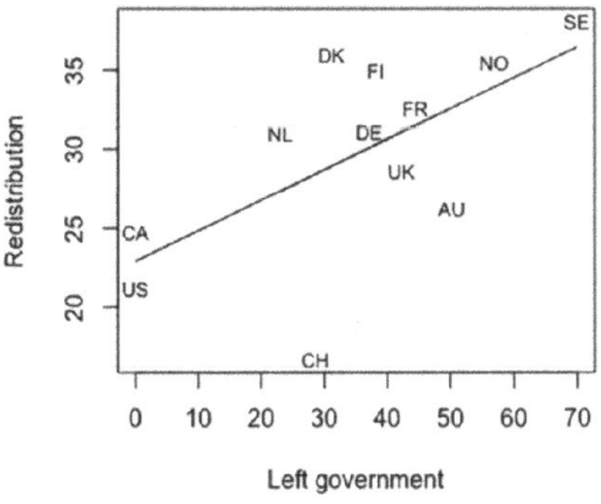

FIGURE 7.13 Average redistribution and left incumbency, 1980 to 2010
Note: r = 0.621, sig @ 0.01

Sources: Table 7.1 and Armingeon et al. (2018).

This raises an important question: How do the redistribution preferences of individuals filter into the electoral arena and affect partisanship, and ultimately policy outcomes? Rueda (2018: 238) finds that individuals who support redistribution are more likely to vote for a Left party—he estimates 70% more likely. A key takeaway of his analysis is that welfare chauvinism, which is often whipped up by the populist right, has not weakened the support for redistribution among lower-income individuals and, accordingly, not undermined their political affiliation with Left parties. Lupu and Pontusson (2011) argue that middle-income individuals—who are the pivotal actors in their study—are more likely to back Left parties and espouse pro-redistribution policies when the income distance between them and the poor is smaller than the income distance between them and the affluent. Alternatively, when bottom-half inequality is greater than top-half inequality, the voting tendencies of middle-income voters favor Right parties, reflecting their opposition to redistribution. In short, as Lupu and Pontusson (2011: 332) remark, "the structure of inequality shapes the coalitional proclivities and policy preferences of middle-income voters."

Ansell (2014) contends that during periods of home price appreciation, right-wing homeowners are much more likely to support cutbacks in redistribution than left-identifying homeowners even though house price booms have made both more affluent. Accordingly, because Right parties draw more support from homeowners than Left parties and the opinions of these potential voters are now more permissive of lowering redistributive spending, a home price boom "creates a greater electoral opportunity" for Right parties to undertake this policy change which would have been more difficult to do under different housing market circumstances (ibid: 387).

Voter turnout plays a crucial role in translating individual preferences into policy outcomes such as compensatory redistribution. The MRR model's predictive power hinges on the condition that all eligible voters actually vote, which would presumably heighten the government's responsiveness to the preferences of low-income voters. Voter turnout also figures in the power-resources theory, for the ability of unions to impact policy and of Left parties to win elections depends on the electoral participation of low-income voters. Kenworthy and Pontusson (2005) point out that welfare state regimes are more responsive to the preferences of low-income workers when voter turnout is high.

Scholars have long claimed that the political clout of low-income citizens is enhanced when voter turnout is high. Underlying this claim is the notion that there are income-based disparities in electoral turnout (Mahler et al. 2014). The income skew decreases (increases) as average turnout increases (decreases). Accordingly, when turnout is high elected officials are much more inclined to be responsive to the preferences of low-income citizens. One of the policy implications is that the redistribution effect of the welfare state should be higher in countries with higher turnout to reflect the higher favorability for redistribution among low-income voters (and middle-income voters under different risk-related circumstances). Figure 7.14 plots average voter turnout against average redistribution between the early 1980s and early 2010s. A positive association exists between voter turnout and redistribution: higher levels of redistribution coincide with higher rates of voter turnout. Using panel data, Iversen (2005), Kenworthy and Pontusson (2005), Lupu and Pontusson (2011), and Mahler et al. (2014) also find evidence of a robust positive connection.

Particular types of skills formation systems and electoral rules can be more conducive to higher redistribution levels than others. Countries with extensive vocational training systems such as the Netherlands, Norway, and Sweden tend to have higher redistribution levels than countries with educational systems geared toward general skills formation such as Australia, Canada, the United Kingdom, and the United States. The reason for this association is that specific skills are usually more prevalent in economies with extensive vocational training. Therefore, in these economies public demand for compensatory redistribution is likely to be higher because those who possess specific skills are more vulnerable to labor market risks. Empirical studies by Cusack et al. (2006) and Iversen (2005) find that vocational training systems have a positive effect on redistribution.

Redistribution levels are likely to be higher (and less prone to major cutbacks) in proportional representation (PR) systems than in majoritarian electoral systems. There are two reasons for this association. First, as Iversen and Soskice (2006a) note, PR is conducive to the formation of center-left party coalitions, which are more disposed to promoting compensatory redistribution given that many of their

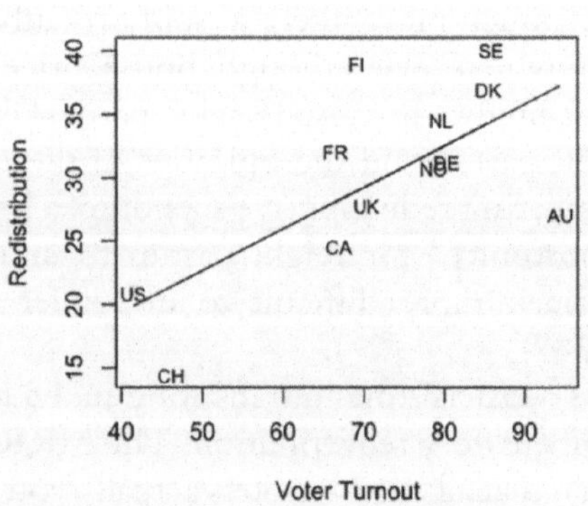

FIGURE 7.14 Average voter turnout and redistribution, early 1980s to early 2010s
Note: r = 0.684, sig @ 0.01
Sources: Table 7.1 and Armingeon et al. (2018).

core constituents are exposed to the unemployment risk. Second, PR systems help parties commit credibly to long-term social protection schemes; the presence of multiple parties, some of which wield veto power, makes it difficult to undertake major policy changes as we discussed in Chapter 3. Therefore, PR facilitates continuity in redistribution spending or smaller spending cuts when PR interacts with Left cabinets. The claim that PR is positively linked to redistribution has been corroborated in empirical studies by Cusack et al. (2006), Iversen (2005), and Mahler et al. (2014), although Lupu and Pontusson's (2011) findings contradict such a claim.

Globalization and redistribution

How does economic globalization affect redistribution? There are two schools of thought regarding the redistribution effect of globalization. The efficiency argument holds that globalization pressures governments to trim public spending and taxation rates. This argument rests on two key pillars. First, a trade-off exists between public spending and market competition. A large public sector requires either higher taxation levels or borrowing or some combination. Higher taxes add to the cost of production by increasing labor cost, decrease corporate profitability, and hurt economic growth. Public sector borrowing diverts money away from the private sector where it could fund investment ("crowding out" effect) and raises interest rates. Thus, higher taxes and public borrowing undermine corporate growth and competitiveness. Second, because globalization enhances factor mobility, governments are forced to refrain from pursuing interventionist policies out of concern that such measures might embolden investors and companies to move to another country. In short, the efficiency theory holds that globalization will lower redistribution over time (Garrett 1998a).

On the other hand, the compensation argument holds that redistribution (of income and risk) is necessary to make economic globalization possible from both a political and economic standpoint. The argument that redistribution is a precondition for globalization rests on two important pillars. First, governments elicit popular support for economic openness by providing compensatory redistribution to its citizens. As we discussed earlier, redistribution functions often as a form of public insurance against labor market risks. To the extent that globalization exposes more people to more market risks, provoking support for protectionism, redistribution counteracts both by buffering individuals against adverse market conditions. Second, redistribution (defined broadly to include public services) generates positive economic effects. Companies gain from redistribution because public provision of education and active labor market policies expand the supply of skilled labor and increase worker productivity, enabling firms to improve their global competitiveness (Boix 1998, 2011). Further, redistribution efforts indirectly help companies' bottom lines by shoring up the disposable income of low-income households and, in turn, bolstering private consumption. In sum, a "virtuous circle" exists between government redistribution and economic globalization (Garrett 1998a; Hays et al. 2005).

Figure 7.15 looks at the association between trade globalization and redistribution on a decade basis starting from the 1980s to the 2010s. The data on trade globalization come from the KOF globalization index (Gygli et al. 2019). Trade globalization, rather than financial globalization, is examined here because the compensation

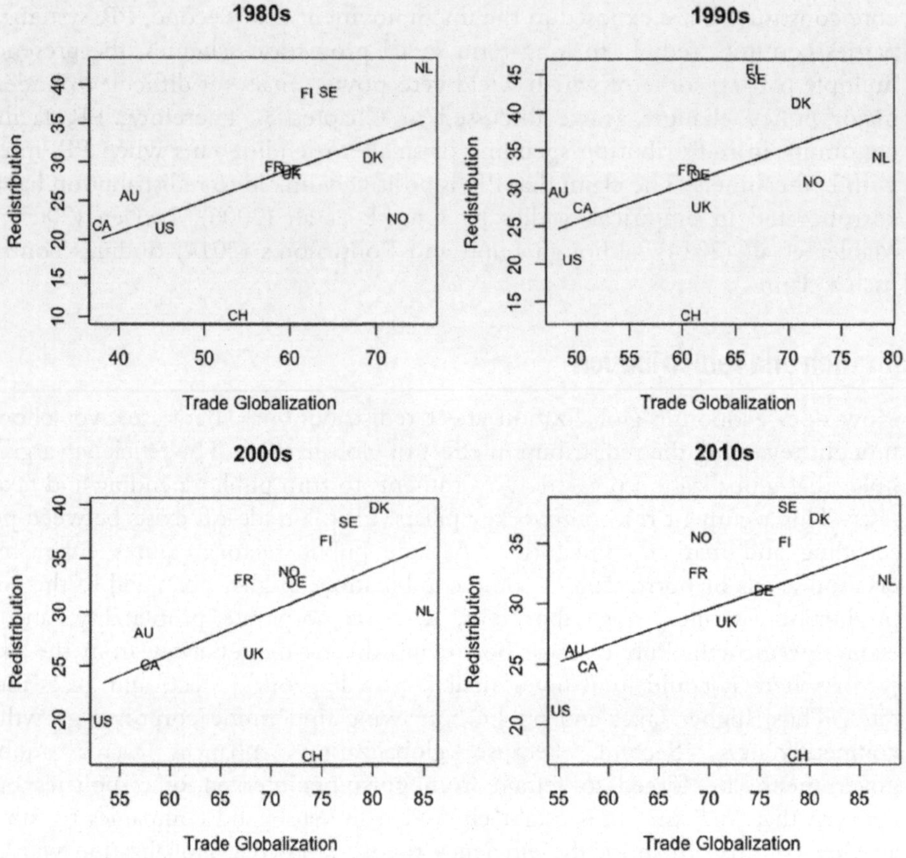

FIGURE 7.15 Trade globalization and redistribution, 1980s to 2010s
Note: averages calculated by the author.
Sources: Table 7.1 and Gygli et al. (2019).

argument is commonly assessed using this measure (see Busemeyer 2009; Cameron 1979; Hays et al. 2005; Rehm 2011; Rodrik 1998). In general, government redistribution and economic openness are positively related, a pattern that Cameron (1979) and Rodrik (1998) found in their widely referenced studies. The countries that have consistently recorded the highest levels of trade globalization such as Denmark, Finland, the Netherlands, Norway, and Sweden have also had some of the highest levels of redistribution between the 1980s and 2010s. Economic openness in these small European countries, Cameron notes, "is the best single predictor of the growth . . . in the scope of the public economy." Similarly, Rodrik (1998: 1028) remarks that "the scope of government has been larger, not smaller, in economies taking greater advantage of world markets." In contrast, Australia, Canada, and the United States consistently have had the lowest levels of economic openness and some of the lowest redistribution levels.

As figure 7.15 illustrates, this positive association has not vanished as trade globalization has increased from the 1980s to 2010s, an observation largely corroborated by pooled time-series analyses. In their study of 17 OECD countries from 1960 to 2000, Hays et al. (2005) find that imports as a percentage of GDP have a substantively and statistically significant positive effect on public social spending. Focusing on a period from 2001 to 2004, Rehm's (2011) panel data analysis also uncovers a positive, statistically significant link between trade openness and unemployment benefit generosity. However, Busemeyer's (2009) work reveals that the positive connection between trade openness and public social spending has weakened over time, losing "much of its explanatory power" between 1995 and 2000.

Although figure 7.15 and empirical studies suggest that economic openness and compensatory redistribution go hand in hand, there are two developments that support insights related to the efficiency argument. First, taxation levels have become less progressive in rich OECD countries. Because of the increased mobility of capital and of high-skilled workers, governments have cut corporate and top-income taxes as a way to attract and retain them (Boix 2011; Cusack and Beramendi 2006). In order to address the persistent demand for social protection and public social services while collecting less corporate and high-income tax revenue, governments have increasingly relied on taxes on labor and consumption to finance social spending. Egger et al. (2019) find that the reallocation of tax burden has fallen heavily on the less mobile segments of the population. The result is that the taxation system has become less effective in achieving redistribution.

Another development is that governments have become more committed to the idea of fiscal conservatism and expanding market governance in general. This shift is partly attributed to government concerns about the risk of capital flight and higher public borrowing costs. This change in the direction of public policy has not translated necessarily to lower public social spending, as illustrated in table 7.2. However, it has led governments to reduce welfare generosity, contain spending on cash transfer benefits, and lower the replacement rate of unemployment insurance—the primary source of income stabilization for the unemployed.

Conclusion

The advances in the study of redistribution since the MRR model surfaced shed valuable light on why the level of redistribution is not always responsive to changes in income distribution. The research that explores the microfoundations of redistribution preferences tells us that individuals' attitudes toward redistribution is not determined simply by their current income. Insurance models of redistribution suggest that individuals' redistribution preferences are also shaped by their current and expected exposure to labor market risks. Moreover, personal attitudes towards redistribution can be influenced by social affinity considerations. A key takeaway of this research is that people who are not likely to benefit from redistribution programs may still support these programs knowing that they and the programs' beneficiaries share a common identity. Another strand of literature links popular support for redistribution to people's fairness perceptions (see Limberg 2020; Scheve and Stasavage 2016). Historically, increased support for raising taxes on the rich has occurred in the face of events such as the two world wars and the Great Recession of 2007–2009, which imposed unequal burdens between ordinary people and the affluent class. These events triggered growing support for tax progressivity on compensatory fairness grounds.

In addition to exploring the factors that influence people's redistribution preferences, this chapter investigated the sources of cross-national differences in the magnitude of redistribution. The variations in the redistribution levels among the three country clusters are partly attributed to the different configurations of their welfare states. Despite the welfare state reforms that have taken place since the 1970s, the Nordic welfare states have continued to be more redistributive even though their taxation systems have relied increasingly on regressive taxes. Countries with long-term Left government incumbencies, higher voter turnout, proportional representation electoral systems, and non-general skills formation systems tend to have higher levels of redistribution. The evidence we examined suggests that these patterns have been resilient in the face of globalization.

Key terms

Cash benefits

Progressive tax

Redistribution

Regressive tax

Right-skewed income distribution

Robin-Hood paradox

Social affinity

Welfare state

Discussion questions

- What does the MRR model argue, and does the empirical evidence support it?
- Describe the redistribution trends in the Nordic, continental, and Anglo countries since the 1980s.
- What factors influence individual preferences for redistribution?
- How can we explain the cross-national differences in the level of redistributive spending?

Further reading

Alesina, Alberto, and Edward L. Glaser. 2004. *Fighting Poverty in the US and Europe: A World of Difference*. Oxford: Oxford University Press.

Discusses different explanations used to account for the cross-Atlantic differences in the level of redistribution.

Huber, Evelyne, and John D. Stephens. 2001. *Development and Crisis of the Welfare State: Parties and Policies in Global Markets*. Chicago: The University of Chicago Press.

Analyzes the historical development of welfare states in advanced political economies.

Rueda, David, and Daniel Stegmueller. 2019. *Who Wants What? Redistribution Preferences in Comparative Perspective*. New York: Cambridge University Press.

Argues that individual preferences for redistribution are shaped by expected future income, concern with crime fueled by inequality, and considerations of social affinity.

Scheve, Kenneth, and David Stasavage. 2016. *Taxing the Rich: A History of Fiscal Fairness in the United States and Europe*. Princeton, NJ: Princeton University Press.

Argues that, in the twentieth century, popular demand to compensate for the unequal sacrifices in mass warfare led to significant increases in the top marginal rates of income and inheritance taxation.

CHAPTER

8

Conclusion—current directions in CPE

In surveying the field of comparative political economy, this book has intentionally kept the varieties of capitalism approach on the sidelines for the most part. This might seem like an odd choice to readers who have come to view the VoC approach as the dominant CPE paradigm since the 2000s. However, as one of my colleagues once pointed out, "there's so much more to CPE than the VoC approach." After reading some or all of the previous chapters, I hope readers have developed an appreciation of the various areas of inquiry to which CPE scholars have devoted their attention. Still, the book, as it stands, is likely to disappoint some for what it does not say about recent research frontiers in CPE. The aim of this concluding chapter is to discuss some of those research frontiers.

There are several recent research endeavors that have emerged in response to the VoC approach. Here, we will focus on two in particular. One of those research endeavors concerns investigating patterns of liberalization in advanced political economies. While many VoC scholars contend that the institutional arrangements that differentiate LMEs and CMEs have been resilient and resistant to change, critics of this view have argued that the process of liberalization in advanced political economies has transformed over time the way in which coordination takes place in the realms of industrial relations, corporate governance, labor market relations, finance, and other spheres of the national political economy. This debate has spawned research that seeks to understand how liberalization, as a common trajectory of change, has transformed national political economic institutions and whether it has brought about convergence between the two types of capitalism.

Another research frontier reflects the renewed interest in exploring the "demand drivers" of growth and employment. By assigning primacy to supply-side institutions—for example, skills development and industrial relations systems—VoC scholars have often overlooked the effects of household consumption, government spending, and exports on macroeconomic outcomes. This strand of scholarship has found a variety of "growth models" in advanced political economies, distinguished by their unique demand-side dynamics and distributional effects. In the first section of this chapter, we will elaborate on these two research frontiers.

DOI: 10.4324/9780429199462-8

This chapter will also survey the emerging literature on populism. The rise of populism in advanced democracies has prompted scholars to investigate its roots and effects. Comparativists have been particularly interested in determining the importance of economic drivers of populism relative to cultural drivers. Whereas some scholars are of the view that economic hardship brought on by global trade, technological change, and the financial crisis of 2007–2009 has fueled voter support for populists, others claim that it is people's hostilities toward immigration, multiculturalism, or racial and gender equality that have inclined them to support populists. Moreover, scholars have devoted more attention to the political and economic effects of populism now that populists have been in national parliaments as well as in governments for more than a decade. We explore these two areas of analysis in the second part of the chapter.

Beyond varieties of capitalism

Liberalization as gradual change

At the heart of the VoC approach is the premise that the institutional practices which distinguish LMEs and CMEs have not converged despite facing common trends like globalization and technological change. Proponents of the VoC perspective argue that the deep historical roots of these divergent institutional modes of economic coordination have enabled them to survive past and present challenges. Their enduring stability and resiliency are the product of employers' continued preference to coordinate their actions with other actors through indigenous institutions. VoC scholars, of course, acknowledge that both systems have witnessed institutional changes over time. However, they are of the view that such changes have been introduced by employers as means of adapting, not replacing, existing institutions to help them cope better with changing economic conditions. Institutional changes have amounted to modifications that reinforce the institutional practices by which actors have coordinated their actions, thus preserving the divergent coordination logics characteristic of LMEs and CMEs.

On the other hand, critics of the VoC approach argue that the emergence of common trends across advanced political economies has unhinged the institutional arrangements that made strategic coordination possible in CMEs (see Baccaro and Howell 2017; Streeck 2009). The result is that CMEs now feature institutional practices and political-economic outcomes that look increasingly like those found in LMEs. In the realm of industrial relations, employers have sought to expand their discretion over wage determination, human resource decisions, and workplace organization, leading to decentralized and flexible management-labor arrangements. In the realm of corporate governance, the practice of maximizing shareholder value is now prevalent in firms across CMEs, a development largely owed to the fact that these firms are increasingly relying on capital markets to meet their funding needs. In their efforts to increase returns on equity, firms have downsized their workforce and relied more on markets to organize their relations with other economic actors. Moreover, social protections in CMEs, which have been complementary to strategic coordination particularly with respect to skills development, have been reduced. In sum, according to this line of argument, these liberalization changes have fundamentally transformed CMEs to such an extent that their institutions are no longer conducive to strategic coordination.

Following the pioneering work of Streeck and Thelen (2005) and Thelen (2009), a new wave of scholarship has emerged in the past decade that seeks to sort out the two competing viewpoints described earlier. The main criticism it levels against the continuity argument is that it overlooks the evidence pointing to the transformative effects of incremental change in different areas of the national political economy. The main criticism of the discontinuity argument is that it neglects the evidence suggesting that CMEs have followed different trajectories of liberalization, leading to different institutional reconfigurations and distributional effects. Rather than converging toward LMEs, liberalization in CMEs has taken on different forms, proceeded at different speeds, and produced different results. Next, we briefly elaborate each point.

Streeck and Thelen (2005: 8) caution against the tendency to link "incremental with adaptive and reproductive minor change," as this "tends to reduce most or all observable changes to adjustment for the purpose of stability." In fact, as Streeck and Thelen point out, slow moving changes such as liberalization often produce transformative effects over time, something that some VoC proponents have overlooked given their tendency to equate small changes with institutional maintenance. Liberalization, a type of political economic change in which market dynamics are allowed increasingly to govern economic transactions, has occurred incrementally and continuously for the most part across advanced political economies since the late 1970s. Although some measures to liberalize economic transactions proved anything but subtle, such as Prime Minister Thatcher's sweeping deregulation of Great Britain's labor market in the late 1970s/early 1980s, liberalization has often been undertaken by actors in a discreet and piecemeal fashion by exploiting the inherent ambiguities and malleability of the institutions within which they interact. These actors have redefined the functions of institutional arrangements so that they better serve their interests or have subverted institutional rules when they undermine their interests. What these endogenous changes have in common is that they have, to varying degrees, rendered political economic institutions more market-accommodating.

IN FOCUS BOX 8.1 TYPES OF GRADUAL INSTITUTIONAL CHANGE

Scholars have identified four different modes of gradual change: displacement, layering, drift, and conversion (Streeck and Thelen 2005). Change through displacement involves the substitution of new rules for old ones. Displacement often takes on the form of deregulation: when existing rules in a particular realm of a national political economy are gradually replaced—via a succession of policy reforms—by more market-accommodating ones (Thelen 2014). Change through layering involves the addition of new rules or institutions on top of existing ones, leading to changes in the operation of and in the level of public support for the original rules or institutions. For example, private retirement account options have been introduced alongside the public pension system in many advanced political economies. According to Hacker (2005), the growth of 401(k)s and IRA private retirement accounts in the United States has had the effect of shifting political support away from Social Security, making it more difficult to pass reforms that address the long-term sustainability of the public pension system.

Change through drift occurs when a set of rules is not updated in the face of changing external conditions. By failing to upkeep an existing institution as external conditions change, that institution's performance may shift as time passes and cause it to produce disparate outcomes over time. Powerful actors who become dissatisfied with an institution can deliberately neglect its maintenance, hoping that this strategy of "passive aggression" will erode over time the constraints that an institution imposes on their actions. As we discussed in Chapter 2, the liberalization of Germany's industrial relations arrangements has occurred largely via institutional drift. In the face of changing circumstances—German reunification and deindustrialization—German employers have opted not to extend traditional industrial relations practices to the eastern part of the country or to the emerging service sector. As a result, collective bargaining covers a much smaller share of Germany's workforce, leading to wider disparities in income distribution.

Lastly, change through conversion involves repurposing institutions to achieve objectives that are not part of their original design. Like drift, conversion keeps formal rules unchanged thus creating the appearance of institutional stability. In fact, the changes that both modes of gradual change produce are "subterranean": whereas drift leads to changes in the effects of institutional rules, conversion amounts to changes in the interpretation of formal rules (Hacker et al. 2015). Conversion has been detected in various political economic domains across advanced political economies. For example, Levy's (2008) work on the French political economy shows that the state's interventionist capacity, which played a crucial role in the modernization of the country's industries in the post-WWII period, was redeployed in the 1980s to address labor market challenges. Not only has institutional conversion reduced the state's direct presence in the economy, it has rendered industrial adjustment much more market driven since the 1980s.

CPE scholars have made major progress in understanding the dynamics of liberalization across advanced capitalist democracies thanks to the conceptual toolkit that Streeck and Thelen (2005) developed. However, their work left several analytical questions unanswered which recent scholarship has sought to address. One area that has received much more attention relates to the question of why and when different modes of gradual change occur. Although CPE scholars have had conceptual tools to describe specific episodes of gradual and cumulative changes, what has been missing until recently are accounts specifying the conditions under which different modes of gradual change are likely to occur (Béland and Powell 2016; Hacker et al. 2015). A key insight from the literature that seeks to explain patterns of institutional change is that the political context and attributes of the targeted institutions matter (Hacker et al. 2015). In political environments that foster a status quo bias due to the presence of multiple veto points, proponents of change are more likely to resort to strategies of drift and conversion because they obviate the need to enact new rules or policies or to repeal them. Institutions that have precise rules and strong enforcement capacity limit actors' ability to reinterpret or repurpose institutions thus making conversion less probable. Moreover, when policies are entrenched because they are backed by well-organized constituents or entail long-term commitments to their beneficiaries, reformers are more likely to maneuver around these popular policies using a strategy of layering or drift.

Another area of research that builds on Streeck and Thelen's (2005) work seeks to link different types of gradual and cumulative institutional change to different trajectories of liberalization. Thelen's (2014) work identifies three different trajectories of liberalization, associating each one with a different mode of institutional change. Deregulation is a path of liberalization that is pushed along by the replacement of old political economic institutions with market-conforming ones. This type of liberalization has occurred largely in Anglo countries and has resulted in greater socioeconomic inequality and more company reliance on market coordination. Dualization, a pattern of liberalization whereby institutional practices conducive to strategic coordination are not diffused evenly throughout the economy, is associated with drift. Witnessed in Germany, this trajectory of liberalization has worsened inequality between labor market insiders and outsiders, but not necessarily degraded firms' ability to coordinate strategically. Finally, embedded flexibilization, a type of liberalization that expands market governance, is backstopped by a social safety net that provides more active labor market assistance—such as training and job placement help—in addition to generous income maintenance support. Seen in Denmark and Sweden, this form of liberalization, to a certain degree, has eroded employers' capacity to strategically coordinate but has not brought about the kind of inequality seen in Germany or the United Kingdom. In sum, as Thelen (2014) and others have noted, although liberalization has been a common trend throughout advanced political economies since the early 1980s, there remains much institutional diversity between LMEs and CMEs. Moreover, one could argue that there is more diversity among CMEs after decades of liberalization.

Bringing macroeconomics back in

The first wave of CPE research (from the early 1970s to early 1980s) sought to explain cross-national differences in macroeconomic outcomes such as economic growth, inflation, and unemployment. Insights from Keynesian macroeconomic theory figured prominently in leading CPE approaches at the time. Hibbs's (1977) partisan model, for example, held that leftist and rightist parties exploited the Phillips curve trade-off between unemployment and inflation to promote the material interests of their core supporters (for more, see Chapter 4). The neo-corporatist literature explored how macroeconomic outcomes were shaped by the strategic interaction among employers, labor, and government. To maintain high employment levels and low inflation, governments in neo-corporatist political economies used fiscal and social policies to induce labor to accept wage restraint. At the center of these approaches was the idea that the active management of aggregate demand generated real macroeconomic effects.

The loss of interest in the politics of macroeconomic management starting in the 1980s coincided with the growing influence of neoclassical economics in political science. This school of economic thought called into question the government's ability to shape macroeconomic outcomes in the medium- and long-term (Iversen and Soskice 2006b; Baccaro and Pontusson 2016). In light of the emerging consensus that Keynesian policies of demand management produced no sustainable effects on employment and output, CPE scholars shifted their attention to supply-side dynamics in advanced capitalist economies. The focus was on explaining how different configurations of supply-side institutions shaped the competitiveness of firms and why countries ended up with distinct supply-side institutions. The novelty of the VoC approach stemmed from its integration of the burgeoning supply-side-oriented CPE research with new institutional economics.

Recent efforts to "bring macroeconomics back in" stem in part from the limitations of the VoC informed literature. First, as Pontusson and Baccaro (2020) have remarked, the question of why divergent macroeconomic performance exists across advanced political economies is central to defining CPE. Yet, the VoC approach, which has dominated the subfield since the early 2000s, does not provide much analytical leverage on that classic question because it overlooks the contribution of different demand drivers of macroeconomic outcomes. Second, the VoC literature sheds little light on the economic implications of the changes in the distribution of income between labor and capital—particularly its effects on economic growth. Finally, the VoC scholarship has lacked the conceptual tools and insights to account for why divergent growth patterns have emerged since the 1980s not just between LMEs and CMEs but also among countries in the latter group.

The growth model perspective developed by Baccaro and Pontusson (2016) and Pontusson and Baccaro (2020) focuses on demand-side determinants of economic growth in the post-Fordist era and on the interaction effects between shifts in income distribution and growth patterns. Accordingly, this new CPE approach is well suited to address the drawbacks we elaborated earlier. There are two key features of the growth model perspective that distinguish it from other "modern macroeconomics" approaches which have recently emerged in CPE (see Iversen and Soskice 2006b; Hope and Soskice 2016). First, different growth models rely on different combinations of aggregate demand drivers such as household consumption, investment, and net exports. The interaction of different demand drivers has led to the formation of distinct post-Fordist growth trajectories across advanced political economies. We will briefly elaborate them later.

The second key feature of the growth model perspective is that it focuses on the co-evolution of distributional shifts and growth trajectories (Baccaro and Pontusson 2016). On the one hand, the distribution of income between labor and capital—measured as labor compensation as a percentage of GDP—has a profound impact on aggregate demand. This is the case because lower-income individuals have a higher marginal propensity to consume as a percentage of their current income than affluent individuals. As a result, an increase in labor's share of the total national income boosts household consumption and aggregate demand. The dominant growth model in advanced political economies during the Fordist era hinged on real wage growth. Labor's increased share of GDP, which coincided with increases in labor productivity, spurred household consumption as well as investment as firms sought to expand their production capacity to meet growing demand. However, the gradual drop in labor's national income share starting in the 1970s, as Baccaro and Pontusson (2016: 10–11) note, thrust on advanced political economies "the problem of finding a replacement for wage-driven growth." Thus, although each post-Fordist growth model has relied on a different mix of demand drivers, they emerged in response to a common distributional shift. On the other hand, proponents of this approach argue that different growth models generate different distributive outcomes. For example, consumption-driven growth models have tended to witness smaller increases in inequality in the lower half of the income distribution than export-driven ones.

IN FOCUS BOX 8.2 POST-FORDIST GROWTH MODELS

Focusing on the period from 1994 to 2008, Bacarro and Pontusson's empirical analysis reveals three post-Fordist growth models—consumption-led growth experienced in the United Kingdom, export-led growth witnessed in Germany, and a combination of consumption and export-led growth seen in Sweden. The United Kingdom's consumption-led growth was made possible thanks to the country's vibrant financial sector. The inflow of foreign capital during this period eased access to credit which in turn buoyed household consumption. Strong domestic demand kept employment levels relatively high and translated into real wage gains that spread to low-wage service workers, helping keep low-income inequality relatively stable. The UK's growth strategy led to rising household debt and current account deficits—two macroeconomic outcomes linked to consumption-led growth models.

Germany's export sector has served as the main engine of growth since the early 1990s. The size of the country's export sector as a percentage of GDP increased quickly in the wake of reunification, making it possible for that sector to become the main locomotive for the economy thereafter. Moreover, wage moderation achieved via coordinated bargaining in export-oriented manufacturing industries coupled with relatively low levels of household consumption helped keep inflation low, preserving the price competitiveness of German exports. The export-led growth model has been associated with lower household debt, which reflects the model's bias against spurring domestic consumption. It is also linked to rising low-income inequality due to the efforts of German export firms to prevent wage gains in the export sector from spreading to the service sector. In fact, as hourly labor compensation in Germany grew moderately in the export-oriented manufacturing sector, it was virtually stagnant in low-end services such as wholesale and retail trade and hotels and restaurants between 1994 and 2007. As Baccaro and Pontusson (2016) observe, Germany's export-led growth proved highly sensitive to price changes. This made it imperative for exporters to keep the country's labor cost as low as possible to ensure exports stayed competitively priced.

Sweden's economic growth was fueled by a blend of household consumption and exports. Unlike Germany's exports, Sweden's ICT-intensive and high value-added service exports were less price elastic. This made it possible to promote household consumption via wage increases without undermining global demand for Sweden's exports. Consumption was buoyed not only by real wage gains but also by household borrowing. The increase in household indebtedness between the 1990s and 2000s was similar to Great Britain's. Moreover, real wages increased in both high-end manufacturing and low-end services, which helped keep inequality in the upper and lower halves of the income distribution largely stable. The continued strength of labor organization in the manufacturing and the service sector played an important role in shaping Sweden's post-Fordist growth model. As Pontusson and Baccaro (2020: 18) note, labor "acted as a beneficial constraint" insofar as forcing Swedish firms to shift into less price-sensitive activities in order to remain competitive. It also ensured that productivity gains translated into economy-wide real wage increases.

The growth model perspective has sparked renewed interest in exploring demand-side determinants of macroeconomic trends. Several avenues of research have emerged recently that draw on its analytical insights. By embracing both supply- and demand-side drivers of output, inequality, and employment, the growth regime approach seeks to offer a more comprehensive political economic analysis of macroeconomic trends in advanced political economies. As Hassel et al. (2020) note, a growth regime "encompasses the institutional, policy, and organizational frameworks that shape the specialization of firms and the consumption and saving patterns of the population, as well as the use of technology and work organization." This strand of research pays close attention to the interaction among three aspects of growth regimes: the sectors that act as the locomotive of growth; the institutions organizing the economy such as industrial relations, social protection regime, and skill-formation system; and components of aggregate demand.

Another avenue of research explores the political foundations of growth models. Baccaro and Pontusson (2019) have argued that growth models rest on "social blocs," alliances of groups differentiated by sectoral and class interests. These cross-class coalitions, dominated by a key sector or combination of sectors, have a vested interest in maintaining the pillars on which growth models rest. Thelen (2019) shows that the divergent evolution of growth models in advanced political economies since the 1970s has been attributed to differences in the producer-group landscape in which the interests of certain sectors are magnified over others. For example, Thelen (2019) observes that the continued political dominance of the coalitional alignment between employers and labor in the manufacturing sector explains to a large extent why Germany's export profile (specialization in automobiles and capital goods such as machines and auto parts) has changed very little since the 1980s. In contrast, the diversification of Sweden's export profile—that is, the specialization in ICT-intensive and business-related services as well as in traditional manufacturing—was made possible thanks to a social coalition that encompassed cross-sectoral interests.

The binary distinction between consumption-led and export-led growth models has prompted many CPE scholars to caution against oversimplifying the political economic realities across advanced capitalist democracies. Accordingly, several scholars have investigated more systematically the institutional and policy distinctions between the two models but also the variations within each model. To gain a better understanding of the scope of commonalities and diversity, more scholars are focusing on differences regarding the level of financialization; patterns of income inequality; patterns of financial imbalances in household, corporate, and government sectors; and national product market profiles (Behringer and Treeck 2019; Hassel et al. 2020).

Populism

Populism is on the rise in many advanced political economies. Throughout Europe, populist parties and politicians have not only redefined the key policy narratives shaping electoral competition, their campaign strategies, which often focus on issues of identity and culture, have propelled many into positions of power. Consider these quick facts about the electoral rise of right- and left-wing European populist parties.

Between 1982 and 2019, the vote share of right-wing populist parties (RWPPs) increased from 1% to 16.1%. After dropping from 9.9% in 1981 to 3.7% in 2010, the vote share of left-wing populist parties (LWPPs) rebounded to 7% in 2019 due to their electoral successes in Cyprus, Greece, Italy, and Spain. These vote shares have enabled Europe's populist parties not only to obtain parliamentary seats but also to be in the government. In 2017, 17.5% (1,342 seats) of the combined seats in European national parliaments (7,843 seats) were controlled by populist parties. In the same year, populist parties were in government as coalition partners or as the ruling party in Austria, Finland, Greece, Hungary, Latvia, Norway, Poland, Slovakia, and Switzerland (TIMBRO 2019).

Researching the rise of populist forces in capitalist democracies and its consequences on policies and democratic institutions has become a cottage industry in the social sciences. Political scientists and economists have been particularly interested in explaining why people are receptive to populist discourse and why the appeal of populism varies across countries and across regions within countries. Another set of questions that has gained more attention now that populist forces have had electoral successes and taken part in governments concerns the public policy effects of RWPPs. The burgeoning scholarship provides crucial insights into these questions. Next, we briefly discuss that literature and, in the process, draw out the different points of contention that have emerged in the expanding research on populism.

What is populism?

Until recently, ambiguity about the meaning of populism hindered the development of a comparative research platform upon which new scholarship on populism could build. As Mudde and Rovira Kaltwasser (2018) have noted, some definitions of populism are too narrow to be used in comparative research. Scholars who approach populism from a political-strategic viewpoint highlight the role of strong, charismatic leaders and their penchant to develop direct connections with their followers. However, this conceptual approach overlooks the fact that the rise of populist forces in several European countries has not hinged on charismatic political entrepreneurs. Alternatively, populism has been defined as a style of politics aimed at defying conventional codes of demeanor and oratory in order to signal to the people that populist politicians are agents of change, willing to take on the status quo. The drawback with this conceptual approach is that not all populist politicians use inflammatory and divisive rhetoric to attract public attention, and displays of unprofessional behavior are limited to a few. Moreover, left-wing populism usually avoids racially charged narratives, and populist politicians are as inclined as mainstream politicians to moderate their demands and compromise once they are voted into office.

There is an emerging consensus among scholars that populism should be understood as a set of ideas or a belief system. At the heart of this belief system is the assertion that society is divided between "the people" and "enemies of the people" such as the elites and foreigners, and that politics must reflect consistently the will of "the people." This is what gives populism its anti-establishment and anti-elite characteristic—the notion that those who have been in positions of authority have led society astray from a general vision of an ideal society. Moreover, its focus on empowering "the people" explains why populists have been critical of unelected bodies such as courts, central banks, and bureaucratic institutions who are blamed for promoting values and policies that clash with the will of the people.

There are several advantages in using this minimalist definition, which accounts for why it has become widely used by scholars. Here we focus on two in particular. First, because populism does not provide a worldview, it is rendered actionable when it is connected with other belief sets such as socialism, liberalism, nationalism, or conservatism. This explains why we encounter left-wing and right-wing versions of populism around the world. Left-wing populism depicts "the people" as the socioeconomic underdogs. For LWPPs, the essence of political struggle involves the masses wresting control from the business and financial elites who are perceived to have leveraged their privileged positions to enrich themselves at the people's expense. On the other hand, right-wing populism defines "the people" based on a common racial-ethnic ("native") identity. It characterizes political struggle as one where natives must take back control from political elites whose multicultural and post-material policy views are perceived to have benefited immigrants and minorities while eroding the social status of the dominant native group.

The other advantage of using this conceptual approach to populism is that it lends itself well to the investigation of the demand-side and the supply-side of populism. Demand-side research aims to uncover the reasons why people are attracted to populism. Recent scholarship, some of which we will briefly cover later, has discovered that certain attitudes and feelings at the individual and community levels are associated with higher support for populism. This strand of scholarship tells us that populist views, whether latent or salient, exist within society independent of what political entrepreneurs do. Supply-side analysis draws attention to how political entrepreneurs respond and adjust to changes in the economic and social circumstances facing voters. Part of why populist parties have garnered more popular support over time is that they have refined their campaign messages, slogans, and platforms in ways that tap better the economic anxieties of voters. Another reason for their political ascent, notably RWPPs, is that they have developed campaign strategies that prime latent racial-ethnic sensitivities, attracting voters whose economic circumstances would otherwise draw them to another party. Still another factor contributing to their electoral success is that many voters have felt that their concerns and worries have fallen on deaf ears among established parties, creating an opportunity for challenger parties to fill the representation gap.

Economic and cultural determinants of populism

There are two schools of thought about why populism has gained popularity. Economic explanations hold that people and communities who have been negatively affected by globalization, deindustrialization, technological change, and low-wage competition from immigrants are more likely to support populist movements than those who have benefited from these economic changes. A common version of this argument is that the trade shocks caused by the surge in imports from China and other emerging economies have inflicted economic pain in import-competing, manufacturing regions of advanced political economies. In their widely referenced work on the impact of the China shock on the American economy, Autor and colleagues (2013) note that communities exposed to Chinese competition since the end of the 1980s—particularly the Midwest region of the country known as the "industrial belt"—have witnessed declining employment rates and wages. Broz et al. (2020) and Colantone and Stanig (2019), among others have found evidence suggesting that the China shock has produced equally large displacement effects throughout Europe. The deindustrialization of those regions is marked not only by the bleak job prospects and income loss of former industrial workers. These regions also face population flight, lower property value, deteriorating public services caused by declining tax revenue, and higher rates of morbidity and drug abuse. Like globalization, technological changes and low-cost competition from immigrants have had distributional consequences. Technological innovation has complemented high-skilled workers but has substituted routine middle-income jobs. Individuals in low-wage, low-skilled jobs are more likely to face competition from immigrants than those in high-skilled professions (Broz et al. 2020).

In short, globalization, technological advances, and immigration can cause economic anxieties and insecurities at the individual level by exposing people to labor market dislocations and related financial woes. Moreover, the unequal geographical effects of the globalization shock can engender community-level feelings of being left behind as other regional economies that rely on professional services, export-oriented manufacturing, and information-communication technologies grow. In hard-hit regions, pessimistic sociotropic sentiments tend to be expressed by people who have and have not faced personal hardship (Hays et al. 2019). These individual and community-level effects have political implications. The research that focuses on economic drivers of populism suggests that disaffected workers and voters in hard-hit regions punish incumbent parties for promoting economic policies that cause personal and community hardships and reward populists for standing against economic globalism and immigration.

Cultural explanations provide insights into two empirical patterns that economic explanations have difficulty accounting for. First, why do people support RWPPs even though their personal economic circumstances suggest they would not gain materially from such a choice? Second, why is the upsurge in the support for RWPPs more widespread than that of LWPPs even though the latter's focus on redistribution would be materially beneficial to regions and individuals affected by economic dislocation? The cultural roots of populism draw attention to the primacy of identity in the formation of individual beliefs and political choices. A prominent version of the cultural explanation is the status threat argument. This argument holds that a growing number of white citizens in Western democracies feel that the promotion of multiculturalism, protections for religious and racial minorities, and gender equality by political and social elites threaten their dominant position within the social hierarchy (Inglehart and Norris 2017; Gidron and Hall 2017). RWPPs have been especially effective at fueling white voters' fears of being socially displaced by fashioning cultural frames that not only emphasize the need to protect traditional values and cultural homogeneity but also foment a political backlash against economic globalization and immigration.

Recent studies have found evidence supporting the perceived status threat explanation for the rise of the populist right. In their cross-national study of

20 countries from 1990 to 2014, Gidron and Hall (2017) find that the perceived social status of men without a college degree dropped in most countries. The sharpest declines occurred after 2009 as the fallout of the global financial crisis set in. Moreover, they find that when individuals feel that their social standing has diminished, they are more likely to support right-wing populism. This association remains robust after controlling for other variables that are known to affect electoral behavior such as occupation and income. Margalit (2019) points to a number of studies showing that cultural grievances affect people's attitudes toward immigration and globalization. One finding is that individuals who express concerns about the erosion of national identity are more likely to emphasize the negative economic effects of immigration. Another finding is that people who worry about the cultural consequences of globalization tend to be more pessimistic about the economic effects of globalization. People who express these personal attitudes are more likely to support the populist right.

Before we move to the consequences of populism, it should be noted that several scholars of populism have rejected the view that economic and cultural determinants of populism are mutually exclusive. As Franzese (2019) remarks, "the question 'status threat *or* economic hardship?' is logically ill-formed" because an individual's vote choice "is a multifactor consideration." One approach that some scholars have taken is to explore how cultural and economic factors interact and condition each other (see Broz et al. 2020; Colantone and Stanig 2019; Gidron and Hall 2017, 2020; Hays et al. 2019; Margalit 2019). For example, the association between the decline in manufacturing employment and support for Trump in 2016 was conditional on the racial profile of counties: the correlation between support for Trump and manufacturing layoffs was positive in counties with white majorities and among white voters, but negative in culturally diverse counties and among non-whites (Broz et al. 2020).

Another approach is to distinguish between levels of and changes in the support for populist movements (Rodrik 2020). Because economic shocks are more dynamic than cultural transformation, scholars interested in explaining increases in the vote share of populist candidates and parties might find that economic variables such as globalization shocks offer more analytical leverage than cultural factors. As Rodrik (2020: 2) notes, "culture generally transforms slowly, and a constant cannot explain a change" therefore "culture is unlikely to do a good job answering the question in changes form." Hays et al. (2019) find no evidence that trade shocks alone influence the level of support for populism. Instead, exposed communities tend to express anti-immigration sentiments and other social grievances; it is these attitudes that are closely aligned with support for RWPPs.

Policy consequences of populism

The continued electoral successes of the populist right in Western democracies have prompted scholars to devote more attention to the question of how the presence of populist politicians in the legislature and in government influences the direction of policies. Populists can impact policies indirectly or directly. For example, center-right and social democratic parties have increasingly taken a harder line on immigration as a way to prevent supporters who are worried about the effects of immigration from joining populist movements. In other words, electoral competition can force mainstream parties to adopt certain policy stances endorsed by populists. Of note, RWPPs have appealed to working-class voters who have typically supported either social democratic or Christian democratic parties as well as attracted middle-class voters aligned with mainstream right-wing parties. Populist politicians might also be able to exert direct policy influence by virtue of being part of a government. In Europe, due to ideological proximity, RWPPs have joined coalition governments led by Christian democratic or conservative parties.

The policy agenda that RWPPs compete on is typically influenced by nativism—that is, their policy prescriptions are biased in favor of the native population and premised on a narrow conception of national identity. Accordingly, they have taken a hard line on immigration and integration issues—the latter focusing on residency and naturalization requirements. Moreover, they have promoted welfare chauvinism, a position that calls for restricting immigrants' access to social benefits. Anti-elitism and anti-establishment also pervade their economic policy agenda. In particular, RWPPs have been critical of economic regulations that protect "insider" networks which favor organized business and labor. This has led them to support privatization and market deregulation as means of curtailing the market privileges of organized economic interests (Röth et al. 2018; Mudde and Rovira Kaltwasser 2018).

Studies have found some evidence of RWPPs' indirect and direct influence on policy outcomes. Akkerman (2012) finds that Europe's increasingly restrictive immigration and integration policies since the 1990s are owed in large part to the fact that established right-wing parties have moved closer to RWPPs' cultural protectionist position regardless of whether these parties are in the government. This suggests that RWPPs exercise some indirect influence over right-wing parties, but much less on social democratic parties which have been less inclined to endorse cultural protectionism. On the issue of deregulation, Röth et al.'s (2018) analysis of 17 European countries between 1970 and 2010 shows that the presence of RWPPs in right-wing coalitions does not led to more deregulation of "insider" friendly labor market policies or privatization. In fact, right-wing coalitions that do not include RWPPs engage in more deregulation on average. This suggests that the material interests of RWPPs' working-class supporters may be given greater consideration than those of their middle-class supporters when these parties are part of a government.

Finally, a growing body of literature has found strong evidence supporting the claim that the political rise of RWPPs has led to more welfare chauvinist reforms. Focusing on a period from 1975 to 2015, Swank and Betz (2019) find that the participation of RWPPs in government leads to an increase in the generosity of key social insurance programs such as pension and unemployment benefits which disproportionately benefit native citizens. Röth et al. (2018) find a similar result as well. On the other hand, Swank and Betz's study reveals that electoral gains by RWPPs have inclined Christian democratic governments, not social democratic ones, to retrench social assistance (e.g., reductions in income replacements rates) and cut back on some social services which are disproportionately utilized by immigrants. They conclude that since the late 1990s, the direct and indirect influences of RWPPs have played contributing roles in reprogramming Europe's welfare states in ways that have only intensified the differential treatment of natives and immigrants.

Conclusion

To be sure, there is much we do not know about the political and economic effects of the current rise of the populist right. This area of inquiry remains underexplored in comparison to investigations of the roots of populism. Scholars have broached several important questions: What effects will the populist right's anti-pluralist and xenophobic position have on the protections of minority rights, multiculturalism, and freedom of expression? What effects will the populist movement have on economic policies, on macroeconomic performance, and on the material well-being of individuals? Will the rise of populism in general render democratic politics more responsive to and representative of the views of average people? What effects will populism have on the international liberal economic order? There is certainly not a lack of interest in addressing these questions. Progress in these areas is only limited by the short history of the current populist movement.

Key concepts

Growth model

Liberalization

Populism

Discussion questions

- What is liberalization? Describe how liberalization is reshaping advanced political economies.
- Elaborate on the economic and cultural roots of populism.
- What do proponents of "bringing macroeconomics back in" seek to contribute to the study of comparative political economy?

Further reading

Hassel, Anke, and Bruno Palier. 2021. *Growth and Welfare in Advanced Capitalist Economies: How Have Growth Regimes Evolved?* New York: Oxford University Press.

Explores how growth regimes in advanced capitalist democracies have evolved since the early 1990s.

Mudde, Cas, and Cristóbal Rovira Kaltwasser. 2017. *Populism: A Very Short Introduction*. New York: Oxford University Press.

A succinct yet thorough analysis of populism.

Streeck, Wolfgang. 2009. *Re-forming Capitalism: Institutional Change in the German Political Economy*. Oxford: Oxford University Press.

Investigates how institutional changes have transformed the German political economy.

Bibliography

Achen, Christopher, and Larry Bartels. 2017. *Democracy for Realists: Why Elections do not Produce Responsive Government*. Princeton, NJ: Princeton University Press.

Adolph, Christopher, Christian Breunig, and Chris Koski. 2020. "The Political Economy of Budget Trade-off." *Journal of Public Policy* 40(1): 25–50.

Akkerman, Tjitske. 2012. "Comparing Radical Right Parties in Government: Immigration and Integration Policies in Nine Countries (1996–2010)." *West European Politics* 35(3): 511–529.

Aklin, Michaël, and Andreas Kern. 2020. "The Side Effects of Central Bank Independence." *American Journal of Political Science*. Early View (December 22).

Alesina, Alberto, and Edward L. Glaser. 2004. *Fighting Poverty in the US and Europe: A World of Difference*. Oxford: Oxford University Press.

Alesina, Alberto, Nouriel Roubini, and Gerald Cohen. 1997. *Political Cycles and the Macroeconomy*. Cambridge, MA: The MIT Press.

Alesina, Alberto, and Lawrence H. Summers. 1993. "Central Bank Independence and Macroeconomic Performance: Some Comparative Evidence." *Journal of Money, Credit, and Banking* 25(2): 151–162.

Almond, Gabriel A. 1991. "Capitalism and Democracy." *PS: Political Science & Politics* 24(3): 467–474.

Alt, James E. 1985. "Political Parties, World Demand, and Unemployment: Domestic and International Sources of Economic Activity." *American Political Science Review* 79(4): 1016–1040.

Alt, James E., and K. Alec Chrystal. 1983. *Political Economics*. Sussex: Wheatsheaf Books Ltd.

Alt, James E., David Dreyer Lassen, and Joachim Wehner. 2014. "It Isn't Just about Greece: Domestic Politics, Transparency and Fiscal Gimmickry in Europe." *British Journal of Political Science* 44(4): 707–716.

Alt, James E., David Lassen, and John Marshall. 2016. "Credible Sources and Sophisticated Voters: When Does New Information Induce Economic Voting?" *The Journal of Politics* 78(2): 327–342.

Alvarez, R. Michael, Geoffrey Garrett, and Peter Lange. 1991. "Government Partisanship, Labor Organization, and Macroeconomic Performance." *American Political Science Review* 85(2): 539–556.

Amable, Bruno, Ekkehard Ernst, and Stefano Palombarini. 2005. "How Do Financial Markets Affect Industrial Relations: An Institutional Complementarity Approach." *Socio-Economic Review* (3): 311–330.

Anderson, Christopher. 2000. "Economic Voting and Political Context: A Comparative Perspective." *Electoral Studies* 19(2): 151–170.

———. 2007. "The End of Economic Voting? Contingency Dilemmas and the Limits of Democratic Accountability." *Annual Review of Political Science* 10: 271–296.

Anderson, Christopher, and Pablo Beramendi. 2008. "Income, Inequality, and Electoral Participation." In Pablo Beramendi and Christopher Anderson, eds., *Democracy, Inequality, and Representation*. New York: Russell Sage Foundation, pp. 278–311.

Anderson, Christopher, and Jason D. Hecht. 2012. "Voting When the Economy Goes Bad, Everyone is in Charge, and No One is to Blame: The Case of the 2009 German Election." *Electoral Studies* 31: 5–19.

———. 2014. "Crisis of Confidence? The Dynamics of Economic Opinions during the Great Recession." In Nancy Bermeo and Larry Bartels, eds., *Mass Politics in Tough Times: Opinions, Votes, and Protest in the Great Recession*. New York: Oxford University Press, pp. 40–71.

Ansell, Ben W., J. Lawrence Broz, and Thomas Flaherty. 2018. "Global Capital Markets, Housing Prices, and Partisan Fiscal Policies." *Economics & Politics* 30(3): 307–339.

Ansell, Benjamin. 2014. "The Political Economy of Ownership: Housing Markets and the Welfare State." *American Political Science Review* 108(2): 383–402.

Armingeon, Klaus, Virginia Wenger, Fiona Wiedemeier, Christian Isler, Laura Knöpfel, David Weisstanner, and Sarah Engler. 2018. *Comparative Political Data Set 1960–2016* (Update 2018). Zurich: Institute of Political Science, University of Zurich.

Autor, David H., David Dorn, and Gordon H. Hanson. 2013. "The China Syndrome: Local Labor Market Effects of Import Competition in the United States." *American Economic Review* 103(6): 2121–2168.

Autor, David H., Lawrence F. Katz, and Melissa S. Kearney. 2006. "The Polarization of the U.S. Labor Market." *The American Economic Review* 96(2): 189–194.

———. 2008. "Trend in U.S. Wage Inequality: Revising the Revisionists." *The Review of Economics and Statistics* 90(2): 300–323.

Baccaro, Lucio, and Chris Howell. 2011. "A Common Neoliberal Trajectory: The Transformation of Industrial Relations in Advanced Capitalism." *Politics & Society* 39(4): 521–563.

———. 2017. *Trajectories of Neoliberal Transformation: European Industrial Relations since the 1970s*. New York: Cambridge University Press.

Baccaro, Lucio, and Jonas Pontusson. 2016. "Rethinking Comparative Political Economy: The Growth Model Perspective." *Politics & Society* 44(2): 175–207.

———. 2019. "Social Blocs and Growth Models: An Analytical Framework with German y and Sweden as Illustrative Cases." Unequal Democracies Working Paper No. 7. University of Geneva.

Baker, Dean, Andrew Glyn, David R. Howell, and John Schmitt. 2005. "Labor Market Institutions and Unemployment: Assessment of the Cross-Country Evidence." In David Howell, ed., *Fighting Unemployment: The Limits of Free Market Orthodoxy*. Oxford: Oxford University Press, pp. 72–118.

Baldwin, Peter. 1990. *The Politics of Social Solidarity: Class Bases of the European Welfare State 1875–1975*. Cambridge: Cambridge University Press.

Bartels, Larry M. 2008. *Unequal Democracy: The Political Economy of the New Gilded Age*. Princeton, NJ: Princeton University Press.

———. 2014. "Ideology and Retrospection in Electoral Responses to the Great Recession." In Nancy Bermeo and Larry M. Bartels, eds., *Mass Politics in Tough Times: Opinions, Votes, and Protest in the Great Recession*. New York: Oxford University Press, pp. 185–223.

———. 2017. "Political Inequality in Affluent Democracies: The Social Welfare Deficit." Working Paper 5–2017. Center for the Study of Democratic Institutions, Vanderbilt University.

———. 2018. *Unequal Democracy: The Political Economy of the New Gilded Age*. 2nd edition. Princeton, NJ: Princeton University Press.

Bebchuk, Lucian Arye, and Jesse M. Fried. 2003. "Economic Compensation as an Agency Problem." *Journal of Economic Perspectives* 17(3): 71–92.

Beck, Nathaniel. 1982. "Parties, Administrations, and American Macroeconomic Outcomes." *American Political Science Review* 76: 83–93.

———. 1987. "Elections and the Fed: Is There a Political Monetary Cycle?" *American Journal of Political Science* 31: 194–216.

Behringer, Jan, and Till van Treeck. 2019. "Income Distribution and Growth Models: A Sectoral Balances Approach." *Politics & Society* 47(3): 303–332.

Béland, Daniel, and Martin Powell. 2016. "Continuity and Change in Social Policy." *Social Policy & Administration* 50(2): 129–147.

Bélanger, Éric, and François Gélineau. 2010. "Does Perceived Competence Matter? Political Parties and Economic Voting in Canadian Federal Elections." *Journal of Elections, Public Opinion and Parties* 20(1): 83–101.

Beramendi, Pablo, and Thomas R. Cusack. 2008. "Economic Institutions, Partisanship, and Inequality." In Pablo Beramendi and Christopher Anderson, eds., *Democracy, Inequality, and Representation*. New York: Russell Sage Foundation, pp. 127–168.

———. 2009. "Diverse Disparities: The Politics and Economics of Wage, Market, and Disposable Income Inequalities." *Political Research Quarterly* 62(2): 257–275.

Beramendi, Pablo, Silja Häusermann, Herbert Kitschelt, and Hanspeter Kriesi. 2015. "Introduction: The Politics of Advanced Democracies." In Pablo Beramendi, Silja Häusermann, Herbert Kitschelt, and Hanspeter Kriesi, eds., *The Politics of Advanced Capitalism*. New York: Cambridge University Press, pp. 1–66.

Beramendi, Pablo, and Philipp Rehm. 2016. "Who Gives, Who Gains? Redistribution and Preference Formation." *Comparative Political Studies* 49(4): 529–563.

Beramendi, Pablo, and David Rueda. 2014. "Inequality and Institutions: The Case of Economic Coordination." *Annual Review of Political Science* 17: 251–271.

Birchfield, Vicki, and Markus M.L. Crepaz. 1998. "The Impact of Constitutional Structures and Collective and Competitive Veto Points on Income Inequality in Industrialized Democracies." *European Journal of Political Research* 34: 175–200.

Blanchard, Olivier, and Justin Wolfers. 2000. "The Role of Shocks and Institutions in the Rise of European Unemployment." *Economic Journal* 110: C1–C33.

Blyth, Mark. 2009. "An Approach to Comparative Analysis or a Subfield within a Subfield? Political Economy." In Mark I. Lichbach and Alan Zuckerman, eds., *Comparative Politics: Rationality, Culture, and Structure*. New York: Cambridge University Press, pp. 193–219.

Boix, Carles. 1997. "Political Parties and the Supply Side of the Economy: The Provision of Physical and Human Capital in Advanced Economies, 1960–90." *American Journal of Political Science* 41(3): 814–845.

———. 1998. *Political Parties, Growth and Equality: Conservative and Social Democratic Economic Strategies in the World Economy*. New York: Cambridge University Press.

———. 2011. "Redistribution Policies in a Globalized World." In Marion Jansen and Marc Bachetta, eds., *Making Globalization Socially Sustainable*. Geneva: WTO-ILO, pp. 261–295.

———. 2019. *Democratic Capitalism at the Crossroads: Technological Change and the Future of Politics*. Princeton, NJ: Princeton University Press.

Bonica, Adam, Nolan McCarty, Keith T. Poole, and Howard Rosenthal. 2013. "Why Hasn't Democracy Slowed Rising Inequality?" *Journal of Economic Perspectives* 27(3): 103–124.

Bowman, John R. 2014. *Capitalisms Compared: Welfare, Work, and Business*. Thousand Oaks: CQ Press.

Bradley, David, Evelyne Huber, Stephanie Moller, François Nielsen, and John D. Stephens. 2003. "Distribution and Redistribution in Postindustrial Democracies." *World Politics* 55(1): 193–228.

Bradley, David, and John D. Stephens. 2007. "Employment Performance in OECD Countries: A Test of Neoliberal and Institutional Hypotheses." *Comparative Political Studies* 40(12): 1486–1510.

Brady, David, Evelyne Huber, and John D. Stephens. 2020. *Comparative Welfare States Data Set.* University of North Carolina and WZB Berlin Social Science Center.

Broz, J. Lawrence. 2013. "Partisan Financial Cycles." In Miles Kahler and David Lake, eds., *Politics in the New Hard Times: The Great Recession in Comparative Perspective.* Ithaca: Cornell University Press, pp. 75–101.

Broz, J. Lawrence, Jeffry Frieden, and Stephen Weymouth. 2020. "Populism in Place: The Economic Geography of the Globalization Backlash." Working Paper. May.

Busemeyer, Marius. 2009. "From Myth to Reality: Globalisation and Public Spending in OECD Countries Revisited." *European Journal of Political Research* 48: 455–482.

Calmfors, Lars, and John Driffill. 1988. "Bargaining Structure, Corporatism and Macroeconomic Performance." *Economic Policy* 3(6): 13–61.

Cameron, David R. 1979. "The Expansion of the Public Economy: A Comparative Analysis." *American Political Science Review* 72(4): 1243–1261.

———. 1984. "Social Democracy, Corporatism, Labour Quiescence and the Representation of Economic Interest in Advanced Capitalist Society." In John H. Goldthorpe, ed., *Order and Conflict in Contemporary Capitalism: Studies in the Political Economy of Western European Nations.* New York: Oxford University Press, pp. 143–178.

Campbell, Angus, Philip E. Converse, Warren E. Miller, and Donald E. Stokes. 1960. *The American Voter.* New York: John Wiley.

Canes-Wrone, Brandice, and Jee-Kwang Park. 2012. "Electoral Business Cycles in OECD Countries." *American Political Science Review* 106(1): 103–122.

Carey, David, and Harry Tchilinguirian. 2000. "Average Effective Tax Rates on Capital, Labour and Consumption." OECD Economics Department Working Papers No. 258. Paris: OECD.

Carpenter, Daniel, and David A. Moss. 2013. "Introduction." In Daniel Carpenter and David A. Moss, eds., *Preventing Regulatory Capture: Special Interest Influence and How to Limit It.* New York: Cambridge University Press, pp. 1–22.

Chappell, Jr., Henry W., and William R. Keech. 1985. "A New View of Political Accountability for Economic Performance." *American Political Science Review* 79: 10–27.

Chappell, Jr., Henry and Linda Viega. 2000. "Economics and elections in western Europe: 1960-1997." *Electoral Studies* 19: 183-97.

Cheibub, José Antonio. 2007. *Presidentialism, Parliamentarism, and Democracy.* Cambridge: Cambridge University Press.

Cheibub, José Antonio, and Adam Przeworski. 1999. "Democracy, Elections, and Accountability for Economic Outcomes." In Adam Przeworski, Susan C. Stokes, and Bernard Manin, eds., *Democracy, Accountability, and Representation.* New York: Cambridge University Press, pp. 222–250.

Cioffi, John W., and Martin Höpner. 2006. "The Political Paradox of Finance Capitalism: Interests, Preferences, and Center-Left Party Politics in Corporate Governance Reform." *Politics & Society* 34(4): 463–502.

Clark, William Roberts. 2005. *Capitalism, not Globalism: Capital Mobility, Central Bank Independence, and the Political Control of the Economy.* Ann Arbor: The University of Michigan Press.

Clark, William Roberts, and Vincent Arel-Bundock. 2013. "Independent but not Indifferent: Partisan Bias in Monetary Policy at the Fed." *Economics & Politics* 25(1): 1–26.

Clark, William Roberts, Sona N. Golder, and Paul Poast. 2013. "Monetary Institutions and the Political Survival of Democratic Leaders." *International Studies Quarterly* 57: 556–567.

Clark, William Roberts, and Mark Hallerberg. 2000. "Mobile Capital, Domestic Institutions, and Electorally Induced Monetary and Fiscal Policy." *American Political Science Review* 94(2): 323–346.

Clarke, Harold D. and Euel Elliott. 1989. "New Models of Presidential Approval: Carter, Reagan and their Predecessors." *European Journal of Political Economy* 5: 551–569.

Colantone, Italo, and Piero Stanig. 2018. "Global Competition and Brexit." *American Political Science Review* 112(2): 201–218.

———. 2019. "The Surge of Economic Nationalism in Western Europe." *Journal of Economic Perspectives* 33(4): 128–151.

Converse, Philip E. 1964. "The Nature of Belief Systems in Mass Publics." In David Apter, ed., *Ideology and Discontent*. New York: Free Press, pp. 206–261.

Cox, Gary W., and Mathew McCubbins. 2001. "Political Structure and Economic Policy: The Institutional Determinants of Policy Outcomes." In Stephen Haggard and Mathew McCubbins, eds., *Presidents, Parliaments, and Policy*. Cambridge, UK: Cambridge University Press, pp. 21–63.

Coyle, Diane. 2020. *Markets, State, and People: Economic for Public Policy*. Princeton, NJ: Princeton University Press.

Crepaz, Markus L. 1996. "Constitutional Structures and Regime Performance in 18 Industrialized Democracies: A Test of Olson's Hypothesis." *European Journal of Political Research* 29: 87–104.

Crepaz, Markus L., and Ann W. Moser. 2004. "The Impact of Collective and Competitive Veto Points on Public Expenditures in the Global Age." *Comparative Political Studies* 37(3): 259–285.

Cruz, Cesi, Philip Keefer, and Carlos Scartascini. 2016. "Database of Political Institutions Codebook, 2015 Update (DPI2015)." Inter-American Development Bank.

Culpepper, Pepper, and Raphael Reinke. 2014. "Structural Power and Bank Bailouts in the United Kingdom and the United States." *Politics & Society* 42: 427–454.

Culpepper, Pepper, and Kathleen Thelen. 2008. "Institutions and Collective Action in the Provision of Training: Historical and Cross-National Comparisons." In Karl Ulrich Mayer and Heike Solga, eds., *Skill Formation: Interdisciplinary and Cross-National Perspectives*. New York: Cambridge University Press, pp. 21–49.

Cusack, Thomas R. 2001. "Partisanship in the Setting and Coordination of Fiscal and Monetary Policies." *European Journal of Political Research* 40: 93–115.

Cusack, Thomas R., and Pablo Beramendi. 2006. "Taxing Work." *European Journal of Political Research* 45(1): 43–73.

Cusack, Thomas R., Torben Iversen, and Philipp Rehm. 2006. "Risks at Work: The Demand and Supply Sides of Government Redistribution." *Oxford Review of Economic Policy* 22(3): 365–389.

Dahl, Robert. 1971. *Polyarchy: Participation and Opposition*. New Haven: Yale University Press.

Dassonneville, Ruth, and Michael S. Lewis-Beck. 2014. "Macroeconomics, Economic Crisis and Electoral Outcomes: A National European Pool." *Acta Politica* 49: 372–394.

———. 2019. "A Changing Economic Vote in Western Europe? Long-Term vs. Short-term Forces." *European Political Science Review* 11(1): 91–108.

Diermeier, Daniel, and Timothy Feddersen. 1998. "Cohesion in Legislatures and the Vote of Confidence Procedure." *American Political Science Review* 92(3): 83–116.

Dimick, Matthew, David Rueda, and Daniel Stegmueller. 2018. "Models of Other-Regarding Preferences, Inequality, and Redistribution." *Annual Review of Political Science* 21: 24.1–24.20.

Dincecco, Mark. 2017. *State Capacity and Economic Development: Present and Past*. New York: Cambridge University Press.

Dixit, Avinash. 1998. *The Making of Economic Policy: A Transaction Cost Politics Perspective*. Cambridge, MA: The MIT Press.

Downs, Anthony. 1957. *An Economic Theory of Democracy*. New York: Harper & Row.

Drazen, Allan. 2000. *Political Economy in Macroeconomics*. Princeton, NJ: Princeton University Press.

Drazen, Allan, and Marcela Eslava. 2010. "Electoral manipulation via voter-friendly spending: Theory and evidence." *Journal of Development Economics* 92(1): 39–52.

Duch, Raymond, and Randolph Stevenson. 2008. *The Economic Vote: How Political and Economic Institutions Condition Election Results*. New York: Cambridge University Press.

Duverger, Maurice. 1964. *Political Parties: Their Organization and Activity in the Modern State*. 3rd edition. London: Methuen & Co.

Ebbinghaus, Bernhard, and Jelle Visser. 1999. "When Institutions Matter: Union Growth and Decline in Western Europe, 1950–1995." *European Sociological Review* 15(2): 135–158.

Egger, Peter, Sergey Nigal, and Nora Strecker. 2019. "The Taxing Deed of Globalization." *The American Economic Review* 109(2): 353–390.

Esping-Andersen, Gøsta. 1990. *The Three Worlds of Welfare Capitalism*. Princeton, NJ: Princeton University Press.

———. 1999. "Politics without Class: Postindustrial Cleavages in Europe and America." In Herbert Kitschelt, Peter Lange, Gary Marks, and John Stephens, eds., *Continuity and Change in Contemporary Capitalism*. New York: Cambridge University Press, pp. 293–316.

Estevez-Abe, Margarita, Torben Iversen, and David Soskice. 2001. "Social Protection and the Formation of Skills: A Reinterpretation of the Welfare State." In Peter Hall and David Soskice, eds., *Varieties of Capitalism*. New York: Oxford University Press, pp. 145–183.

Fair, Ray C. 1978. "The Effect of Economic Events on Votes for President." *Review of Economics and Statistics* 60: 159–173.

Faricy, Christopher. 2016. "The Distributive Politics of Tax Expenditures: How Parties Use Policy Tools to Distribute Federal Money to the Rich and the Poor." *Politics, Groups, and Identities* (4): 110–125.

Fearon, James D. 1999. "Electoral Accountability and the Control of Politicians: Selecting Good Types versus Sanctioning Poor Performance." In Adam Przeworski, Susan Stokes, and Bernard Manin, eds., *Democracy, Accountability, and Representation*. New York: Cambridge University Press, pp. 55–97.

Ferejohn, John. 1986. "Incumbent Performance and Electoral Control." *Public Choice* 50(6): 5–25.

Fiorina, Morris. 1981. *Retrospective Voting in American National Elections*. New Haven: Yale University Press.

Fontenot, Kayla, Jessica Semega, and Melissa Kollar. 2018. *Income and Poverty in the United States: 2017*. U.S. Census Bureau, Current Population Reports, P60–263. Washington, DC: U.S. Government Printing Office.

Franzese, Jr., Robert J. 2002. "Electoral and Partisan Cycles in Economic Policies and Outcomes." *Annual Review of Political Science* 5: 369–421.

———. 2019. "The Comparative and International Political Economy of Anti-Globalization Populism." In *Oxford Research Encyclopedia of Politics*. Oxford: Oxford University Press.

Franzese, Jr., Robert J., and Peter A. Hall. 2000. "Institutional Dimensions of Coordinating Wage Bargaining and Monetary Policy." In Torben Iversen, Jonas Pontusson, and David Soskice, eds., *Unions, Employers, and Central Banks: Macroeconomic Coordination and Institutional Change in Social Market Economies*. New York: Cambridge University Press, pp. 173–204.

Freeman, Richard B. 1980. "Unionism and the Dispersion of Wages." *Industrial and Labor Relations Review* 34(1): 3–23.

———. 2012. "(Some) Inequality is Good for You." In David Grusky and Tamar Krichell-Katz, eds., *The New Gilded Age: The Critical Inequality Debate of Our Time*. Stanford: Stanford University Press, pp. 63–87.

Gabaix, Xavier and Augistin Landier. 2008. "Why Has CEO Pay Increased so Much? *Quarterly Journal of Economics* 123(1): 49–100.

Garbinti, Bertrand, Jonathan Goupille-Lebret, and Thomas Piketty. 2018. "Income Inequality in France, 1900–2014: Evidence from Distributional National Accounts (DINA)." *Journal of Public Economics* 162: 63–77.

Garfinkel, Irwin, Lee Rainwater, and Timothy M. Smeeding. 2006. "A Re-examination of Welfare States and Inequality in Rich Nations: How In-Kind Transfers and Indirect Taxes Change the Story." *Journal of Policy Analysis and Management* 25(4): 897–919.

Garrett, Geoffrey. 1998a. "Global Markets and National Politics: Collision Course or Virtuous Circle?" *International Organization* 52(4): 787–824.

———. 1998b. *Partisan Politics in the Global Economy*. New York: Cambridge University Press.

Gerring, John, Strom C. Thacker, and Carola Moreno. 2009. "Are Parliamentary Systems Betters?" *Comparative Political Studies* 42(3): 327–359.

Gidron, Noam, and Peter Hall. 2017. "The politics of social status: economic and cultural roots of the populist right." *The British Journal of Sociology* 68: S57–S84.

———. 2020. "Populism as a problem of social integration." *Comparative Political Studies* 53(7): 1027–1059.

Gilens, Martin. 2005. "Inequality and Democratic Responsiveness." *Public Opinion Quarterly* 69(5): 778–796.

Gilens, Martin, and Benjamin Page. 2014. "Testing Theories of American Politics: Elites, Interest Groups, and Average Citizens." *Perspectives on Politics* 12(3): 564–581.

Gingrich, Jane, and Ben Ansell. 2015. "The Dynamics of Social Investment: Human Capital, Activation, and Care." In Pablo Beramendi, Silja Häusermann, Herbert Kitschelt, and Hanspeter Kriesi, eds., *The Politics of Advanced Capitalism*. New York: Cambridge University Press, pp. 82–304.

Golden, David G., and James M. Poterba. 1980. "The price of popularity: the political business cycle reexamined." *American Journal of Political Science* 24(4): 696–714.

Golden, Miriam. 1993. "The Dynamics of Trade Unionism and National Economic Performance." *American Political Science Review* 87(2): 439–454.

Golden, Miriam, and John B. Londregan. 2006. "Centralization of bargaining and wage inequality: A correction of Wallerstein." *American Journal of Political Science* 50(1): 208–213.

Golden, Miriam, Michael Wallerstein, and Peter Lange. 2008. "Postwar Trade-Union Organization and Industrial Relations in Twelve Countries." In David Austen-Smith, Jeffry A. Frieden, Miriam A. Golden, Karl Ove Moene, and Adam Przeworski, eds., *Selected Works of Michael Wallerstein: The Political Economy of Inequality, Unions, and Social Democracy*. New York: Cambridge University Press, pp. 173–211.

Goldin, Claudia, and Lawrence F. Katz. 2009. "The Race between Education and Technology: The Evolution of U.S. Educational Wage Differentials, 1890 to 2005." Working Paper 12984. National Bureau of Economic Research.

Gomez, Brad T., and J. Matthew Wilson. 2006. "Cognitive Heterogeneity and Economic Voting: A Comparative Analysis of Four Democratic Electorates." *American Journal of Political Science* 50: 127–145.

Gottschalk, Peter, and Timothy M. Smeeding. 1997. "Cross-National Comparisons of Earnings and Income Inequality." *Journal of Economic Literature* 35(2): 633–687.

Gourevitch, Peter A. 1996. "The Macropolitics of Microinstitutional Differences in the Analysis of Comparative Capitalism." In Suzanne Berger and Ronald Dore, eds., *National Diversity and Global Capitalism*. Ithaca: Cornell University Press, pp. 239–259.

Gourevitch, Peter A., and James Shinn. 2005. *Political Power & Corporate Control: The New Global Politics of Corporate Governance*. Princeton, NJ: Princeton University Press.

Grigoli, Francesco, and Adrian Robles. 2017. "Inequality Overhang." IMF Working Paper 17/76. International Monetary Fund.

Gygli, Savina, Florian Haelg, Niklas Potrafke, and Jan-Egbert Sturn. 2019. "The KOF Globalisation Index—Revisited." *The Review of International Organizations* 14: 543–574.

Hacker, Jacob. 2005. "Policy Drift: The Hidden Politics of US Welfare State Retrenchment." In Wolfgang Streeck and Kathleen Thelen, eds., *Beyond Continuity: Institutional Change in Advanced Political Economies*. Oxford: Oxford University Press, pp. 40–82.

Hacker, Jacob, and Paul Pierson. 2010. "Winner-Take-All Politics: Public Policy, Political Organization, and the Precipitous Rise of Top Incomes in the United States." *Politics and Society* 38(2): 152–204.

———. 2011. *Winner-Take-All Politics: How Washington Made the Rich Richer—And Turned Its Back on the Middle Class*. New York: Simon & Schuster Paperbacks.

———. 2016. *American Amnesia: How the War on Government Led Us to Forget What Made America Prosper*. New York: Simon & Schuster.

Hacker, Jacob, Paul Pierson, and Kathleen Thelen. 2015. "Drift and Conversion: Hidden Faces of Institutional Change." In James Mahoney and Kathleen Thelen, eds., *Advances in Comparative-Historical Analysis*. Cambridge: Cambridge University Press, pp. 180–208.

Hall, Peter A. 1986. *Governing the Economy: The Politics of State Intervention in Britain and France*. New York: Oxford University Press.

Hall, Peter A., and Daniel Gingerich. 2004. "Varieties of Capitalism and Institutional Complementarities in the Political Economy: An Empirical Analysis." MPIfG Discussion Paper 04/5.

Hall, Peter A., and David Soskice, eds. 2001. *Varieties of Capitalism: The Institutional Foundations of Comparative Advantage*. New York: Oxford University Press.

Hall, Peter A., and Rosemary C.R. Taylor. 1996. "Political Science and the Three New Institutionalisms." *Political Studies* 44: 936–957.

Hall, Peter A., and Kathleen Thelen. 2009. "Institutional Change in Varieties of Capitalism." *Socio-Economic Review* 7(1): 7–34.

Hassel, Anke, Bruno Palier, and Sonja Avlijaš. 2020. "The Pursuit of Growth: Growth Regimes, Growth Strategies and Welfare Reforms in Advanced Capitalist Economies." *Stato e mercato* 118(April): 41–77.

Haynes, Stephen E., and Joe A. Stone. 1989. "An Integrated Test for Electoral Cycles in the US Economy." *The Review of Economics and Statistics* 71(3): 426–434.

Hays, Jude C. 2003. "Globalization and Capital Taxation in Consensus and Majoritarian Democracies." *World Politics* 56: 79–113.

Hays, Jude C., Sean Ehrlich, and Clint Peinhardt. 2005. "Government Spending and Public Support for Trade in the OECD: An Empirical Test of the Embedded Liberalism Thesis." *International Organization* (Spring): 473–494.

Hays, Jude C., Junghyun Lim, and Jae-Jae Spoon. 2019. "The path from trade to right-wing populism in Europe." *Electoral Studies* 60: 102038.

Hellwig, Timothy. 2001. "Interdependence, Government Constraints, and Economic Voting." *The Journal of Politics* 63(4): 1141–1162.

———. 2010. "Elections and the Economy." In Lawrence LeDuc, Richard Niemi, and Pippa Norris, eds., *Comparing Democracies 3: Elections and Voting in the 21st Century*. London: Sage Publications, pp. 184–201.

———. 2014. *Globalization and Mass Politics: Retaining the Room to Maneuver*. New York: Cambridge University Press.

Hellwig, Timothy, Yesola Kweon, and Jack Vowles. 2020. *Democracy Under Siege? Parties, Voters, and Elections After the Great Recession*. New York: Oxford University Press.

Hellwig, Timothy, and David Samuels. 2007. "Voting in Open Economies: The Electoral Consequences of Globalization." *Comparative Political Studies* 40(3): 283–306.

Hibbs, Douglass A. 1977. "Political Parties and Macroeconomic Policy." *American Political Science Review* 71: 1467–1487.

———. 1987. *The American Political Economy: Macroeconomics and Electoral Politics*. Cambridge, MA: Harvard University Press.

Hicken, Allen, Shanker Satyanath, and Ernest Sergenti. 2005. "Political Institutions and Economic Performance: The Effects of Accountability and Obstacles to Policy Change." *American Journal of Political Science* 49(4): 897–907.

Hicks, Alexander, and Lane Kenworthy. 1998. "Cooperation and Political Economic Performance in Affluent Democratic Capitalism." *American Journal of Sociology* 103(6): 1631–1672.

Hope, David, and Angelo Martelli. 2019. "The Transition to the Knowledge Economy, Labor Market Institutions, and Income Inequality in Advanced Democracies." *World Politics* 71(2): 236–288.

Hope, David, and David Soskice. 2016. "Growth Models, Varieties of Capitalism, and Macroeconomics." *Politics & Society* 44(2): 209–226.

Höpner, Martin. 2005. "What Connects Industrial Relations and Corporate Governance? Explaining Institutional Complementarity." *Socio-Economic Review* (3): 331–358.

Huber, Evelyne, Jingjing Huo, and John D. Stephens. 2017. "Power, Policy, and Top Income Shares." *Socio-Economic Review* 12(2): 245–267.

Huber, Evelyne, and John D. Stephens. 2001. *Development and Crisis of the Welfare State: Parties and Policies in Global Markets*. Chicago: The University of Chicago Press.

———. 2014. "Income Inequality and Redistribution in Post-industrial Democracies: Demographic, Economic and Political Determinants." *Socio-Economic Review* 12: 245–267.

———. 2015. "Postindustrial Social Policy." In Pablo Beramendi, Silja Häusermann, Herbert Kitschelt, and Hanspeter Kriesi, eds., *The Politics of Advanced Capitalism*. New York: Cambridge University Press, pp. 259–281.

Huber, Evelyne, John D. Stephens, and Kaitlin Alper. 2020. "The Varied Sources of Increasing Wage Dispersion." In Romana Careja, Patrick Emmenegger, and Nathalie Giger, eds., *The European Social Model under Pressure*. New York: Springer, pp. 231–252.

Ibsen, Christian Lyhne, and Kathleen Thelen. 2017. "Diverging Solidarity: Labor Strategies in the New Knowledge Economy." *World Politics* 69(3): 409–447.

Inglehart, Ronald, and Pippa Norris. 2017. "Trump and the Populist Authoritarian Parties: The Silent Revolution in Reverse." *Perspectives on Politics* 15(2): 443–454.

International Monetary Fund (IMF). 2020. "Database of Fiscal Policy Responses to COVID-19." www.imf.org/en/Topics/imf-and-covid19/Fiscal-Policies-Database-in-Response-to-COVID-19.

Iversen, Torben. 2005. *Capitalism, Democracy, and Welfare*. New York: Cambridge University Press.

Iversen, Torben, and David Soskice. 2001. "An Asset Theory of Social Policy Preferences." *American Political Science Review* 95(4): 875–893.

———. 2006a. "Electoral Institutions and the Politics of Coalitions: Why Some Democracies Redistribute More Than Others." *American Political Science Review* 100(2): 165–181.

———. 2006b. "New Macroeconomics and Political Science." *Annual Review of Political Science* 9: 425–453.

———. 2009. "Distribution and Redistribution: The Shadow of the Nineteenth Century." *World Politics* 61(3): 438–486.

Jaumotte, Florence, and Carolina Osorio Buitron. 2015. "Rising Income Inequality: Technology, or Trade and Financial Globalization? *IMF Economic Review* 61(2): 271–309.

Kaplan, Steven N., and Joshua Rauh. 2013. "It's the Market: The Broad-Based Rise in the Return to Top Talent." *Journal of Economic Perspectives* 27(3): 35–56.

Katz, Lawrence, and Kevin M. Murphy. 1992. "Changes in Relative Wages, 1963–1987: Supply and Demand Factors." *The Quarterly Journal of Economics* 107(1): 35–78.

Katzenstein, Peter J. 1985. *Small States in World Markets: Industrial Policy in Europe*. Ithaca: Cornell University Press.

Kayser, Mark Andreas. 2014. "The Elusive Economic Vote." In Lawrence LeDuc, Richard Niemi, and Pippa Norris, eds., *Comparing Democracies: Elections and Voting in a Changing World*. London: Sage Publications, pp. 112–132.

Kayser, Mark Andreas, and Christopher Wlezien. 2011. "Performance Pressure: Patterns of Partisanship and the Economic Vote." *European Journal of Political Research* 50: 365–394.

Keech, William R. 2013. *Economic Politics in the United States: The Costs and Risks of Democracy*. 2nd edition. New York: Cambridge University Press.

Keech, William R., and Kyoungsan Pak. 1989. "Electoral Cycles and Budgetary Growth in Veterans' Benefit Programs." *American Journal of Political Science* 33: 901–911.

Keister, Lisa A. 2014. "The One Percent." *Annual Review of Sociology* 40: 347–367.

Kenworthy, Lane. 2008. *Jobs with Equality*. Oxford: Oxford University Press.

Kenworthy, Lane, and Jonas Pontusson. 2005. "Rising Inequality and the Politics of Redistribution in Affluent Countries." *Perspectives on Politics* 3(3): 449–472.

Keys, V.O. 1966. *The Responsible Electorate: Rationality in Presidential Voting, 1936–1960*. Cambridge, MA: Harvard University Press.

Kinder, Donald R., and D. Roderick Kiewiet. 1979. "Economic Discontent and Political Behavior: The Role of Personal Grievances and Collective Economic Judgments in Congressional Voting." *American Journal of Political Science* 23(2): 495–527.

———. 1981. "Sociotropic Politics: The American Case." *British Journal of Political Science* 11: 129–161.

Kjellberg, Anders. 2009. "The Swedish Ghent System and Trade Unions under Pressure." *Transfer—European Review of Labour and Research* 15(3–4): 481–504.

Knutsen, Carl Henrik. 2011. "Which Democracies Prosper? Electoral Rules, Form of Government and Economic Growth." *Electoral Studies* 30: 83–90.

Kramer, Gerald H. 1971. "Short-Term Fluctuations in U.S. Voting Behavior, 1896–1964." *American Political Science Review* 65: 131–143.

———. 1983. "Ecological Fallacy Revisited: Aggregate- versus Individual-level Findings on Economics and Elections, and Sociotropic Voting." *American Political Science Review* 77: 92–111.

Kwak, James. 2014. "Cultural Capture and the Financial Crisis." In Daniel Carpenter and David Moss, eds., *Preventing Regulatory Capture: Special Interest Influence and How to Limit It*. Cambridge: Cambridge University Press, pp. 71–98.

Lange, Peter, and Geoffrey Garrett. 1985. "The Politics of Growth: Strategic Interaction and Economic Performance in the Advanced Industrial Democracies, 1974–1980." *The Journal of Politics* 47(3): 792–827.

Lebarz, Claire. 2015. "Income Inequality and Household Debt Distribution: A Cross-Country Analysis using Wealth Surveys." LWS Working Paper Series # 20. Luxembourg Income Study.

LeDuc, Lawrence, and Jon H. Pammett. 2013. "The Fact of Governing Parties in Times of Economic Crisis." *Electoral Studies* 32: 494–499.

Lehmbruch, Gerhard. 1984. "Concertation and the Structure of Corporatist Networks." In John H. Goldthorpe, ed., *Order and Conflict in Contemporary Capitalism: Studies in the Political Economy of Western European Nations*. New York: Oxford University Press, pp. 60–80.

Levi, Margaret. 2000. "The Economic Turn in Comparative Politics." *Comparative Political Studies* 33(6/7): 822–844.

Levy, Frank, and Peter Temin. 2007. "Inequality and Institutions in 20th Century America." Working Paper 13106. National Bureau of Economic Research. May.

Levy, Jonah D. 2008. "From the *Dirigiste* State to the Social Anesthesia State: French Economic Policy in the *Longue Durée*." *Modern & Contemporary France* 16(4): 417–435.

Lewis-Beck, Michael S. 1986. "Comparative Economic Voting: Britain, France, Germany, Italy." *American Journal of Political Science* 30(2): 315–346.

Lewis-Beck, Michael S., and Glen Mitchell. 1990. "Transnational Models of Economic Voting: Tests from a Western European Pool." *Revista del Instituto de Estudios Economicos* 4: 65–81.

Lewis-Beck, Michael S., and Martin Paldam. 2000. "Economic Voting: An Introduction." *Electoral Studies* 19: 113–121.

Lewis-Beck, Michael S., and Mary Stegmaier. 2013. "The VP-function Revisited: A Survey of the Literature on Vote and Popularity Functions after over 40 Years." *Public Choice* 157: 367–385.

Lijphart, Arend. 2012. *Patterns of Democracy: Government Forms and Performance in Thirty- Six Countries*. 2nd edition. New Haven: Yale University Press.

Limberg, Julian. 2020. "What's Fair? Preferences for tax progressivity in the wage of the financial crisis." *Journal of Public Policy* 40: 171–193.

Lindsey, Brink, and Steven M. Teles. 2017. *The Captured Economy: How the Powerful Enrich Themselves, Slow Down Growth, and Increase Inequality*. New York: Oxford University Press.

Lindvall, Johannes. 2014. " 'The Electoral Consequences of Two Great Crises." *European Journal of Political Research* 53(4): 747–765.

Lindvall, Johannes, and David Rueda. 2013. "The Insider-Outsider Dilemma." *British Journal of Political Science* 44(2): 460–475.

Lizzeri, Alessandro, and Nicola Persico. 2001. "The Provision of Public Goods Under Alternative Electoral Incentives." *The American Economic Review* 91(1): 225–239.

Lupu, Noam, and Jonas Pontusson. 2011. "The Structure of Inequality and the Politics of Redistribution." *American Political Science Review* 105(2): 316–336.

MacKuen, Michael B., Robert S. Erikson, and James A. Stimson. 1992. "Peasants or Bankers? The American Electorate and the U.S. Economy." *American Political Science Review* 86(3): 597–611.

Mahler, Vincent A., David K. Jesuit, and Piotr R. Paradowski. 2014. "Electoral Turnout and State Redistribution: A Cross-National Study of Fourteen Developed Countries." *Political Research Quarterly* 67(2): 361–373.

Mahler, Vincent A., David K. Jesuit, and Douglas Roscoe. 1999. "Exploring the Impact of Trade and Investment on Income Inequality: A Cross-National Sectoral Analysis of the Developed Countries." *Comparative Political Studies* 32: 233–256.

Manin, Bernard, Adam Przeworski, and Susan C. Stokes. 1999a. "Introduction." In Adam Przeworski, Susan C. Stokes, and Bernard Manin, eds., *Democracy, Accountability, and Representation*. Cambridge, UK: Cambridge University Press, pp. 1–27.

———. 1999b. "Elections and Representation." In Adam Przeworski, Susan C. Stokes, and Bernard Manin, eds., *Democracy, Accountability, and Representation*. Cambridge, UK: Cambridge University Press, pp. 29–54.

Mansbridge, Jane. 2009. "A 'Selection Model' of Political Representation." *Journal of Political Philosophy* 17(4): 369–398.

Mares, Isabela. 2006. *Taxation, Wage Bargaining, and Unemployment*. New York: Cambridge University Press.

Margalit, Yotam. 2019. "Economic Insecurity and the Causes of Populism, Reconsidered." *Journal of Economic Perspectives* 33(4): 152–170.

Martin, Cathie Jo, and Alexander Hertel-Fernandez. 2014. "How Sweden Fights Inequality—without Soaking the Rich." *Vox,* October 8.

Martin, Cathie Jo, and Duane Swank. 2012. *The Political Construction of Business Interests: Coordination, Growth, and Equality*. New York: Cambridge University Press.

McCarty, Noland, Keith Poole, and Howard Rosenthal. 2016. *Polarized America: The Dance of Ideology and Unequal Riches*. 2nd edition. Cambridge, MA: The MIT Press.

McManus, Richard, and F. Gulcin Ozkan. 2018. "Who does Better for the Economy? Presidents versus Parliamentary Democracies." *Public Choice* 176: 361–387.

Meltzer, Allan H., and Scott F. Richard. 1981. "A Rational Theory of the Size of Government." *Journal of Political Economy* 89(5): 914–927.

Menz, Georg. 2017. *Comparative Political Economy: Contours of a Subfield*. New York: Oxford University Press.

Metz, Neil, and Mariya Burdina. 2016. "Neighbourhood Income Inequality and Property Crime." *Urban Studies* 55(1): 133–150.

Milesi-Ferretti, Gian Maria, Roberto Perotti, and Massimo Rostagno. 2002. "Electoral Systems and Public Spending." *The Quarterly Journal of Economics* 117(2): 609–657.

Mishel, Lawrence, and Alyssa Davis. 2015. "Top CEOs Make 300 Times More Than typical Workers." EPI Issue Brief # 399. Economic Policy Institute, June 21.

Mitchell, William, and Michael Munger. 1991. "Economic Models of Interest Groups: An Introductory Survey." *American Journal of Political Science* 35(May): 512–546.

Moene, Karl Ove, and Michael Wallerstein. 2008a. "Inequality, Social Insurance, and Redistribution." In David Austen-Smith, Jeffry A. Frieden, Miriam A. Golden, Karl Ove Moene, and Adam Przeworski, eds., *Selected Works of Michael Wallerstein: The Political Economy of Inequality, Unions, and Social Democracy*. New York: Cambridge University, pp. 285–319.

———. 2008b. "Earnings Inequality and Welfare Spending: A Disaggregated Analysis." In David Austen-Smith, Jeffry A. Frieden, Miriam A. Golden, Karl Ove Moene, and Adam Przeworski, eds., *Selected Works of Michael Wallerstein: The Political Economy of Inequality, Unions, and Social Democracy*. New York: Cambridge University Press, pp. 409–442.

———. 2008c. "Social Democracy as a Development Strategy." In David Austen-Smith, Jeffry A. Frieden, Miriam A. Golden, Karl Ove Moene, and Adam Przeworski, eds., *Selected Works of Michael Wallerstein: The Political Economy of Inequality, Unions, and Social Democracy*. New York: Cambridge University pp. 443–466.

———. 2008d. "How Social Democracy Worked: Labor-Market Institutions." In David Austen-Smith, Jeffry A. Frieden, Miriam A. Golden, Karl Ove Moene, and Adam Przeworski, eds., *Selected Works of Michael Wallerstein: The Political Economy of Inequality, Unions, and Social Democracy*. New York: Cambridge University, pp. 378–408.

Mudde, Cas, and Cristóbal Rovira Kaltwasser. 2018. "Studying Populism in Comparative Perspectives: Reflections on the Contemporary and Future Research Agenda." *Comparative Political Studies* 51(13): 1667–1693.

Nadeau, Richard, and Michael S. Lewis-Beck. 2001. "National Economic Voting in U.S. Presidential Elections." *The Journal of Politics* 63(1): 159–181.

Nadeau, Richard, Michael S. Lewis-Beck, and Éric Bélanger. 2012. "Economic and Elections Revisited." *Comparative Political Studies* 46(5): 551–573.

Nadeau, Richard, Richard G. Niemi, David P. Fan, and Timothy Amato. 1999. "Elite Economic Forecasts, Economic News, Mass Economic Judgments, and Presidential Approval." *The Journal of Politics* 61(1): 109–135.

Nadeau, Richard, Richard G. Niemi, and Antoine Yoshinaka. 2002. "A Cross-national Analysis of Economic Voting: Taking Account of the Political Context across Time and Nations." *Electoral Studies* 21: 403–423.

Nannestad, Peter, and Martin Paldam. 1994. "The VP-function: A Survey of the Literature on Vote and Popularity after 25 Years." *Public Choice* 79: 213–245.

———. 2000. "Into Pandora's Box of Economic Evaluations: A Pooled Cross-Section Study of Economic Voting in Denmark, 1986–92." *Electoral Studies* 19: 123–140.

Nickell, Stephen. 1997. "Unemployment and Labor Market Rigidities: Europe versus North America." *The Journal of Economic Perspectives* 11(3): 55–74.

Nickell, Stephen, Luca Nunziata, and Wolfgang Ochel. 2005. "Unemployment in the OECD since the 1960s. What do we Know?" *The Economic Journal* 115(January): 1–27.

Nordhaus, William D. 1975. "The Political Business Cycle." *Review of Economic Studies* 42(1): 169–190.

Norpoth, Helmut. 1996. "Presidents and the Prospective Voter." *The Journal of Politics* 58(3): 776–792.

Okun, Arthur. 1975. *Equality and Efficiency: The Big Tradeoff*. Washington, DC: Brookings Institute.

Olson, Mancur. 1982. *The Rise and Decline of Nations: Economic Growth, Stagflation, and Social Rigidities*. New Haven: Yale University Press.

Organization for Economic Cooperation and Development. 1997. *Making Work Pay: Taxation, Benefits, Employment, and Unemployment*. Paris: OECD.

———. 2019a. "Social Expenditure Database (SOCX)." www.oecd.org/social/expenditure.htm.

———. 2019b. "Income Distribution Database (IDD)." www.oecd.org/social/income-distribution-database.htm.

———. 2019c. "Tax Database: Table I.7 Dataset." https://stats.oecd.org/Index.aspx?DataSet Code= TABLE_I7.

Pacek, Alexander. 1994. "Macroeconomic Conditions and Electoral Politics in East Central Europe." *American Journal of Political Science* 38(3): 723–744.

Paldam, Martin. 1991a. "How Robust is the Vote Function? A Study of Seventeen Nations over Four Decades." In Helmut Norpoth, Micheal Lewis-Beck, and Jean-Dominique Lafay, eds., *Economics and Politics: The Calculus of Support*. Ann Arbor: The University of Michigan Press, pp. 9–32.

———. 1991b. "Macroeconomic Stabilization Policy: Does Politics Matter?" In Arye L. Hillman, ed., *Markets and Politicians: Politicized economic choice*. New York: Springer Science, pp. 63–91.

Palmer, Harvey D., and Guy D. Whitten. 2000. "Government Competence, Economic Performance and Endogenous Election Dates." *Electoral Studies* 19: 413–426.

Paul, Pascal. 2018. "Historical Patterns of Inequality and Productivity around Financial Crises." Federal Reserve Bank of San Francisco Working Paper 2017–23.

Perrson, Torsten, Gérard Roland, and Guido Tabellini. 2000. "Comparative Politics and Public Finance." *Journal of Political Economy* 108(6): 1121–1161.

Persson, Torsten, and Guido Tabellini. 1990. *Macroeconomic Policy, Credibility, and Politics*. Chur, Switzerland: Harwood Academic Publishers.

———. 2003. *The Economic Effects of Constitutions*. Cambridge, MA: The MIT Press.

———. 2004a. "Constitutional Rules and Fiscal Policy Outcomes." *The American Economic Review* 94(1): 25–45.

———. 2004b. "Constitutions and Economic Policy." *Journal of Economic Perspectives* 18(1): 75–98.

Philippon, Thomas, and Ariell Reshef. 2012. "Wages and Human Capital in the U.S. Finance I Industry: 1909–2006." *Quarterly Journal of Economics* 127(4): 1551–1609.

Pickett, Kate E., and Richard G. Wilkinson. 2015. "Income Inequality and Health: A Causal Review." *Social Science & Medicine* 128: 316–326.

Pierson, Paul. 1996. "The New Politics of the Welfare State." *World Politics* 48(2): 143–179.

———. 2000. "Increasing Returns, Path Dependence, and the Study of Politics." *American Political Science Review* 94(2): 251–267.

———. 2001a. "Post-industrial Pressures on the Mature Welfare States." In Paul Pierson, ed., *The New Politics of the Welfare State*. Oxford: Oxford University Press, pp. 80–104.

———. 2001b. "Coping with Permanent Austerity: Welfare State Restructuring in Affluent Democracies." In Paul Pierson, ed., *The New Politics of the Welfare State*. Oxford: Oxford University Press, pp. 410–456.

Piketty, Thomas. 2013. *Capital in the Twenty-First Century*. Cambridge, MA: Harvard University Press.

Piketty, Thomas, and Emmanuel Saez. 2006. "The Evolution of Top Incomes: A Historical and International Perspective." *AEA Papers and Proceedings* 96(2): 200–205.

Piketty, Thomas, Emmanuel Saez, and Stefanie Stantcheva. 2011. "Optimal Taxation of Top Labor Incomes: A Tale of Three Elasticities." Working Paper 17616. National Bureau of Economic Research.

Piketty, Thomas, Emmanuel Saez, and Gabriel Zucman. 2016. "Distributional National Accounts: Methods and Estimates for the United States Data Appendix." WID.world Working Paper Series N° 2016/4. Wealth & Income Database.

Pitkin, Hanna Fenichel. 1972. *The Concept of Representation*. Berkeley: University of California Press.

Pontusson, Jonas. 2005. *Inequality and Prosperity: Social Europe vs. Liberal America*. Ithaca: Cornell University Press.

———. 2013. "Unionization, Inequality and Redistribution." *British Journal of Industrial Relations* 51(4): 797–825.

Pontusson, Jonas, and Lucio Baccaro. 2020. "Comparative Political Economy and Varieties of Macroeconomics." In *Oxford Research Encyclopedia of Politics*. Oxford: Oxford University Press.

Pontusson, Jonas, David Rueda, and Christopher R. Way. 2002. "Comparative Political Economy of Wage Distribution: The Role of Partisanship and Labour Market Institutions." *British Journal of Political Science* 32: 281–308.

Pontusson, Jonas, and Peter Swenson. 1996. "Labor Markets, Production Strategies, and Wage Bargaining Institutions: The Swedish Employer Offensive in Comparative Perspective." *Comparative Political Studies* 29(2): 223–250.

Pontusson, Jonas, and David Weisstanner. 2018. "Macroeconomic Conditions, Inequality Shocks and the Politics of Redistribution, 1990–2013." *Journal of European Public Policy* 25(1): 31–58.

Powell, G. Bingham, Jr. 1982. *Contemporary Democracies: Participation, Stability, and Violence*. Cambridge, MA: Harvard University Press.

Powell, G. Bingham, Jr., and Guy Whitten. 1993. "A Cross-National Analysis of Economic Voting: Taking Account of the Political Context." *American Journal of Political Science* 37(2): 391–414.

Rae, Douglass W. 1967. *The Political Consequences of Electoral Laws*. New Haven: Yale University Press.

Rajan, Raghuram. 2010. *Fault Lines: How Hidden Fractures Still Threaten the World Economy*. Princeton, NJ: Princeton University Press.

Rehm, Philipp. 2011. "Social Policy by Popular Demand." *World Politics* 63(2): 271–299.

Remmer, Karen L. 1991. "The Political Impact of Economic Crisis in Latin America in the 1980s." *American Political Science Review* 85(3): 777–800.

Rhoads, Steven E. 1985. *The Economist's View of the World: Government, Markets, & Public Policy*. New York: Cambridge University Press.

Riera, Pedro. 2015. "Economy, Type of Government, and Strategic Timing of Elections: Calling Opportunistic Early Elections in OECD Democracies." *West European Politics* 38(6): 1129–1151.

Rodrik, Dani. 1998. "Why Do More Open Economies Have Bigger Governments?" *Journal of Political Economy* 106(5): 997–1032.

———. 2020. "Why Does Globalization Fuel Populism? Economics, Culture, and the Rise of Right-Wing Populism." Research Paper. September.

Rogoff, Kenneth. 1990. "Equilibrium Political Budget Cycles." *American Economic Review* 80: 21–36.

Rogoff, Kenneth, and Anne Sibert. 1988. "Elections and Macroeconomic Policy Cycles." *Review of Economic Studies* 55: 1–16.

Rogowski, Ronald. 1987. "Trade and the Variety of Democratic Institutions." *International Organization* 41(2): 203–223.

Romer, Thomas. 1975. "Individual Welfare, Majority Voting, and the Properties of a Linear Income Tax." *Journal of Public Economics* 4(2): 163–185.

Rosen, Sherwin. 1981. "The Economics of Superstars." *The American Economic Review* 71(5): 845–858.

Röth, Leonce, Alexandre Afonso, and Dennis C. Spies. 2018. "The Impact of Populist Radical Right Parties on Socio-economic Policies." *European Political Science Review* 10(3): 325–350.

Rothstein, Bo. 1992. "Labor-market Institutions and Working-class Strength." In Sven Steinmo, Kathleen Thelen, and Frank Longstreth, eds., *Structuring Politics: Historical Institutionalism in Comparative Analysis*. New York: Cambridge University Press, pp. 33–56.

Rueda, David. 2006. "Social Democracy and Active Labour-Market Policies: Insiders, Outsider and the Politics of Employment Protection." *British Journal of Political Science* 36: 385–406.

———. 2007. *Social Democracy Inside Out: Partisanship & Labor Market Policy in Industrialized Democracies*. New York: Oxford University Press.

———. 2008. "Political Agency and Institutions: Explaining the Influence of Left Government and Corporatism on Inequality." In Pablo Beramendi and Christopher Anderson, eds., *Democracy, Inequality, and Representation*. New York: Russell Sage Foundation, pp. 169–200.

———. 2015. "The State of the Welfare State: Unemployment, Labor Market Policy, and Inequality in the Age of Workfare." *Comparative Politics* 47(3): 296–314.

———. 2018. "Food Comes First, Then Morals: Redistribution Preferences, Parochial Altruism and Immigration in Western Europe." *The Journal of Politics* 80(1): 225–239.

Rueda, David, and Jonas Pontusson. 2000. "Wage Inequality and Varieties of Capitalism." *World Politics* 52: 350–383.

Rueda, David, and Stephan Thewissen. 2018. "Automated but Compensated? Technological Change and Redistribution in Advanced Democracies." In Eva Paus, ed., *Emerging Dystopias? The New Technological Revolution and the Future of Work*. Ithaca: Cornell University Press, pp. 134–155.

Sanders, D. 2000. "The Real Economy and the Perceived Economy in Popularity Functions: How Much do Voters Need to Know? A Study of British Data, 1974–97." *Electoral Studies* 19: 275–294.

Scheidel, Walter. 2017. *The Great Leveler: Violence and the History of Inequality from the Stone Age to the Twenty-First Century*. Princeton, NJ: Princeton University Press.

Scheve, Kenneth, and David Stasavage. 2006. "Religion and Preferences for Social Insurance." *Quarterly Journal of Political Science* 1: 255–286.

———. 2009. "Institutions, Partisanship, and Inequality in the Long Run." *World Politics* 61(2): 215–253.

———. 2016. *Taxing the Rich: A History of Fiscal Fairness in the United States and Europe*. Princeton, NJ: Princeton University Press.

Schleiter, Petra, and Margit Tavits. 2016. "The Electoral Benefits of Opportunistic Election Timing." *The Journal of Politics* 78(3): 836–850.

———. 2018. "Voter Reactions to Incumbent Opportunism." *The Journal of Politics* 80(4): 1183–1196.

Schultz, Kenneth A. 1995. "The Politics of the Political Business Cycle." *British Journal of Political Science* 25: 79–99.

Schwander, Hanna. 2019. "Labor Market Dualization and Insider-Outsider Divides: Why This New Conflict Matters." *Political Studies Review* 17(1): 14–29.

Scruggs, Lyle, Jahn Detlef, and Kati Kuitto. 2017. "Comparative Welfare Entitlements Dataset 2." Version 2017–09. University of Connecticut & University of Greifswald.

Shepsle, Kenneth A. 1989. "Studying Institutions: Some Lessons from the Rational Choice Approach." *Journal of Theoretical Politics* 9(2): 131–147.

———. 2006. "Rational Choice Institutionalism." In Sarah Binder, R.A.W Rhodes, and Bert Rockman, eds., *Oxford Handbook of Political Institutions*. Oxford: Oxford University Press, pp. 23–39.

Shonfield, Andrew. 1965. *Modern Capitalism: The Changing Balance of Public and Private Power*. London: Oxford University Press.

Siebert, Horst. 1997. "Labor Market Rigidities: At the Root of Unemployment in Europe." *The Journal of Economic Perspectives* 11(3): 37–54.

Singer, Matthew M., and Ryan Carlin. 2013. "Context Counts: The Election Cycle, Development, and the Nature of Economic Voting." *The Journal of Politics* 75(3): 730–742.

Smith, Alastair. 2003. "Election Timing in Majoritarian Parliaments." *British Journal of Political Science* 33: 397–418.

Soskice, David. 1990. "Wage Determination: The Changing Role of Institutions in Advanced Industrialized Countries." *Oxford Review of Economic Policy* 6(4): 36–61.

Stigler, George J. 1973. "General Economic Conditions and National Elections." *American Economic Review* 63: 160–164.
Stimson, James A. 2004. *Tides of Consent: How Public Opinion Shapes American Politics*. New York: Cambridge University Press.
Streeck, Wolfgang. 2002. "Introduction: Explorations into the Origins of Nonliberal Capitalism in Germany and Japan." In Wolfgang Streeck and Kozo Yamamura, eds., *The Origins of Nonliberal Capitalism: Germany and Japan in Comparison*. Ithaca: Cornell University Press, pp. 1–38.
———. 2009. *Re-forming Capitalism: Institutional Change in the German Political Economy*. Oxford: Oxford University Press.
———. 2011. "The Crisis of Democratic Capitalism." *New Left Review* 71(September/October): 5–29.
Streeck, Wolfgang, and Kathleen Thelen. 2005. "Introduction: Institutional Change in Advanced Political Economies." In Wolfgang Streeck and Kathleen Thelen, eds., *Beyond Continuity: Institutional Change in Advanced Political Economies*. New York: Oxford University Press, pp. 1–39.
Strobl, Daniel, Hanna Bäck, Wolfgang C. Müller, and Mariyana Angelova. 2019. "Electoral Cycles in Government Policy Making: Strategic Timing of Austerity Reform Measures in Western Europe." *British Journal of Political* Science, First View, 1–22.
Swank, Duane. 2002. *Global Capital, Political Institutions, and Policy Change in Developed Welfare States*. Cambridge, UK: Cambridge University Press.
———. 2020. "The Partisan Politics of New Social Risks in Advanced Postindustrial Democracies: Social Protection for Labor Market Outsiders." In Romana Careja, Patrick Emmenegger, and Nathalie Giger, eds., *The European Social Model under Pressure*. New York: Springer, pp. 139–157.
Swank, Duane, and Hans-Georg Betz. 2019. "Do Radical Right Populist Parties Matter? The Case of the European Welfare State." Working Paper.
Swenson, Peter. 1991. "Bringing Capital Back in, or Social Democracy Reconsidered: Employer Power, Cross-Class Alliances, and Centralization of Industrial Relations in Denmark and Sweden." *World Politics* 43(4): 513–544.
Tavits, Margit. 2004. "The Size of Government in Majoritarian and Consensus Democracies." *Comparative Political Studies* 37(3): 340–359.
Tax Policy Center. 2020. "Historical Highest Marginal Income Tax Rates: 1913 to 2020." https://www.taxpolicycenter.org/statistics/historical-highest-marginal-income-tax-rates
Thelen, Kathleen. 1994. "Beyond Corporatism: Toward a New Framework for the Study of Labor in Advanced Capitalism." *Comparative Politics* 27(1): 107–124.
———. 2009. "Institutional Change in Advanced Political Economies." *British Journal of Industrial Relations* 47(3): 471–498.
———. 2014. *Varieties of Liberalization and the New Politics of Social Solidarity*. New York: Cambridge University Press.
———. 2019. "Transitions to the Knowledge Economy in Germany, Sweden, and the Netherlands." *Comparative Politics* 51(2): 295–315.
TIMBRO. 2019. "Authoritarian Populism Index." https://populismindex.com/wp- content/uploads/2019/02/TAP2019C.pdf
Tsebelis, George. 1995. "Decision Making in Political Systems: Veto Players in Presidentialism, Parliamentarism, Multicameralism and Multipartyism." *British Journal of Political Science* 25: 289–325.
Tucker, Joshua A. 2001. "Economic Conditions and the Vote for Incumbent Parties in Russia, Poland, Hungary, Slovakia, and the Czech Republic from 1990 to 1996." *Post-Soviet Affairs* 17(4): 309–331.
Tufte, Edward R. 1978. *Political Control of the Economy*. Princeton, NJ: Princeton University Press.

Visser, Jelle. 2019. "ICTWSS Database." Version 6.0. Amsterdam: Amsterdam Institute for Advanced Labour Studies (AIAS), University of Amsterdam. June.

Vogel, Steven K. 2018. *Marketcraft: How Governments Make Markets Work*. New York: Oxford University Press.

Wallerstein, Michael. 1999. "Wage Setting Institutions and Pay Inequality in Advanced Industrial Societies." *American Journal of Political Science* 43(3): 649–680.

Wallerstein, Michael, and Bruce Western. 2008. "Unions in Decline? What Has Changed and Why." In David Austen-Smith, Jeffry A. Frieden, Miriam A. Golden, Karl Ove Moene, and Adam Przeworski, eds., *Selected Works of Michael Wallerstein: The Political Economy of Inequality, Unions, and Social Democracy*. New York: Cambridge University Press, pp. 212–238.

Western, Bruce. 1997. *Between Class and Market: Postwar Unionization in the Capitalist Democracies*. Princeton, NJ: Princeton University Press.

Western, Bruce, and Jake Rosenfeld. 2011. "Unions, Norms, and the Rise of U.S. Wage Inequality." *American Sociological Review* 76(4): 513–537.

Weymouth, Stephen, and J. Lawrence Broz. 2013. "Government Partisanship and Property Rights: Cross-Country Firm-Level Evidence." *Economics & Politics* 25(2): 229–256.

Wlezien, Christopher, Mark Franklin, and Daniel Twiggs. 1997. "Economic Perceptions and Vote Choice: Disentangling the Endogeneity." *Political Behavior* 19(1): 7–17.

Wolf, Jr., Charles. 1993. *Markets or Governments: Choosing between Imperfect Alternatives*. 2nd edition. Cambridge, MA: The MIT Press.

World Inequality Database (WID). 2019. "World Wealth and Income Database." https://wid.world, accessed March 19, 2019.

Wright, John R. 2012. "Unemployment and the Democratic Electoral Advantage." *American Political Science Review* 106(4): 685–702.

Wüest, Reto, and Jonas Pontusson. 2018. "Descriptive Misrepresentation by Social Class: Do Voter Preferences Matter?" Working Paper. May.

Zysman, John. 1983. *Governments, Markets, and Growth: Financial Systems and the Politics of Industrial Change*. Ithaca: Cornell University Press.

Index

Note: **Bold** pages refer to tables; *italic* pages refer to figures